UBUNTU

Thinking Africa is a series produced by the Department of Political and International Studies at Rhodes University and University of KwaZulu-Natal Press. For more information on the project, visit http://www.ru.ac.za/politics/thinkingafrica/ or write to:

Leonhard Praeg: Series Editor
Thinking Africa
Political and International Studies
Rhodes University
Private Bag 94
Grahamstown 6139
South Africa

Email: L.Praeg@ru.ac.za

Previous series titles:
The Return of Makhanda: Exploring the Legend by Julia C. Wells (2012)
On African Fault Lines: Meditations on Alterity Politics by V-Y Mudimbe (2013)
A Report on Ubuntu by Leonhard Praeg (2014)

UBUNTU
Curating the Archive

Edited by
Leonhard Praeg and Siphokazi Magadla

UNIVERSITY OF KWAZULU-NATAL PRESS

Published in 2014 by University of KwaZulu-Natal Press
Private Bag X01
Scottsville, 3209
Pietermaritzburg
South Africa
Email: books@ukzn.ac.za
Website: www.uknpress.co.za

ISBN: 978-1-86914-265-0

Managing editor: Sally Hines
Editor: Alison Lockhart
Proofreader: Sean Fraser
Typesetter: Patricia Comrie
Indexer: Ethné Clarke
Cover design: MDesign
Cover art: *Awelani* by Tanya Poole

Printed and bound in South Africa by Paarl Media Paarl

CONTENTS

Acknowledgements   ix

Preface   x

Introduction   1
  Leonhard Praeg and Siphokazi Magadla

1 Justice Otherwise: Thoughts on Ubuntu   10
   Lewis R. Gordon

2 The Historical Discourse on African Humanism: Interrogating
   the Paradoxes   27
   Ama Biney

3 Ubuntu Versus the Core Values of the South African Constitution   54
   Ilze Keevy

4 From ubuntu to Ubuntu: Four Historic a Prioris   96
   Leonhard Praeg

5 Ubuntu: Affirming a Right and Seeking Remedies in South Africa   121
   Mogobe B. Ramose

6 *Utu, Usawa, Uhuru*: Building Blocks of Nyerere's Political Philosophy   137
   Issa G. Shivji

7 Ubuntu and the Law: Some Lessons for the Practical Application
   of Ubuntu   150
   Katherine Furman

8 Ubuntu and Subaltern Legality   167
   Drucilla Cornell

9 The Self Become God: Ubuntu and the 'Scandal of Manhood'   176
   Siphokazi Magadla and Ezra Chitando

10 Concluding Reflections: The 'Fierce Urgency of Now'   193
     Danielle Alyssa Bowler

Notes on the Contributors   213
Index   215

To the memory of
Evelyn Macetshane Magadla and Agnes Nozici Tom

'I'm saying that our love is shallow!'
'Could that be because the territory of sorrows which we inhabit is very large?'

— Nuruddin Farah, *Links*

This volume contains the proceedings of the 2012 Thinking Africa colloquium 'Ubuntu: Curating the Archive', hosted by the Department of Political and International Studies at Rhodes University. As such, it would not have been possible without the assistance of our colleagues in the project: Sally Matthews, George Barrett, Phumlani Majavu and Richard Pithouse. We would particularly like to thank those colleagues who travelled considerable distances to join us for this colloquium and who, through their continued support, have contributed to the growth of the project.

We also acknowledge the financial assistance and support offered by Rhodes University's research office, in particular its director, Jaine Roberts, and vice-chancellor, Dr Saleem Badat, who has maintained a much-appreciated enthusiasm and intellectual support for the Thinking Africa project.

We are grateful for all the students who, over the last four years, have participated in and contributed to the postgraduate Ubuntu course in the Department of Political and International Studies: in a very real sense, the colloquium and this volume would not have been possible without their passionate and creative participation.

Lastly, we would like to acknowledge and thank the UKZN Press team – Debra Primo, Louis Gaigher and Sally Hines – for their commitment to and support of this book series. In particular, we thank our editor Alison Lockhart for her excellent work on this manuscript.

If in that second – that is to say, at the last conscious moment before the fit – he had time to say to himself, consciously and clearly, 'Yes, I could give my whole life for this moment,' then this moment by itself was, of course, worth the whole of life. However, he did not insist on the dialectical part of his argument: stupor, spiritual darkness, idiocy stood before him as the plain consequence of those 'highest moments'.

— Fyodor Dostoyevsky, *The Idiot*

The process of preparing for publication the two volumes that mark the culmination of the Thinking Africa project of 2012 – *A Report on Ubuntu* and the proceedings of its annual colloquium, *Ubuntu: Curating the Archive* – commenced in the week that marked the first commemoration of the Marikana massacre. Though the place and meaning of this event in a future South African historiography is already (and always will remain) hotly contested, one thing is already abundantly clear today. The African National Congress's (ANC's) claim to have founded the new South Africa on the *nomos*, or spirit of law, of an extraordinary humanism has bottomed out. After Marikana, no such claim can plausibly be made or sustained. Just as its so-called human-rights-inspired foreign policy revealed itself as a myth soon after it was named as such, any claim by the ANC government to have founded our democratic politico-juridical order on the idea of a shared humanity will and indeed must in future be met with derision.

For this reason alone, it would be the most obvious thing in the world to denote and dismiss, or perhaps embrace, this as the dawn of our post-humanist present, to abandon talk of Ubuntu altogether, to dismiss it as historical artefact or as a passing infatuation with an already exhausted nationalism. In that case, projects such as the *Report* or *Ubuntu: Curating the Archive* would amount to little more than a silly intellectual and economic gamble because they would be a memorial to a history-just-past, a history that was betrayed; testament to a lasting traumatic melancholy that would do no more than make visible, through its very engagement with the topic, the absence of Ubuntu in the postcolony, a sign of a shared recognition of the absence of a shared humanity and the vacuity of any claim to a founding humanist *nomos*.

From another more resilient perspective, however, it seems that what has passed is not the possibility of a humanist *nomos*, per se, as much as its conception in the narrow nationalist terms of an African *nomos*, one that was always driven, less by a concern with our shared humanity than with the violent politics of identity claims, premised on an infatuation with an equally violent logic of cultural and political sovereignty, which historically manifested nowhere so clearly as in the beloved myth of South Africa's so-called miraculous transition – always a function, it was claimed, of something as lasting, because essential, as Africa's exceptional humanism. Of course, this is not to say that there have not always been theorists who contested this Ubuntu-driven nationalism, this nationalist, reductive violation of Ubuntu. There have been many excellent critiques, but even they were always articulated within the confines of a nationalist matrix: a binary juxtapositioning of the old South Africa with the new South Africa, of apartheid with democracy, Eurocentrism with Africanity and so on. Within this matrix, the claims of those who posited Ubuntu as the founding value of a new politico-juridical order were contested by anti-nationalists, who saw in such claims nothing but the vacuous identitarian claims of a bourgeois politics, largely unconcerned with mobilising the radically expansive understanding of justice implicit in Ubuntu as a potent critique of neoliberal constitutionalism. This is to say that the problem was never with Ubuntu as such, but with the politics of Ubuntu, the domestication of humanism to do the necessary, but not therefore less dirty, work of the politics of the day; the tendency to reduce a humanist emphasis on our shared humanity to an ideology, a humanism narrowly conceived in terms of the nationalist project, always premised on the identitarian assumption of a miraculous African subjectivity and its exceptional humanism – in short, the violent reduction of humanism to the logic of identity politics. If, for nationalists, Ubuntu was always simply present as a founding *nomos* of a potentially humanist order, it was only ever considered either as vacuous by those who, through the seductions of neo-racist dismissals of things African, trivialised its potential to found a new order, or as absent by those who could see no need to found a politico-juridical order on anything other than the contractarian axiomatic, the Law of laws, of liberal constitutionalism.

In retrospect, it was to be expected that this nationalist matrix, inspired as it was by the transition as our 'highest moment', should have delivered us onto this post-humanist moment of spiritual darkness and idiocy, that it should have culminated in this paradox of a humanism exhausted by its incarnation as nationalism, the moment at which we suddenly find ourselves disillusioned by the very idea of nationalism and everything that was invoked in order to make it plausible and executable as political project, a moment that will always predetermine as irredeemably apocalyptic the meaning of Marikana in our collective imagination. Marikana was an apocalyptic moment (apocalypse: from the Greek 'unveiling') precisely because it revealed with incontestable clarity the horror of a politico-juridical order that had come adrift from the 'highest moment' of its founding promise. Marikana is a sign of the drift of political Will, of a juridico-political order that has lost its moorings, become detached from its own founding as a political event, excluded from the very promisorial structure that would make of Marikana a political event. There can be few experiences as horrifying as this collective sense of being adrift from the origin for implicit in the founding is always a sense of purpose, of direction and intent immemorially captured by the claim, 'We the people . . .' commit to or believe in this or that, so that for a society to find itself severed from and, as a consequence, adrift from its founding, amounts to recognising the horror of no longer existing with a sense of purpose premised on a founding intent. Existence is reduced to the random outcome of the calculation of fleeting interests. Of course, there is a real sense in which the political is always precisely such a calculation, but what keeps political orders from imploding under the weight of random calculations has always been nothing but a conception of themselves as a lasting iteration of the founding intent, a determination to remain anchored to the sense of purpose that first unified the collective as a 'We'.

But a different response to the present is possible, one that will have to proceed from a temporary suspension (*epoché*) of the nationalist matrix and all the dead-end questions that have resulted from it (What is African about this communitarianism, this humanism, this socialism? What does African mean?), in order to reposition Ubuntu in the more cosmopolitan terms of a critical humanism that must always remain irreducible to the politics of the day, a project that has to return to, in order to retrace, the founding claim that a politics premised on our shared humanity is, after all, perhaps, possible. Such an endeavour will demand of us nothing less than a return to the origin that ushered in our contemporary, postcolonial discourse on Ubuntu, in order to reinterpret its meaning and place, no longer in the narrow binary terms of the nationalist matrix, but in the more universal terms of a pre-nationalist undecidability that has been reduced to simple presence by a nationalist claim to speak on its behalf. If Ubuntu is to be reinvented, yet again, but this time beyond the easy-going seductions of a belated nationalism and its discontents, it is to the inescapable ambivalence of the founding that we have to return, in order to appropriate it as founding trope that was always necessarily going to be both present and absent.

There is therefore an argument to be made that as a critical project, Ubuntu needs to be rethought, or at the very least, that the question of how it interrogates us, and not just us, 'it', must be thought all over again.

We at Thinking Africa can only hope that these two volumes will do some of the urgent conceptual work needed to give discussions on Ubuntu a new philosophical and political life, one in which we may one day, yet again, return to the idea and the possible viability of claiming that contemporary political life is, indeed, the constant iteration of a founding commitment to our shared humanity.

Leonhard Praeg
January, 2014

Introduction

Leonhard Praeg and Siphokazi Magadla

In 2011, the Department of Political and International Studies at Rhodes University in Grahamstown, South Africa, launched an African studies project called Thinking Africa, with the explicit aim of exploring different synergies or counterpoints between research and postgraduate teaching. Every year, one of the department's researchers is given the opportunity, via Thinking Africa, to present a current research project as a postgraduate course for Honours and Master's students. The topic of this research project then becomes the annual Thinking Africa theme. Over the course of a thirteen-week semester, students join the researcher in exploring the theme through an approach to tertiary education that the relevant literature, depending on emphasis, describes either as teaching-led research or research-led teaching. The research course culminates in a colloquium, to which notable international and national scholars are invited. This is not a standard academic conference with multiple streams and parallel sessions, but rather a focused conversation between ten to twelve scholars, open to all and free of charge to the public. The postgraduate students, now well versed in the pertinent literature, attend the colloquium with some actively participating by delivering papers of their own. In addition to presenting papers at the Thinking Africa colloquium, some of the visiting scholars also teach individual seminars, either before or after the colloquium.

As with many other conferences – the more successful ones, anyway – the idea is that the colloquium should be a conversation in which scholars present work-in-progress. In the months after the colloquium, these contributions are reworked into more substantial chapters and published, in book form, as part of the Thinking Africa Series, in association with University of KwaZulu-Natal (UKZN) Press. Although the core business of the book series consists of publishing the proceedings of the annual colloquium, other titles that are considered relevant to the overall intellectual concerns of the project are also published. The series was launched in 2012 with the publication of Julia Wells's *The Return of Makhanda: Exploring the*

1

Legend – a timely re-examination of the historiography of Makhanda, the Xhosa warrior and reputed prophet, who in 1919 led an estimated 10 000 soldiers in a failed assault on British army headquarters in Grahamstown. This publication was followed in 2013 by V-Y Mudimbe's *On African Fault Lines: Meditations on Alterity Politics*, which reformulates the experience of African studies as a concern with Africa's place in today's intellectual, economic and cultural configurations, including the main axes that structure disciplinary practices relating to African difference and in terms of the possibility of understanding being-in-the-world, with reference to alienation, creativity and friendship. In early 2014, the most recent book in the series, Leonhard Praeg's *A Report on Ubuntu*, was published. This book argues for the reappropriation of Ubuntu in the post-nationalist terms of a more cosmopolitan discourse on critical humanism.

The present volume is the outcome of Thinking Africa 2012, conceived and organised around the thematic 'Ubuntu: Curating the Archive'. The aims of this particular research project were twofold: first, to contextualise the debate on Ubuntu – which is often quite a myopic, South African-centred discourse – within the wider historical context of attempts, particularly by the first generation of post-independence African leaders, to rearticulate or reinvent African humanism, either as an autonomous and substantial philosophy and/or as an emancipatory developmental ideology, of which Julius Nyerere's Ujamaa project in Tanzania has probably been the most coherent. The second aim was to situate Ubuntu discourse in the wider historical context of a racist, Western modernity that, in many ways, created black subjectivity as both an exteriorised form of Otherness – a projection that plays itself out in the tired juxtapositioning of so-called Western individualism and so-called African communalism – and as a form of resistance to and a critique of that modernity. In this collection, we start with the latter perspective.

Given these two aims, a comment on the principles we used as guidelines for the spelling of the term 'ubuntu' is important. In 'Ubuntu and the Globalisation of Southern African Thought and Society', Wim van Binsbergen notes the following:

> Over the past twenty years, *ubuntu* (a word from the Nguni language family, which comprises Zulu, Xhosa, Swati, and Ndebele) and the equivalent Shona word *hunhu* have been explored as viable philosophical concepts in the context of majority rule in South Africa and Zimbabwe. In the hands of academic philosophers, *ubuntu/hunhu* has become a key concept to evoke the unadulterated forms of African social life before the European

conquest . . . The form of the word *ubuntu* . . . is purely productive in the morphological linguistic sense. It is the result of coupling the prefix generating abstract words and concepts (i.e. *ubu-*, in the Nguni languages) to the general root *-ntu* which one and a half centuries ago persuaded the pioneering German linguist [Wilhelm] Bleek to recognise a large Bantu-speaking family: the entire group of languages, spoken from the Cape to the Sudanic belt, where the root *-ntu* stands for 'human' (2001: 53).

In terms of this background, the linguistic convention in certain Nguni languages, such as isiZulu, is that when a sentence starts with the word, it should be spelled 'uBuntu'. However, given the aims of this volume, we were guided by the following two principles: one, following the usage introduced by Praeg in *A Report on Ubuntu* (2014), we use 'ubuntu' to refer to the living practice (the 'unadulterated forms of African social life') and 'Ubuntu' to refer to the postcolonial retrodiction of that practice as abstract philosophy and two, since the word is accepted in South African English usage, it is not italicised here.

In the first chapter, Lewis R. Gordon articulates the shared logic of modernities, what he calls the 'script of the relationship of tradition to modernity from antiquity to the present', of which Western modernity is but one recent example. According to this script, colonised peoples are always left with one of two choices: disappearance – 'either through genocide, cultural erasure or assimilation' – or adaptation, through transformation in the form of 'hybridisation and synthesis'. The latter possibility is of particular importance to us because it suggests rethinking Ubuntu in terms of a reinvented tradition or, in Mudimbe's concise description, appropriating it as 'retrodiction' – that is, as both a product of Western modernity and a critique of it. The idea that Ubuntu contains and can be mobilised as a critique of Western modernity generates the more specific question about its emancipatory potential in post-apartheid South Africa.

The three chapters that follow lay the foundation for responding to this challenge and they do so by looking at Ubuntu through three different kinds of lenses that bring into sharper focus different aspects of the relationship between African humanism and the project of emancipation: context, values and history. In terms of context, in Chapter 2, Ama Biney presents a broad historical synopsis of the variants of African humanism and the manner in which it has been deployed to emancipatory ends, more specifically, the first wave of post-independence development projects of Kwame Nkrumah, Kenneth Kaunda and Nyerere. She teases out some of the paradoxes generated by this history: What is the relationship between postcolonial state-formation, developmental humanism and the appalling violence that shadows this history? How do we account for the fascinating nexus of humanism and totalitarianism in the post-independence history surveyed in this chapter? Ambivalences and paradoxes abound in what we can perhaps think of as the political economy of African humanism. Many of these paradoxes relate to the tension that can be argued to exist between historical and contemporary values, between the values of which this humanism was historically a function and the contemporary values – often associated with Christianity, human rights and so on – that it seeks to domesticate and rearticulate. There are two relatively uncritical ways out of this 'messy dialectic' (as Frantz Fanon would call it): an ethnophilosophical denial of the tension, which often glorifies Ubuntu as an expression *avant la lettre* of the essential insights offered by Christianity, human rights and socialism, as if there were nothing by way of axiological residue that was then, as it is now, incompatible with these discourses.

Against this nostalgia is a second response that sees nothing but incompatibility between Ubuntu and the core values embodied by the Constitution. Here, the patriarchal values, of which ubuntu *qua* praxis was a function, combined with the fact that it is fundamentally a religious, not spiritual (in the post-secular sense of the word) world view, renders Ubuntu fundamentally at odds with the requirements of liberal democracy. This is the claim put forward by Ilze Keevy in Chapter 3. It is an important argument because it represents the view of many ordinary South Africans and scholars for whom the emancipatory potential of Ubuntu *qua* African humanism is limited by its own core values. What is the status of these critiques, by which we mean: What conceptions of history, time and culture are presupposed by them? Perhaps, ultimately, that 'things do not change', cultures and traditions do not reinvent themselves or, where they do, it is the prerogative of hegemonic traditions, such as liberal constitutionalism, which, far from being the 'common law' of its own imagination can, from another perspective, be described as nothing but Western customary law. The merit of Keevy's contribution lies in the fact that it pushes to the fore this *archē* contestation over what is hegemonic and what is 'merely' customary. It forces into the open the political question of who and under what conditions can assert the prerogative to reinvent tradition, without *therefore* being dismissed as 'mere' ideological and identitarian imitation. At work in this dismissal – and in fact, we would argue, in the vast majority of critical engagements with Ubuntu – is a failure to distinguish between the historical ubuntu praxis and the contemporary, retrodicted reinvention of Ubuntu philosophy of the postcolonial imagination.

The third lens through which the question of the emancipatory potential of Ubuntu is approached is therefore a philosophical argument for the usefulness and relevance of this distinction. In Chapter 4, Leonhard Praeg considers what he calls the four historical conditions of the possibility for Ubuntu as postcolonial philosophy. In effect, he asks what needed to have happened historically in order for us to ask the kinds of questions about Ubuntu that we do. His analysis of four of these conditions (or a prioris) suggests a difference between, on the one hand, an ubuntu deeply embedded in historical praxis or a political economy of obligation, where what it meant to recognise 'shared humanity' amounted to the mutual reaffirmation of a number of culturally and time-specific values and, on the other hand, a contemporary, postcolonial use of Ubuntu that seeks expansion and application beyond that political economy, in order to engage with questions of justice and belonging presupposed by our imagined community. When, for instance, a contemporary Constitutional Court judge invokes Ubuntu, s/he is deploying an abstract philosophy that, over many decades, has retrodicted this expansion as a result of mutually enriching interfaces with glocal discourses, such as Christian theology and human rights. In this precise sense, Ubuntu is both a function and a critique of Western modernity and therein, Praeg argues, lie both the conditions of its possibility and the limitations of its emancipatory potential.

Having considered the contextual, axiological and philosophical questions generated by the reinvention of Ubuntu, the other chapters engage with the question that comes after this: Now that we understand how we have come to speak about Ubuntu in the way that we do, why bother? What is the emancipatory potential of an Ubuntu so conceived? This question is addressed at two levels: in the first instance, at the level of the big picture, where Ubuntu is invoked to challenge, not the laws of the land, but the conception of justice that informs those laws. In the second instance, two contributions consider Ubuntu more immediately, in terms of its potential as form of ethical activism. Let us briefly outline the main concerns of both approaches.

A number of contributors – Gordon, Drucilla Cornell, Issa G. Shivji, Katherine Furman and M.B. Ramose – ask a very similar question that can be summarised as follows: Is the concept of justice projected by the contractual axiomatic of the Constitution adequate for a postcolonial South Africa or might Ubuntu, as Gordon argues, amount to a form of potentiated movement into a normative field, where justice so understood is recognised as a political and historical construct, as customary law with (at best) universalising ambitions? And once we have followed this potentiated movement to the originary *archē* of the political, what alternative or complementary conception of justice does Ubuntu offer us?

In Chapter 5, Ramose takes up this challenge by advancing a radical argument: the right to life is inseparable from the right to express the meaning of that life in terms that make sense to the individual. Where a politico-juridical order exists that recognises the former right, but not the latter, the 'right to life' is but an abstraction. For Ramose, this is how we need to understand what it means to have a right: it includes, among other things, the right to development and a livable environment, in addition to the freedom to express, in ethno-specific terms, what having rights means to the individual. This is a holistic and therefore radical, because expansive, understanding of 'rights'; 'expansive' because it insists that although rights may be universal, they still have meaning and this meaning is never simply universal. Rights mean something specific, both phenomenologically – in terms of the construct an individual deploys in making sense of what 'having rights' means – as well as practically, in the sense that rights become inseparable from the conditions of their meaningful and substantial realisation.

This suggestion – which appears radical only to the extent that liberal democratic understandings of both rights and justice have managed to naturalise themselves, along with the distinction they have generated between first- and second-generation rights, between immediately realisable individual rights and the promisorial structure of socio-economic rights – is also echoed in Chapter 6 by Shivji, who reminds us of the equally radical understanding of justice in Nyerere's political philosophy, one that radically subverts the very assumption upon which such distinctions are based. What inspired Nyerere's socialist Ujamaa project was the realisation that the notion of 'equality of rights' captures something essential about the 'juridical outlook' of the bourgeoisie, for whom human beings are considered equal *because they possess equal rights* – a conception of equality that is superimposed on the fundamental social and economic inequalities inherent in the capitalist system. In such a system, our very conception of 'justice' is a function of a double abstraction that makes it possible and that is replicated and sustained by it: The 'individual being' is abstracted from the 'social being' and this 'abstract individual' is then said to possess equal rights. For African philosophers, such as Nyerere and Ramose, the equality of human beings is prior or anterior to any discourse on rights. Equality and (by deduction) justice, does not derive from rights; it is not a function of rights discourse, but rather precedes it. Shivji writes:

Coupled with the idea of *utu* (dignity or humanness), this idea of *usawa* (equality) per force imports the idea of *equity* and *justice*, both of which, in Kiswahili, translate into the word *haki*, which also means rights. Here, rights are not separated from justice – unlike in the bourgeois understanding where 'right' connotes a legal right, so that justice merely translates into 'legal' justice. In Kiswahili, equity, justice and right are all connoted by one word, *haki*, which is often used interchangeably. *Utu* and *usawa* are inseparable in the sense that all are equal in their dignity. *Haki* is not equivalent to the concept of rights in bourgeois philosophy. *Haki* is not justice according to rights, but justice as social justice.

These are fascinating meta-questions – not simply about the justice or just*ness* of laws, but about *the justice of justice* itself, the very conception of justice we invoke when we decide on the justness of laws. However, in this volume, we do not pursue this question any further at a meta-level. Instead, in Chapter 7, Katherine Furman discusses, among other things, the kinds of objections judges regularly encounter when they invoke Ubuntu in an attempt to expand our understanding of justice along these lines. Juxtaposing the jurisprudence of Johan van der Walt's *Law and Sacrifice: Towards a Post-Apartheid Theory of Law* with Drucilla Cornell's 'A Call for a More Nuanced Constitutional Jurisprudence' and 'Ubuntu, Pluralism and the Responsibility of Legal Academics', Furman identifies, in order to refute, three main criticisms routinely levelled at Ubuntu-engaged adjudication: a lack of conceptual clarity, a lack of African particularity and a lack of appropriate cultural context when making use of Ubuntu in the law. Her chapter brings to a conclusion the contributions that deal with Ubuntu's emancipatory potential at a macro-level.

Straddling the transition between this macro-level discourse and the chapters that consider Ubuntu as an activist ethic is Drucilla Cornell's concise argument in Chapter 8, in which she defends Ubuntu on the basis that it engages racist, Western modernity at the totality of the levels at which it presents itself: philosophical, political and juridical. In doing so, she argues, it presents us with a new ethical vision of what being human together can mean and look like. In her account, Ubuntu needs to be taken seriously not simply because it is an African or South African value or philosophy, but because it offers a way of renewing and reinvigorating the philosophical and political project of human solidarity. This it can only do if we take seriously the emancipatory potential for radical transformation embodied by 'revolutionary Ubuntu' – a phrase used by, among others, members of Abahlali baseMjondolo, for whom Ubuntu is irreconcilable with the capitalist system.

The potential of Ubuntu as an ethical force or critique is also the topic of Chapter 9 by Siphokazi Magadla and Ezra Chitando, in which they attempt to reconcile the disjuncture between the formal/legal equality achieved between men and women after apartheid with the harrowing day-to-day cases of sexual and gender-based violence against women in South Africa. The authors examine how, if at all, Ubuntu can/should contribute to reconfiguring masculinities and femininities. They do so specifically because tradition has been used as a basis to articulate the backdrop as to why men use violence to control women, in a context where they presumably perceive legal equality as an attack on their 'traditional' superior role as men, in both the public and private spaces. The authors reveal a complicated relationship between what has until now been a binary representation of this tradition versus legal equality discourse, which sees men represented as using tradition as a tool to preserve male hegemony and ordinary women and/or feminists who perceive the reinvention of tradition as potentially eroding the liberal constitutional values of equality that offer protection to women. Magadla and Chitando argue that Ubuntu does not exclusively belong to the male traditionalists because many women also see themselves as custodians of its associated values. Thus, the argument is that liberal rights discourse is not irreconcilable with traditional values, since it is possible to aspire to legal equality that destroys the gender inequality inherent in the language of tradition, while *also* considering oneself a custodian of the same tradition.

In her concluding reflection in Chapter 10, Danielle Alyssa Bowler argues that the current positioning of Ubuntu in state discourse anticipates a future irrevocably different from the past and, as such, tends to present us with a vision of an easy and uncomplicated road to the future, devoid of the hard work of first finding and insisting on what is truly common in our shared humanity. In its obsession with progress, Ubuntu discourse often fails to address the present *as present* and, in doing so, deprives us of a vision of the future *as future*. The question that should haunt us in this strange temporality that is postcoloniality is: What sort of moment is this in which to pose the question of Ubuntu to the contemporary South African reality? This is a question, Bowler argues, that restores temporality to the present because it insists on the way in which memory and its repetition can pave the road towards the unprecedented.

References

Praeg, L. 2014. *A Report on Ubuntu*. Pietermaritzburg: University of KwaZulu-Natal Press.

Van Binsbergen, W. 2001. '*Ubuntu* and the Globalisation of Southern African Thought and Society'. *Quest* 15 (1–2): 54–89.

CHAPTER 1

Justice Otherwise
Thoughts on Ubuntu

Lewis R. Gordon

The topic of Ubuntu lends itself to so much, primarily because of the shifts and efforts for a native English speaker to grapple with an important concept that oddly speaks to the core of African thought, on the one hand and, as I will argue, to the normative challenges of the modern world, on the other. It is similar to the task of articulating African diasporic philosophy, what is also called Africana philosophy, which I have argued is a fundamentally *modern* philosophy; it brings some of these elements to the fore in ways that question some of the tendencies that would make Ubuntu collapse into the particular, rare and exotic (Gordon 2008: 21–33).

Engaging with a concept of African humanism no doubt stimulates tendencies towards what the late Michel-Rolph Trouillot (2003) calls 'the savage slot', where, the presupposition of a form of premodern, sometimes pristine and noble, other times corrupt and vicious, existence is advanced under the rubric of 'tradition'. Although there are no human communities without traditions, the use of the term has a peculiarly insidious connotation in the study and political debates over and with indigenous peoples. As Franz Boas showed, the tendency is to look at such groups as somehow located outside of modern time, which makes them, to some extent, more like ghosts of the present: effects in the now that belong in the past.[1]

Modernity, modernities
An immediate criticism of the presumption of the premodern temporal location of values is that it requires indigenous people to cease thinking, living and creatively and critically engaging with the world around them at the moment of conquest and colonisation. Frozen at, if not just before, the moment of contact with the 'outside world', which simply means Europe or the 'West', indigenous peoples, in this formulation, hold their breath on their values.

There is, however, another portrait of what transpired in the modern world. As one group of people enforced its portrait of reality on others, an antagonistic relationship emerged in which dominated peoples not only resisted what was imposed on them, but also evaluated their presuppositions about the world. This process took on a dialectical quality of give and take, which led to new problems of value and meaning that also affected the people who dominated them. The modern in this view, then, is not a singular, homogenous event, but instead a variety of tensions through which the present emerged. It is not, however, peculiar in this regard since this story of confluence and synthesis precedes the form of modernity that we have come to treat as the phenomenon itself.

Now, one may object that modernity is an invention of late nineteenth-century French thought and artistic practice. A problem with this view, however, is that it presupposes the particular naming of an event, experience or practice as that which brings its reality into being. An examination of the dynamics of modernist thinking reveals some features that connect it to practices that precede its baptismal moment. Enrique Dussel, for example, has shown that there have in fact been *modernities*, instead of only one modernity and that for the people on whom it is imposed, it often means the catastrophe of a haunted future, of a disruption of time, wherein a new set of problematics of continued existence comes to the fore. Thus, while European triumphalism looks to modernity in terms of modern philosophy or the epistemic rationalisation of the bourgeois revolution from the seventeenth century onwards, the indigenous peoples of the Americas mark it as the beginning of a regime of genocide from the fifteenth century onwards.

The story of modernity shifts, then, when it is read through its colonial correlate. Colonialism imposes a peculiar crisis on colonised peoples, since every colonial regime offers itself as the only viable future for its subjects. Colonised subjects face possible futures of (1) their disappearance, either through genocide or cultural erasure or assimilation and/or (2) their adaptation, through transformation often in the form of hybridisation and synthesis (see Gordon and Gordon 2009: Chapter 5).

Looking to the antiquated past, imagine what Kmt/Egypt looked like to peoples brought into its borders by conquest.[2] That it, too, was colonised by the Greeks who renamed Kmt (using the Greek name for Memphis – Egypt) led to the fusion of worlds made manifest in the region. The Roman Empire, too, offered a vision of no choice to those it conquered, but to become Roman. A familiar example of this is the historical transformation of values that emerged from the conquest of

Judah, which the Romans and Greeks called Judea. The process from Greek to Roman control was one in which Judah had at first expanded into the Hasmonean Empire, which at first led to an expansion of the reach of the laws of Judah. Rome, however, asserted its control, which led to important debates over colonisation, many of which are portrayed in the story of Jesus of Nazareth. Recall, for instance, the famous baiting of Jesus on the matter of taxes, where he encourages the people to give unto Caesar what is his and unto G-d what is G-d's.[3] The more pressing question for the priests, rebels and everyday people of Judah, however, was about which set of laws would prevail, Roman or Judean. In this framework, Rome represented the modern and Judah the traditional.

What followed could be called the script of the relationship of tradition to modernity from antiquity to the present. It may seem odd to talk about ancient modernity, but we should bear in mind what ancient Rome represented politically, sociologically and technologically to those it conquered. As the asserted centre of the world, it was also its presumed future and the designation 'eternal city' was a reflection of this aspiration. So, for the people of Judah, the dilemma was about being 'purely' Judean or becoming Roman. Some, however, offered a third way: becoming a hybrid of Rome and Judah. The Roman concepts of *relegere* (go through again, to read over and over, to repeat, as in ritual) and *religare* (to bind), from which emerged the term 'religion', offered conditions of citizenship and other forms of membership, through which gods and state could be separated by systems of taxation and gender-specific lineage of birth. The Israelites of Judah had determined patrilineal conditions of born membership until their transformation under Roman rule into matrilineal membership and what became Rabbinic Judaism.

There were approximately 150 000 Judeans in Rome in the period leading up to the Roman destruction of the Second Temple of Jerusalem. A hundred years later, there were 8 000 000 people under the emerging identity now known as 'Jews'. What happened was a transformation and adaptation of Judean laws (*Halacha*) with Roman laws, a process that included proselytising. Rapid growth in their numbers would have continued had the Emperor Constantine not converted to Christianity, their rival group, in the fourth century ACE, inaugurating the theological-political constellation of Christendom, which brought with it edicts against Jewish proselytising that included capital punishment.[4]

The meeting of Alexandria, Athens, Jerusalem and Rome was not only political and juridical, but also epistemological and cosmological. The world of the Egyptians, Greeks and Romans, governed by a mythopoetics of cyclical permanence and eternity, was fused with that of the Judeans, an eschatological world with a beginning, an ongoing process of perfection and a future end, telos or purpose.

Christendom, mediated by the emergence of Rabbinic Judaism, brought a different problematic to the understanding of history and time. For antiquated histories, as found in the writings of Herodotus, the story was primarily about the past. This newly emerging fusion of Egypt, Greece, Rome and the now diasporic Judah, worked through past, present and future, where rituals of the past were primarily preparations for the future. History came to assume a new form of understanding the present from the perspective of a proposed time to come – a consideration that took a decisive turn when a revolt against religion, in the Roman sense outlined here, emerged in the seventh century with the birth of Islam.

As a critique of religion, of the Romanisation of West Asian laws and values as modernity in the form of the Holy Roman Empire, Islam advanced a conception of law that through conquest also ironically offered itself as a new and better modernism.[5] It was ironic since it was advanced as a return to a truer set of laws beyond religion, but it did so through incorporating itself into the conclusion of the future to come. Thus, it posed a challenge to Christendom in its Afro-Arabic form from northern and western Africa into southern Europe as far north as southern France. To the east, the challenge went all the way to the Indian and Pacific oceans. But central here is that it set in motion the series of conflicts that led to Christendom moving across the Atlantic Ocean in the fifteenth century. This conflict was well under way by the seventh century when Muslim control of trade across the Mediterranean plummeted Christendom into an economic depression. This dire circumstance lasted nearly 800 years, during which the 'higher civilisation' was Islamic and the historical representation of that trauma is characterised in the West as the 'Dark Ages'. The 'reconquest', achieved by Queen Isabella and King Ferdinand in Grenada in January 1492, pushed this conflict into the Atlantic Ocean along the coasts of Africa and across to what became the Caribbean. These events inaugurated both a new epoch and a new world.

The story thus far reveals that 'modernity' is not the right designation, but instead *modernities*. In each instance, the dominating civilisation posed itself to the dominated as no less than the future, hence the dilemmas of extinction or hybridisation. While the people who became Jews resolved this question through Rabbinic Judaism – where *Halacha* fused with much of Roman law – and the

Arab world offered a response to Christendom in the form of *sharia* – whose legal structure incorporated and debated ideas from Greek antiquity, Rabbinic Judaism and the varieties of challenges posed from its own forms of conquest from the Atlantic to the Pacific – a striking shift emerged when Christians, Muslims and Jews encountered people who were none of these formulations, not even in the form of a faint hybridisation. This epistemic challenge was also a rupture at the core of presuppositions of what it means to be a human being, which for Christians was presumed to be Christian; for Muslims, to be people of the Book; and for Jews, more or less the same, with privilege and obligations imposed upon the elected.

The upheavals that followed created crises of justification, as the worlds of indigenous peoples of the New World fought a series of impositions that posed a future completely without them, at worst, or with a modicum of their former numbers, at best. For the invaders, the crisis was at the level of theological naturalism and a theological-epistemic order: With the breakdown of theological rationalisation, other forms of justification became necessary, such as accounting for nature and humanity without the creative intervention of a deity. Without preordination, the future held the possibility of the genuinely new (see Blumenberg 1985). The shift from a theological-naturalistic anthropology to a secular anthropology arose, but the normative underpinnings of theological rationality remained. Thus, the grammar of deification was shifted to epistemic and social orders, which led to a theodicy of the new era. Theodicy is the accounting for the legitimacy of G-d in the presence of injustice and evil. If G-d is omnipotent, omniscient and benevolent, why doesn't He or She do something about injustice and evil? Or worse, given the criterion of omnipotence and omniscience, shouldn't G-d be considered the *source* of injustice and evil? The classic response is to shift responsibility for life's infelicities onto humanity through at least two arguments: (1) human beings are finite and are thus not able to grasp the greater good of G-d's will and (2) G-d endowed human beings with free will, which they have abused. Both formulations place the blame on humankind – the first, in terms of perception and the second, in terms of deed.[6]

The deification of an epistemic or social order has similar results, in the sense that the integrity of the system depends on externalising its contradictions. Thus, proponents of the imposed order regard poverty, disease, high mortality and social misery as intrinsic to the condition of conquered peoples, instead of as afflictions imposed on them. The result is an anthropology of 'problem people'. The modernity marked by this process differs from prior modernities precisely in the manner in which its philosophical anthropology did not only place whole groups of people outside of ongoing time, but also transformed the idea of the dominating group into a geographical reach that was genuinely global, *while* locating the dominated group outside of that terrain in what Frantz Fanon called the 'zone of nonbeing' (see, for example, Dussel 1995, 1996, 2013; Gordon 2008: Chapter 1, Chapter 2; Mignolo 2012; Robinson 2001). In anthropological terms, 'Christendom' was changed into 'Europe' (which transformed the lives of Christians who were not north of the Mediterranean) and Europeans, deified but still asserting a mythos of the heavens above, became 'men' below, against whom was now posited the rest of humanity. As sub-humanity, the anthropological order of modern racialisation took its now well-known course.

People did not, however, stop living, thinking and fighting in the 'zone of nonbeing', neither did this struggle always assume the form of cultural authenticity. In some instances, it was more a matter of building on normative resources at hand with which to deal with the new, imposing epoch and which also challenged the theodicean presumptions of that system. Thus, as peoples across the globe faced the question of European laws versus so-called 'traditional laws', they also interrogated the problems of the age that inaugurated such dilemmas. Such inquiry led not only to a transformation of their indigenous concepts, but also to those that were being imposed on them. This is because, as scholars of Africana thought and decolonial studies have shown, the underside of modern life reveals its contradictions and thereby offers a broader picture of the epoch.[7]

Let us call this phenomenon 'potentiated double consciousness', a term coined by Paget Henry, who, through his engagement with the thought of W.E.B. Du Bois, pointed out that there are at least two kinds of double consciousness: (1) first-stage double consciousness, where one sees oneself as constructed by the eyes of the (often hostile) Other and (2) the second stage, where one realises the errors of that false construction of the self and the society that cultivates it (see Henry 2005; Gordon 2000: Chapter 4). Realising the contradictions produced by a society that makes people into problems, critical reflection then turns to the society or social system. This movement brings the original presupposition of universality into question and particularises it. The result is a subversion of false universality that proceeds by unmasking its actual particularity – a movement through which claims to universality are assessed with humility by distinguishing between *universalising* and *universal* practices.[8]

Potentiated double consciousness raises a question of the kind of critique the underside of modernity offers our understanding of not only the epistemic claims of the modern world, but also its normative claims.

Modern Ubuntu because Ubuntu is modern

Ubuntu in the contemporary South African context is a serious matter on which not only case law, but also human lives depend. According to Percy Mabogo More:

> In one sense *ubuntu* is a philosophical concept forming the basis of relationships, especially ethical behaviour. In another sense, it is a traditional politico-ideological concept referring to socio-political action. As a moral or ethical concept, it is a point of view according to which moral practices are founded exclusively on consideration and enhancement of human well-being; a preoccupation with 'human'. It enjoins that what is morally good is what brings dignity, respect, contentment, and prosperity to others, self and the community at large.
>
> . . . *uBuntu* is a demand for respect for persons no matter what their circumstances may be.
>
> In its politico-ideological sense it is a principle for all forms of social or political relationships. It enjoins and makes for peace and social harmony by encouraging the practice of sharing in all forms of communal existence (2006: 149, 156–7).

Ubuntu has descriptive and prescriptive dimensions.[9] Descriptively, there is its history and the empirical elements, as part of the moral anthropology of norms in the southern African context, often referred to as 'traditional law'.[10] (Oddly enough, British traditional law is simply called 'common'.) On the other hand, it is the articulation of a critical philosophical position on norms offering not only its internal meta-critique, but also one by which norms of the West, which European settlers presumptively asserted as norms of humanity, could be brought under scrutiny. As Drucilla Cornell and Nyoko Muvangua (2012) point out, in terms of its relation to Hobbesian and Kantian expectations of social order – the former premised on necessary conditions for social order and the latter on regulative ideals for freedom – Ubuntu offers a humanistic critique and constructive demand of whether human worth and dignity are indeed maintained through conceptions of rationality and reason, the consequence of which has been human subordination.

A rational being includes, but is not reducible to, human beings and since there are dimensions of human beings that are outside the purview of rationality, any system that measures human worth solely in rationalist terms is bound to encounter the human being as a problem of systemic limitation and insubordination.

The descriptive course also reveals affinities with ancient struggles against and with imperialism. As seen in the discussion of ancient Judaism, such efforts affect normative systems of regulation, such as *Halacha* or Jewish law. The normative framework for Jews was one in which the ethical face of G-d is the responsibility of the human being and this face takes the form of human dignity, exemplified in the rabbinic positions that emerged on, for instance, death.[11] It was not always the case that Jewish burials required simplicity. Once lavish and ornate, the price of burying a loved one became so expensive that some families abandoned the deceased's remains. Such a development was surely not the ethical face of G-d, reasoned the early medieval rabbis and they offered rules covering Jewish burial, premised on this mandate of dignity, which became *Halachic*.

Ubuntu, born of the normative debates of different African communities in what became known as South Africa, raises the question of the ethical face of humanity from people who faced the negation of dignity under conditions of colonisation. Since colonisation poses a crisis of indigenous values, critical reflection on those values reaches meta-normative levels where the colonised peoples of South Africa (and, in truth, all colonised peoples) have to face not only their values and the responsibility for those values, but also the responsibility for responsibility. This raises a variety of philosophical questions, including that of human evasion or bad faith. A first-order conception of responsibility rests, for instance, on simply adhering to a command or following the normative rules. Valuing such rules, however, demands self-reflection and where there is no external source of value, the responsibility for such a value falls on the shoulders of the valuing agent. Such a burden may be too much for some of us to bear and we may attempt an escape through the denial of our responsibility for values in the first place. This effort, however, is premised on the conditions that brought about such an onus – the ability to accept or reject them, in other words, *choice* – which make it a form of self-denial or bad faith.[12] This conclusion depends not only on self-accountability, but also on accountability in itself, a public phenomenon that transcends the self. In the realm of ethics, this amounts to realising that the radicalisation of oneself as an exception becomes an assault on sociality, with the performative contradiction of relying on the social, in order to be an exception in the first place. One cannot be an exception to a rule without there being rules. Thus, whether as the only point of view or as the rejection of being a point of view at all, the meaning of either requires a point of view from which to be differentiated from the other.

Put differently, any human effort to be in a non-human relation is already thwarted because of its being a human aspiration in the first place. A danger consists, however, in making the rules into a fetish, one that collapses rules into what existentialists call seriousness, where one makes oneself forget that human responsibility for rules also requires knowing when such rules should be broken.[13] To evade sociality – and, by extension, the conditions of evidence and accountability – also requires, then, attempting the same in relation to humanity. It would be a mistake, however, as Cornell and Muvangua have pointed out, to presume that the assertion or acknowledgement of sociality entails the affirmation of humanity (2012: 9–10, 14, 30). The Kantian model premised on 'rational beings' could, as some of us have argued, affirm a 'Kingdom of Ends', a universal community that may not necessarily be a humane one.[14]

Take, for example, the liberal, neo-Kantian political philosopher John Rawls's theory of justice as fairness (1971).[15] Rawls raised the importance of thinking through justice at the level of the basic institutions of a society, with the goal of constructing a just society. Justice, he claims, is the basic virtue of all social institutions. This concern of Rawls is taken for granted as a project of universal import primarily because of the presumption of the universal translatability of the English word 'justice', even though, as anyone working through the concepts even within the Indo-European linguistic framework would attest, such translation is an extraordinarily presumptive one. Is 'justice' as Rawls and many of us in the English language use it, mediated by its French usage, really identical to the Latin *iustitia*, which in turn was from *iustus*, often not mentioned in philosophical discussions that reach across time to the ancient Greek δίκη (*dikē*) or, when engaged philosophically, δικαιοσύνη (*dikaiosunē*) – that is, the ancient Greek notions? Or how about the Kmt or ancient Egyptian word – symbolised as ∤ (an ostrich feather; at other times also represented as scales or a primeval mound) – *maat* or *ma'at*?[16] As we trudge through the variety of normative concepts with which to examine the proper ordering of a society, why can we not bring to the table normative ideals, that to which to aspire at the societal level, from the elements of a society that reaches out and attempts to speak to the rest of humanity? In other words, what might emerge from reformulating the question not only as one about the justice of Ubuntu, but also of the Ubuntu of justice? Formulated differently, is the scope of justice sufficient to incorporate Ubuntu or might the latter be a form of potentiated movement into a normative field where justice is simply not enough?[17]

This rather odd formulation to some should rightfully suggest a point of continuity and differentiation. For it would be correct to say there are points of normative convergence between justice and Ubuntu, but the extent to which they are identical should occasion pause. I say this for the same reasons of consideration with *dikē* and *ma'at* (although *ma'at* is closer to Ubuntu than *dikē* because of its significance also for *truth*). Here, I am drawing upon an insight from the famed Ghanaian philosopher Kwasi Wiredu who, in his excellent and underappreciated *Cultural Universals and Particulars* (1996), argues simultaneously for universality and specificity, through a focus on the human capacity for communication. Although not all cultural concepts are translatable – that is, there is not complete linguistic isomorphism across human languages – it does not follow that their meanings cannot be *learned*. Anyone who has acquired language can, in principle, learn a concept from another language *in its own terms*. Thus, the significance of Ubuntu is not so much a matter of definition and translation, although that intellectual exercise is not short of importance, but of *understanding*.

Thus oddly enough, although many in the African diaspora were not aware of the term 'Ubuntu', there are early twentieth-century instances of arguing for the substance of that concept. Take, for instance, Charles Houston, who was the mastermind behind the legal stratagem that led to the legislation against segregation in the United States.[18] Houston did not know about Ubuntu, but he thought about humanity and justice and he had formulated principles of justice akin to Rawls's, but with a different outcome from Rawls on the meta-critical question of assessing the principles. Rawls, as is well known, argued that justice in the United States (and possibly all Western liberal democracies) should be ordered according to two principles: one that prioritises civil liberties and another that responds to inequalities and disadvantages.[19] The latter, he contended, is fair if inequalities actually benefit the least advantaged members of the society. If, however, there were a situation in which these two principles were in conflict, Rawls advocated prioritising the first principle over the second. In other words, civil liberties, which Rawls regarded as necessary conditions for the formation of moral persons, must be protected, even at the expense of the least advantaged people.

Houston, who formulated these principles nearly a quarter of a century before Rawls, argued the contrary (see Houston 1935a, 1935b, 1935c, 1936, 1940).[20] Where the two principles conflicted, he defended the material transformation of inequalities over the prioritising of liberties – the second principle over the first. His rationale was interestingly based on the kind of argument that Rawls was also engaged in, namely the articulation of the conditions of possibility for a just society. Houston pointed out that liberties are meaningless without material conditions from which to enact them – which amounts to questioning the formation of moral persons outside of a materially significant framework for sociality and reflection. Rawls argued as though a principle could serve as both necessary and sufficient condition for its manifestation, although this was clearly not his intent, given his overall goal of articulating, through his notion of a basic structure, a just *society*.

We see here different positions on a fundamentally human question. Because Rawls writes from a perspective that imagines the capacity to create material conditions so long as liberty is maintained, his heuristic model is much like that of the once-imagined Robinson Crusoe. What Houston understands, however, is that the Crusoe model is fallacious precisely because it posits the human being in the person of Friday *outside of society*, when the question at hand is about a just *society*. Crusoe's welfare depends on Friday, whose erasure as a human being in the narrative enables Crusoe to appear self-sufficient. That the problem already presupposes a world of others means that the inherent sociality of social conditions has to be taken into account. We are on the road here to another fundamental difference, namely between a conception of the human being as a substance in isolation versus that of being a relationship that presupposes a world of others and in which struggle is required for things that really matter. This is one reason why, in spite of their shared concerns for a just society, Houston's and Rawls's genealogical paths point in different directions. Houston's places him in affinity with revolutionary thinkers on law and society, while Rawls's theory points to reforms of a society that is presumed to be basically decent. Both are premised on fundamentally different philosophical anthropologies. The *relationality* of the human being is, in other words, the task through which not only justice must be cultivated, but also the human being (and human well-being).

That Houston was a jurist brings to the fore his connection to Ubuntu and to Cornell and Muvangua's wider question of its relation to law. The notion of Ubuntu as 'the Law of law', of course raises questions of its meta-normative significance and also, given the postcolonial context in which it is raised, the question of whether it collapses into the neocolonial relations admonished in the thought of Fanon and more recently in Achille Mbembe's reflections in *On the Postcolony* (2001). According to Mbembe, the period of colonial independence is unfortunately not the eradication of colonial relations because there is the continued epistemic and normative structure of a colony without the formal legal apparatus or status. Thus, the postcolony is really a new kind of colony. Mbembe does not use the term 'neocolonialism' because that model offers too neat a picture of agents (former governors) and passive subjects (people of the neocolony). In stream with Fanon, he argues for the analysis of complicit relations, of entangled networks of agents, whose actions constitute a colony that is disavowed as such.

The postcolony raises the problem of what decolonial theorists call 'decolonisation'. This project is often addressed in epistemic terms as challenging also the meaning of material conditions of colonisation. Epistemic decolonisation becomes the focus. The portrait I have been offering here raises an additional level of decolonisation, however. While a necessary condition, epistemic decolonisation is insufficient because of its failure to get at the core of normative life. The decolonisation of normative life is also needed, which is hard to imagine outside of an epistemic framework, precisely because of the scope of epistemological imposition on modern life. This is why I have argued for analyses premised on the fundamental and symbiotic relationships across questions of identity, liberation and critique or, in more formal terms, philosophical anthropology, freedom and meta-critiques of reason.[21]

Returning to Ubuntu, we should consider its similarity to notions such as *Halacha* in Judaism and *sharia* in Islam. The specificity of these, however, is the mediating role of the Roman Empire, the emergence of Judaism, Christianity and Islam, and the Roman concepts of *relegere* (to read again) and *religare* (to bind), through which religion emerges as a category eventually separated from *legis* (genitive of *lex*, 'law'), in the modern separation of state and religion. Ubuntu, however, while posed in the context of colonial imposition and resistance, is *not* a religious notion. It is a calling for a society to rise to a standard beyond those imposed on it. It is, in other words, a realisation that while the illegalisation of apartheid was a form of justice, the cultivation of a post-apartheid society is an ongoing project, through which the responsibility for justice means appealing to a higher standard than those posed by a world in which epistemic and normative practices have been, in a word, colonised.

Addressing the emancipatory potential of Ubuntu, then, requires transcending the expected relativising of it posed by unfortunate epistemic and meta-ethical attitudes towards things African, often posed in patronising terms, such as 'tradition'. It demands, I dare say, taking seriously its *universalising* elements, not simply those elements that are aligned with extant hierarchies, but also those that would enable us to aspire to a better future. This does not suggest an imperial imposition on the rest of the world – which is no threat, given the realities of power and the status of states in the international arena – but instead, simply an encomium from the distinct perspective of struggle in a world that is patently global. It means admitting that the purported universal normative language is limited and that each generation of humanity has the task of raising the standards of what we claim to be the best in all of us. As I have already argued, this means taking seriously Du Bois's theories of double consciousness and potentiated double consciousness. Recall that the first involves understanding the perspective by which Africa is seen in the world, while the second requires a critique of the contradictions of that perspective by bringing global hegemony under investigation and critique. In effect, that critical evaluation particularises hegemonic conceptions of universality in ways that expand knowledge and justice, while also taking into account the fallacy of closure on such efforts. In effect, the practice is universalising without collapsing into closed universality. In other words, it remains open to self-critique and the human capacity to think, act and build otherwise.

A concluding thought

Reading Cornell's *Defending Ideals* (2004), one can easily see why Ubuntu is a concept that she, an Irish-American woman committed to a world of human decency, embraces. Society, she contends, must always strive to become better. I would add to this that the responsibility for that responsibility is a crucial element of any society that takes seriously the question of movement as project. The call to Ubuntu, then, means a scale of accountability that is no less than radical, for it means that it must account not only for the question of its emancipating potential, but also for the subject of such practice and the conditions by which both are taken into account. As such, drawing on the work of Philip Iya, Mabogo More, Yvonne Mokgoro, Albie Sachs and many others, the notion of Ubuntu as 'Law of laws' calls for a consideration dreaded and rebuked in an age of neoconservatism and neoliberalism, namely the radical idea that law and the mechanisms by which society is governed should, at the end of the day, exist for the sake of human well-being.

Notes

1. On this matter of 'ghostlike existence,' see the last chapter – 'Existential Borders of Anonymity and Superfluous Invisibility' – in Gordon (2000) and 'On the Temporality of Indigenous Identity' (Gordon 2013a: 60–78).
2. 'Kmt', sometimes written as 'Kam', 'Kamit' or 'Kemet', meaning 'dark lands', was the original name of what is now known as Egypt, the Greek name for the area (see Gordon 2008: 2).
3. As I am Jewish, I use this convention of not fully spelling out the name since the monotheistic formulation collapses into a proper name instead of a general referent.
4. An excellent history of this process of transformation is offered by Cohen (1999); see also Gordon (2011: 75–82).
5. The debates within Islam, including between various groups, such as the Sunni majority, Shiite minority and the various other sects, are not my main concern here. What they all have in common is the view that Islam offers a better understanding of the human being's place in the universe, which for them requires a critique of Judaism and Christianity (among others). For a treatment similar to some of what I will be arguing here, see Shariati (1981).
6. There are many classic discussions of theodicy. For provocative recent discussions from Africana thinkers, see Pinn (1999) and Jackson (2009). Although theodicean arguments are well beyond Gottfried Wilhelm Leibniz's metaphysical reflections on the subject, as seen in the thought of Saint Augustine in the early Middle Ages, I refer to these two black scholars' recent reflections because of the obvious modern context of anti-black racism.
7. For Africana thought, see Gordon (2008), and for decolonial studies, see for instance, Mignolo (2012) and Maldonado-Torres (2008).
8. For more on this distinction, see for example, Gordon (2012). A similar consideration is made in Buck-Morss (2009), while Jane Anna Gordon also discusses this distinction in *Creolizing Political Theory: Reading Rousseau through Fanon* (forthcoming 2014).
9. Various expanded definitions are offered in Cornell and Muvangua (2012).
10. For a critical discussion of this tendency, see Sachs (2012: 303–16), Serequeberhan (2000) and Gordon (2008: Chapters 1 and 2).
11. For discussion of death in Rabbinic Judaism, see for instance, Schulweis (2001) and Glustrom (1989).
12. For a detailed discussion of this concept, see Gordon (1999).
13. On the spirit of seriousness, see Gordon (1999). On the fetishising of rules in contemporary times, see Comaroff and Comaroff (2006: 1–56).
14. I am referring to Kant's classic discussion of the 'Kingdom of Ends' (1997); see also my critical discussion in Gordon (1999: Part II).
15. Rawls's critics covered every spectrum. They ranged from libertarians of radically different kinds, such as Robert Nozick and Ayn Rand, to welfare-state liberals, such as Ronald Dworkin and Michael Sandel, to Marxists, such as G.E. Cohen and many more. That Rawls prioritised the first over the second principle makes it difficult, however, for his brand of liberalism not to collapse into neoliberalism, the brand of market fundamentalism premised on the preservation of individual liberty and the rejection of group rights. See, for example, the debates in Daniels (1989).

16. For a detailed discussion of *ma'at*, see Karenga (2006). The Greek and Latin concepts have received much attention, but see MacIntyre (1984) for a similar set of critical concerns about presuppositions on justice from antiquity to modernity.
17. Other chapters in this volume offer insights into this debate.
18. For rich discussions of Houston's life and thought, see Conyers (2012).
19. See Rawls (1971) for his classic statement of his position; Rawls (1993) for his revisions, especially along lines of cultural specificity; Rawls (1999) for a later attempt; and Rawls and Kelly (2001) for considerations interestingly in the direction of Houston. For standard debates on Rawls's theory, see for example, Freeman (2002), in addition to Daniels (1989).
20. As is evident from these articles, Houston believed in getting to the point and being brief. For a biography and discussion, see James (2010) and Friedman (2008).
21. I outline these considerations in *An Introduction to Africana Philosophy* (2008) and address them specifically in terms of what I call the decolonisation of normative life in *No Longer Enslaved Yet Not Quite Free* (forthcoming 2014). For related discussion, see also Gordon (2013b: 25–9).

References

Blumenberg, H. 1985. *The Legitimacy of the Modern Age*. Translated by R.M. Wallace. Cambridge: MIT Press.

Buck-Morss, S. 2009. *Hegel, Haiti, and Universal History*. Pittsburgh: University of Pittsburgh Press.

Cohen, S.J.D. 1999. *The Beginnings of Jewishness: Boundaries, Varieties, Uncertainties*. Berkeley: University of California Press.

Comaroff J. and J. Comaroff. 2006. 'Law and Disorder in the Postcolony: An Introduction'. In *Law and Disorder in the Postcolony*, ed. J. Comaroff and J. Comaroff, 1–56. Chicago: University of Chicago Press.

Conyers, J., Jr (ed.). 2012. *Charles H. Houston: An Interdisciplinary Study of Civil Rights Leadership*. Lanham: Lexington Books.

Cornell, D. 2004. *Defending Ideals: War Democracy, and Political Struggles*. New York: Routledge.

Cornell D. and N. Muvangua (eds). 2012. *Ubuntu and the Law: African Ideals and Postapartheid Jurisprudence*. New York: Fordham University Press.

Daniels, N. (ed.). 1989. *Reading Rawls: Critical Studies of Rawls' 'A Theory of Justice'*. Palo Alto: Stanford University Press.

Dussel, E. 1995. *The Invention of the Americans: Eclipse of "the Other" and the Myth of Modernity*. Translated by M. Barber. New York: Continuum.

———. 1996. *The Underside of Modernity: Apel, Ricoeur, Rorty, Taylor, and the Philosophy of Liberation*. Translated by Eduardo Mendieta. Atlantic Highlands: Humanities Press.

———. 2013. 'Anti-Cartesian Meditations: On the Origin of the Philosophical Anti-Discourse of Modernity'. *Journal of Human Architecture: Journal of the Sociology of Self-Knowledge* XI (1): 25–30.

Freeman, S. (ed.). 2002. *The Cambridge Companion to John Rawls*. Cambridge: Cambridge University Press.

Friedman, M.J. 2008. *Free At Last: The U.S. Civil Rights Movement*. Washington, DC: US Department of State, Bureau of International Information Programs. Available at http://www.america.gov/media/pdf/books/free-at-last.pdf#popup.

Glustrom, S. 1989. *The Myth and Reality of Judaism*. West Orange: Behrman House Publishers.

Gordon, J.A. Forthcoming 2014. *Creolizing Political Theory: Reading Rousseau through Fanon*. New York: Fordham University Press.

Gordon, L.R. 1999. *Bad Faith and Antiblack Racism*. Amherst: Humanity Books; originally published by Humanities International, 1995.

———. 2000. *Existentia Africana: Understanding Africana Existential Thought*. New York: Routledge.

———. 2008. *An Introduction to Africana Philosophy*. Cambridge: Cambridge University Press.

———. 2011. 'Réflexions sur la question afro-juive'. *Plurielles: Revue culturelle et politique pour un judaïsme humaniste et laïque* 16: 75–82.

———. 2012. 'Essentialist Anti-Essentialism, With Considerations from Other Sides of Modernity'. *Quaderna: A Multilingual and Transdisciplinary Journal* 1. Available at http://quaderna.org/wp-content/uploads/2012/09/Gordon-essentialist-anti-essentialism.pdf.

———. 2013a. 'On the Temporality of Indigenous Identity'. In *The Politics of Identity: Emerging Indigineity*, ed. M. Harris, M. Nakata and B. Carlson, 60–78. Sydney: UTS ePress.

———. 2013b. 'Thoughts on Dussel's "Anti-Cartesian Mediations"'. *Human Architecture* XI (1): 25–9.

———. Forthcoming 2014. *No Longer Enslaved Yet Not Quite Free*. New York: Fordham University Press.

Gordon, L.R. and J.A. Gordon. 2009. *Of Divine Warning: Reading Disaster in the Modern Age*. Boulder: Paradigm Publishers.

Henry, P. 2005. 'Africana Phenomenology: Its Philosophical Implications'. *C.L.R. James Journal* 11 (1): 7–12.

Houston, C. 1935a. 'Cracking Closed University Doors'. *Crisis* 42 (December): 364.

———. 1935b. 'Educational Inequalities Must Go'. *Crisis* 42 (October): 300.

———. 1935c. 'The Need for Negro Lawyers'. *Journal of Negro Education* 4 (January): 49.

———. 1936. 'Glass Aided School Inequalities'. *Crisis* 43 (January): 15.

———. 1940. 'Saving the World for Democracy'. A series for *The Pittsburgh Courier*, 20, 27 July; 2, 17, 24, 31 August; 7, 14, 21, 28 September and 5, 12 October.

Jackson, S.A. 2009. *Islam and Black Suffering*. New York: Oxford University Press.

James, R. Jr. 2010. *Root and Branch: Charles Hamilton Houston, Thurgood Marshall, and the Struggle to End Segregation*. New York: Bloomsbury Press.

Kant, I. 1997. *Groundwork of the Metaphysics of Morals*. Edited and translated by Mary Gregor. Cambridge: Cambridge University Press.

Karenga, M. 2006. *Maat: The Moral Ideal in Ancient Egypt; A Study in African Ethics*. Los Angeles: University of Sankore Press; hardback edition published in 2004 by Routledge.

MacIntyre, A.C. 1984. *After Virtue: A Study in Moral Theory*. 2nd edition. South Bend: Notre Dame University Press.

Maldonado-Torres, N. 2008. *Against War: Views from the Underside of Modernity*. Durham: Duke University Press.

Mbembe, A. 2001. *On the Postcolony*. Berkeley: University of California Press.

Mignolo, W. 2012. *The Darker Side of Western Modernity: Global Futures, Decolonial Options*. Durham: Duke University Press.

More, P.M. 2006. 'South Africa under and after Apartheid'. In *A Companion to African Philosophy*, ed. K. Wiredu, 148–60. Oxford: Blackwell.

Pinn, A.B. 1999. *Why, Lord? Suffering and Evil in Black Theology*. New York: Continuum.

Rawls, J. 1971. *A Theory of Justice*. Cambridge: Harvard University Press.

———. 1993. *Political Liberalism*. New York: Columbia University Press.

———. 1999. *The Law of Peoples*. Cambridge: Harvard University Press.

Rawls, J. and E. Kelly (eds). 2001. *Justice as Fairness: A Restatement*. Cambridge: Harvard University Press.

Robinson, C. 2001. *An Antrhopology of Marxism*. Aldershot: Ashgate.

Sachs, A. 2012. 'Towards the Liberation and Revitalization of Customary Law'. In *Ubuntu and the Law: African Ideals and Postapartheid Jurisprudence*, ed. D. Cornell and N. Muvangua, 303–16. New York: Fordham University Press.

Schulweis, H.M. 2001. *Finding Each Other in Judaism: Meditations on the Rites of Passage from Birth to Immortality*. New York: UAHC Press.

Serequeberhan, T. 2000. *Our Heritage: The Past in the Present of African-American and African Existence*. Lanham: Rowman & Littlefield.

Shariati, A. 1981. *Man and Islam*. Translated by Fatolla Marjani. North Haledon: Islamic Publications International.

Trouillot, M-R. 2003. *Global Transformations: Anthropology and the Modern World*. New York: Palgrave Macmillan.

Wiredu, K. 1996. *Cultural Universals and Particulars*. Bloomington: Indiana University Press.

CHAPTER 2

The Historical Discourse on African Humanism
Interrogating the Paradoxes

Ama Biney

. . . at the very time when it most often mouths the word, the West has never been further from being able to live a true humanism – a humanism made to the measure of the world.

— Aimé Césaire, *Discourse on Colonialism*

We believe that in the long run the special contribution to the world by Africa will be in this field of human relationship. The great powers of the world may have done wonders in giving the world an industrial and military look, but the great gift still has to come from Africa – giving the world a more human face.

— Steve Biko, *I Write What I Like*

We have held, and we still hold, that Africa's gift to world culture must be in the field of Human Relations.

— Kenneth Kaunda, *Humanism in Zambia*

The contemporary African postcolonial state is a schizophrenic state. It is wholly uncertain of its identity because it is a product of colonial rule and continues to be legitimated and controlled, not primarily by its citizens, but by outside interests that are largely in tension with the interests of African people themselves (Mbembe 2001). For the last 50 years – that is, since formal decolonisation – Africa has been engulfed by a crisis of identity, state-sponsored wars against its citizens, the consequences of 'maldevelopment' (Ake 1987; Mutua 2002: 112; Amin 1990), deteriorating living standards, which have given rise to hunger and famine on many parts of the continent, and various forms of neocolonial subordination. As Claude Ake writes: 'Ordinary people are terrorized daily by wanton display of state power and its instruments of violence' (1987: 7). The Frankenstein postcolonial

African state has proved to be just as brutal towards its citizens and in much the same manner as the behemoth colonial state that was its predecessor.

There are many dimensions to the crisis currently confronting the African continent, other than the economic and the political. While Ake argues that the political dimension to the crisis is 'critical' and 'may well be the most decisive factor' (1987: 7), another equally grave dimension is the psychological aspect of internalised colonial racism. The consequences of anti-black racism have affected the psyche or self-esteem of *many* colonised black Africans (not all Africans are people of African descent) who find themselves psychologically disfigured by an inferiority complex typical of mental enslavement. The psychological scarring of colonised human beings has resulted in a form of dehumanisation to which black Africans often contributed, since white supremacy operates through manufactured collusion by the oppressed in their own oppression and subjugation. Some individuals and groups of oppressed people are oblivious to their own collaboration in the structures, systems and values that continue to dehumanise them. Harriet Tubman, the African-American 'Black Moses', declared: 'I freed a thousand slaves. I could have freed a thousand more. If only they knew they were slaves.'[1]

An argument can and indeed has been made that present-day capitalism, neocolonialism and neoliberalism continue to present themselves as the norm, with no alternative – as a result of which human beings are not encouraged to question the roots of their oppression nor the system that continues to dehumanise them. This chapter argues that Ubuntu or African humanism can offer an alternative to that norm. It explores some of the tensions, contradictions or paradoxes between Ubuntu/African humanism as a philosophy or mode of critique and its empirical reality or manifestation in postcolonial politics. It addresses the following questions: First, how do we define African humanism or Ubuntu? How has it been defined in the past, particularly by African leaders of the early period of post-independence? I seek to present a broad and cursory historical synopsis of the variants of African humanism across the African continent within postcolonial discourse, in order to contest the argument that Ubuntu is something new and unique to South Africa. In addition, I argue that African humanism was as vital to nation-building in the era of the 1960s as some would argue Ubuntu is in the context of contemporary South Africa.

Second, how can Africans harness humanism towards a genuine emancipatory project in the interests of the dispossessed and poor? To put the question differently, how can Africans continue to assert their humanity when they find themselves up against authoritarian and neoliberal states that speak the language of mirage? While there is a particular rhetoric of African humanism that has been advanced by African leaders and intellectuals, the lived reality of ordinary Africans is often quite the opposite of such declarations. This paradox is most evident when we look at the record of human rights in Africa, particularly the translation (or not) of human rights in the lives of the majority of African people – demonstrated vividly by the manner in which Thabo Mbeki's government responded to the HIV and AIDS crisis in South Africa. In short, a paradox appears to shadow the ideal of humanism as lived and experienced by ordinary human beings.

Third, to what extent can the presently constructed Western discourse on human rights be reconciled with an African humanist philosophy? Are the prevailing notions of 'human rights' and the entire human rights discourse inextricably linked to neoliberal imperialist interests and the objective of advancing Western political liberal democracy? Or is Ubuntu a means by which Africans can redefine the relevance of human rights to an African context and reassert their humanity in a dehumanising world? I begin with the first of these three questions.

Curating African humanism (Ubuntu)

Elusiveness and contestation surround definitions of Ubuntu in particular and African humanism in general. The work of Christian Gade (2011: 307–8) on the historiography of the concept of Ubuntu prior to 1980 illustrates its varied interpretations and meanings. Some have defined Ubuntu to mean 'human quality' and 'humanness'. Others have referred to Ubuntu as a philosophy or 'ethics' (Ramose 1998), a world view and value system. It is broadly encapsulated in the often-repeated maxim of the Nguni peoples of South Africa, *'umuntu ngumuntu ngabantu'* – that is, a person is a person through other persons. For the purposes of this chapter, I adhere to the generalised definition that Ubuntu or African humanness/humanism is a philosophical world view that emanates values and principles about human beings, their modes of interaction and their relationship to one another. It includes the natural and spiritual world. The terms 'Ubuntu' and 'African humanism' are used interchangeably, but it must be recognised that Ubuntu is a profoundly southern African manifestation, although it shares some parallels with the articulation of African humanism in other African contexts. Among the commonly agreed upon values and principles enshrined in this philosophy of Ubuntu or African humanism are: interdependence, dignity, self-respect, respect for others, co-operation or communalism, forgiveness, sharing and equality.

While accepting this broad definition, one must avoid an essentialist concept of humanism (Gibson 2011: 201–2), for Ubuntu must be defined by communities of human beings who constantly give it relevance and meaning in relation to their own lives.

On Heritage Day, 24 September 2005, President Mbeki made the following reference to Ubuntu in his speech:

> A close examination of the central tenets of the values that drive the behaviour and approach of the Afrikaner, Indian and Jewish communities reveal that there are many elements that are consistent with the value-system of Ubuntu . . . However, *we have not done enough to articulate and elaborate on what Ubuntu means as well as promoting this important value-system* in a manner that should define the *unique identity of South Africans*. Indeed, there has not been a campaign to ensure that *Ubuntu becomes synonymous with being South African* . . . Clearly, we have a responsibility to utilise the many positive attributes of Ubuntu to build a non-racial, non-sexist and united South Africa. We also have to use to better effect the values and ethos of Ubuntu in our Moral Regeneration Campaign (Mbeki 2005, emphasis added).

Contrary to Mbeki, my argument is that Ubuntu is not unique to the identity of South Africans and that there are striking historical parallels between Ubuntu in a specifically South African context and the African humanism we find in other parts of the African continent. For example, during the euphoria of nationalist independence, Kwame Nkrumah referred to it as 'philosophical consciencism'; Léopold Sédar Senghor upheld *négritude* and African socialism; Kenneth Kaunda referred to 'Zambian humanism'; Julius Nyerere coined 'Ujamaa' and in Zimbabwe, the Samkanges referred to Hunhuism during the 1980s (Gade 2011: 306). In short, all these earlier definitions of African humanism, narrated through what Gade, following Leonhard Praeg (2000), aptly describes as 'narratives of return' (304), are embedded in cultural precepts, norms and orientations of the precolonial period that provide a philosophical paradigm for the creation of a future society. Viewed as narratives, they allow us to curate the various meanings that African humanism has assumed over historical time and in different contexts. It is therefore useful to examine the interpretations of African humanism in the writings of Nkrumah, Nyerere and Kaunda.[2]

In the wake of political independence, Nkrumah characterised African society as comprising three 'segments': the 'traditional way of life', 'the presence of the Islamic tradition in Africa' and 'the infiltration of the Christian tradition and culture of Western Europe into Africa that used colonialism and neo-colonialism as its primary vehicles' (1964: 68). The traditional, Islamic and Euro-Christian – or what Ali Mazrui (2004) refers to as 'the triple heritage' – coexisted with 'competing ideologies' that threatened harmony and societal social cohesion. (In certain African countries today, for example, Sudan, Mali, Mauritania and Nigeria, these 'segments' continue to generate acute conflicts among diverse communities.) Nkrumah believed: 'In the traditional African society, no sectional interest could be regarded as supreme; nor did legislative and executive power aid the interests of any particular group. The welfare of the people was supreme' (1964: 69). The 'traditional African society' was, in Nkrumah's view, centred on the human being who was part of a clan and community in which all were equal and responsibility and welfare were collectively upheld and revered. The individual was not only a spiritual being, but also possessed 'dignity, integrity and value' (68). Relations between individuals were essentially socialist (69) and therefore Nkrumah considered capitalism 'irreconcilable with those basic principles which animate the traditional African society. Capitalism is unjust; in our newly independent countries it is not only too complicated to be workable, it is also alien' (76). For Nkrumah, 'under socialism, however, the study and mastery of nature has *a humanist impulse*, and is directed not towards a profiteering accomplishment, but the affording of ever-increasing satisfaction for the material and spiritual needs of the greatest number' (emphasis added). It appears that for Nkrumah, humanism, communalism and socialism were antithetical to greed and the exploitation of human beings because as an ideology or philosophy, African humanism was orientated towards fulfilling the needs of human beings.

For Nkrumah, the intrusion of colonialism, with its economic and political subjugation of African people, meant that 'a new harmony needs to be forged, a harmony that will allow the combined presence of traditional Africa, Islamic Africa and Euro-Christian Africa, *so that this presence is in tune with the original humanist principles underlying African society*' (1964: 70, emphasis added). To reiterate, the humanist principles Nkrumah refers to that should be mobilised in forging a contemporary African society include an emphasis on the welfare of the collective, as opposed to the advancement of the individual, and the prioritising of dignity, integrity, equality and the value of each individual:

Our society is not the old society, but a new society enlarged by Islamic and Euro-Christian influences. A new emergent ideology is therefore required, an ideology which can solidify in a philosophical statement, but at the same time *an ideology which will not abandon the original humanist principles of Africa*. Such a philosophical statement will be born out of the crisis of the African conscience confronted with the three strands of present African society. Such a philosophical statement I propose to name *philosophical consciencism*, for it will give the theoretical basis for an ideology whose aim shall be to contain the African experience of Islamic and Euro-Christian presence as well as the experience of the traditional African society, and, by gestation, employ them for the harmonious growth and development of that society (Nkrumah 1964: 70, emphasis added).

The decade of the 1960s witnessed the rise of socialist experiments around the globe and the term 'African socialism' was increasingly employed by some African leaders to describe this new kind of postcolonial African society. Senghor and Nyerere are most closely associated with the term and, erroneously, so is Nkrumah. In 'African Socialism Revisited', Nkrumah critiques the concept of 'African socialism' and Senghor's use of the term and writes that it 'tends to obscure our fundamental socialist commitment' (1972: 443). Moreover, it is a term imbued with a dangerous nostalgia and oversimplification. As Nkrumah has often been incorrectly associated with the concept of 'African socialism', it is important to cite him directly:

Today the phrase 'African Socialism' seems to espouse the view that *the traditional African society was a classless society imbued with the spirit of humanism* and to express a nostalgia for that spirit. Such a conception of socialism makes a fetish of the communal African society. But an idyllic, African classless society (in which there were no rich and no poor) enjoying a drugged serenity is certainly a facile simplification; there is no historical or even anthropological evidence for any such society . . . All available evidence from the history of Africa up to the eve of the European colonisation, shows that African society was neither classless nor devoid of a social hierarchy. Feudalism existed in some parts of Africa before colonisation; and feudalism involves a deep and exploitative social stratification, founded on the ownership of land (1972: 440, emphasis added).

For Nkrumah, the precolonial era was not 'an African Golden Age or paradise' and therefore 'a return to the pre-colonial African society is evidently not worthy of the ingenuity and efforts of our people'. However, as an African nationalist, he also recognises that

> all this notwithstanding, one could still argue that the basic organisation of many African societies in different periods of history manifested a certain communalism and that *the philosophy and humanist purposes behind that organisation are worthy of recapture*. A community in which each saw his well-being in the welfare of the group certainly was praiseworthy, even if the manner in which the well-being of the group was pursued makes no contribution to our purposes. Thus, *what socialist thought in Africa must recapture is not the structure of the 'traditional African society' but its spirit, for the spirit of communalism is crystallised in its humanism and in its reconciliation of individual advancement with group welfare*. Even if there is incomplete anthropological evidence *to reconstruct the 'traditional African society' with accuracy, we can still recapture the rich human values of that society* (1972: 441, emphasis added).

Nkrumah raises an important question for us: How do Africans in the twenty-first century recapture the spirit of humanism imbued in past 'traditional communities' and reconcile it with economic advancement, in order to address the current challenges of neocolonialism, imperialism and neoliberalism on the African continent? Is the reconciliation of 'individual advancement with group welfare' that Nkrumah refers to, reconcilable with Western individualism or in tension with it?

Nkrumah emphasises the egalitarian principles on which the 'traditional African society' was founded and insists that 'any meaningful humanism must begin from egalitarianism and must lead to objectively chosen policies for safeguarding and sustaining egalitarianism. Hence, socialism. Hence, also, scientific socialism' (1972: 442). He does not advocate a return to an idyllic communalistic past which, in his view, never existed and which he chastised African socialists (and Senghor in particular) for advocating. According to Nkrumah, 'we know that the "traditional African society" was founded on principles of egalitarianism. In its actual workings, however, it had various shortcomings' (441). Nkrumah does not elaborate on these shortcomings, but insists that 'its humanist impulse, nevertheless, is something that continues to urge us towards our all-African socialist reconstruction'. He argues:

The way out is certainly not to regurgitate all Islamic or Euro-colonial influences in a futile attempt to recreate a past that cannot be resurrected. The way out is only forward, forward to a higher and reconciled form of society, *in which the quintessence of the human purposes of traditional African society reassert itself* in a modern context – forward, in short, to socialism, through policies that are scientifically devised and correctly applied (1972: 443, emphasis added).

Nkrumah considers socialism to be a restitution of the humanist values of Africa's past. He calls for a social revolution in Africa, of which an intellectual revolution would be a prerequisite – '[a] revolution in which our thinking and philosophy are directed towards the redemption of our society' (1964: 78). Furthermore, he argues:

The philosophy that must stand behind this social revolution is that which I have once referred to as philosophical consciencism; consciencism is the map in intellectual terms of the disposition of forces which will enable African society to digest the Western and the Islamic and the Euro-Christian elements in Africa, and develop them in such a way that they fit into the African personality. *The African personality is itself defined by the cluster of humanist principles which underlie the traditional African society* (1964: 79, emphasis added).

Nyerere, a contemporary of Nkrumah, also considered the construction of a socialist society as congruent with the 'traditional' values of African humanism and communalism. Unlike Nkrumah, however, Nyerere defined himself as an African socialist and believed that 'there will even be variations of African Socialism' (1968: 18). In '*Ujamaa*: The Basis of African Socialism', Nyerere contends: 'Socialism, like democracy, is an attitude of mind. In a socialist society it is the socialist attitude of mind, and not the rigid adherence to a standard political pattern, which is needed to ensure that the people care for each other's welfare' (162). For Nyerere, socialism is inseparable from the achievement of human dignity, equality and equity – in short, what we can and do refer to as Ubuntu. Nyerere argues that 'a socialist society would seek to uphold human dignity everywhere; and however limited its capacity in this respect, it could never act in such a manner as to be itself responsible for the denial of any man's humanity' (5). For Nyerere (and Nkrumah), Karl Marx cannot be said to have invented socialism, 'for the universality of socialism does not imply a single, world-wide uniformity of social institutions, social habits, or social language' (3). Rather, Nyerere posits that 'traditional Tanzanian society had many socialist characteristics' (16) and that 'the people did not call themselves socialists, and they were not socialists by deliberate design. But all people were workers, there was no living off the sweat of others.' Furthermore, 'success in a socialist society will imply that a man has earned the respect, admiration, and love of his fellow citizens, by his desire to serve, and by the contribution he has made to the well-being of the community' (9).

Despite their significant ideological differences, we can say that for both Nyerere and Nkrumah, 'socialism involved building on the foundation of our past, and building also to our own design' (Nyerere 1968: 2). In January 1967, the 'Arusha Declaration', which enshrines the core principles of Nyerere's ideology, was published. Essentially it emphasises education for self-reliance and places the human being at the centre of socialist construction. Ujamaa and African socialism and the dignity of the human being became the most explicit systematisation of Nyerere's vision of a more humane and egalitarian society, premised on historical – that is, precolonial – African values.

While Nkrumah emphasises that African society has to 'remould' itself in a socialist direction so that 'the humanism of traditional African life reassert[s] itself in a modern technical community' (1972: 439), Nyerere takes a different stance on how the regeneration of these values was to be gained, by considering the family unit as the institutional basis upon which Ujamaa ('familyhood' in Kiswahili) would become the unit of social organisation of production in creating a socialist society. As Steven Metz argues:

> While allowing for some degree of technologically derived change, Nyerere argued that the institutions which first bred these old values must be recreated. In effect, he felt that changes in the social organisation of production could be *reversed* through will and leadership. Nkrumah, on the other hand, from the perspective of dialectical materialism, believed that change could be encouraged and channelled in a certain direction, but never reversed. While [Nkrumah] agreed that the ethics of African communalism remained valid, he felt that they would not re-emerge by copying the structures which originally produced them. For Nkrumah, only 'progressive' changes were real (1982: 383).

In the wake of political independence in 1964, Kaunda proclaimed humanism as the ideology of the newly formed nation-state of Zambia. Like Nkrumah and Nyerere, Kaunda (n.d.: 5) also drew substantially from the positive features of inclusivity inherent in 'traditional [African] community', which he defines as 'a mutual aid society . . . organised to satisfy the basic human needs of all its members and [in which], therefore, individualism was discouraged'. Kaunda captures the logic of the by-now-familiar '*umuntu ngumuntu ngabantu*' in the following argument:

> On a higher plane of human development the Common Man philosophy we would say is a question of doing the right thing to a fellow human being simply because he was human and one is supposed to serve one's fellow men. On a lower or more selfish level – better still on a more understandable and appreciable level, in human terms – the question could simply be IT COULD BE YOU in that unfortunate position (n.d.: 33).

Intrinsic to 'Zambian humanism' was a profound religious belief and commitment to social morality. Kaunda's contemporaries, Nkrumah and Nyerere, also emphasised the spiritual and social dimensions of humanism in Africa. As a Christian humanist, Kaunda did not believe that the teachings of the Christian faith were its monopoly. As he puts it:

> I take with the utmost seriousness, the power of every great religion to inspire it its followers the highest qualities. Our nation badly needs such qualities which are not necessarily inherent in any political philosophy, even nationalism . . . so Zambian humanism which makes the welfare of Man the central aim of national policy invites all religious believers to harness the power inherent in their faith for socially desirable ends. Humanism is neither anti-religious, nor some super religion (in Dillon-Malone 1989: 20).

Kaunda defines humanism as 'a political philosophy which endeavours to devise a social, political and economic order which is based on Man's truth rather than on Man's untruth' (n.d.: 4). As such, it is a philosophy that seeks 'to rid this world of the evils of capitalism, imperialism, colonialism, neo-colonialism, fascism and racism on the one hand, and poverty, hunger, ignorance, disease, crime and the exploitation of man by man on the other' (n.d.: 5). Yet, in the world view of Kaunda and his contemporary male nationalists, it appears that patriarchial domination was somehow not understood as a form of exploitation that also needed to be confronted – just as much of the contemporary Ubuntu discourse seems to celebrate our 'shared humanity' by obscuring the tensions and fissures in society between men and women, young and old, homosexual and heterosexual.

Kaunda recognised some tensions in this philosophy when, in 1964, he posed the following pertinent question: 'How does an individual in Zambia today remain mutual aid society-minded and at the same time function in a society that is emerging from a so-called economy which has been born out of capitalism?' Similarly, he questions: 'How do we preserve what is good in our traditions, and at the same time allow ourselves to benefit from the science and technology of our friends from both the West and the East' (n.d.: 9)? Again, he claims:

> This high valuation of MAN and respect for human dignity which is a legacy of our tradition should not be lost in the new Africa. However, 'modern' and 'advanced' in a Western sense this young nation of Zambia may become, we are fiercely determined that this humanism will not be obscured (n.d.: 32).

These questions of how Africa and Africans can acquire material and technological progress, as opposed to materialism, while preserving the principles of African humanism remain very relevant to human beings in general and to postcolonial Africa in particular. Another pertinent question relates to what sense we should make of the manner in which Ubuntu has been co-opted by management theory under 'Ubuntu capitalism' (McDonald 2010: 143), not only in South Africa, but also elsewhere on the African continent. Currently the discourse on Ubuntu in South Africa is devoid of any link with socialism despite the fact that African humanism was linked to socialism during the nationalist era of the 1960s. The current neoliberal order and ethos that prevails on the African continent is a wholly different ideological climate than it was during the Cold War of the 1960s, in which capitalism was ideologically challenged by socialism. So the question we must pose to the contemporary discourse on Ubuntu is whether its incorporation into management theory amounts to being co-opted or whether it is, as some claim, a form of humanised capitalism, a form of emancipatory praxis.

Either way, the legacy of this humanism is complex. Like Mbeki, Kaunda considered Zambian humanism unique. Kaunda also envisioned that this humanism should inform the caring role of the state:

Zambia can say with pride that its humanism is original, based very much on the importance of Man. *In this case the State cares for Man, the Person. He, in return, as an individual will, or at least is expected to, care for his neighbour* . . . The oft-declared principles of non-tribalism, non-racialism, no discrimination based on religion and creed is very much part of the principles embodied in the importance of the Common Man (n.d.: 12, emphasis added).

However, the litany of experiences in Africa in the decades that followed independence, were to reveal the diametrical opposite of a caring state. That 'non-tribalism' was advocated by nationalist leaders of the 1960s did not prevent countries such as Nigeria, the Democratic Republic of the Congo, Uganda, Burundi, Sudan, Mali and others from descending into bloody ethnic conflicts in the wake of independence, conflicts marred by the most extreme, unimaginable and inhumane forms of violence. How is this contradiction between a humanist philosophy and inhumane politics to be explained?

A troubling development in the era of physical decolonisation was the creeping authoritarianism in these new countries, bound to what Basil Davidson critically refers to as the 'burden' of 'the nation-statist project' (1992: 197) – a rejection of traditional African self-governing institutions with the embrace of the European/ Westphalia project of nation-statism. This was as a result of the fact that 'the fifty or so states of the colonial partition, each formed and governed as though their peoples possessed no history of their own, became fifty or so nation-states formed and governed on European models, chiefly the models of Britain and France' (10). In short, 'liberation thus produced its own denial. Liberation led to alienation.' This alienation played out in various ways. While Nyerere sought via Ujamaa to restore the sense of family as new social unit of production, he also later embraced 'developmentalist authoritarianism' (Cooper 2002: 89), as did Senghor, Nkrumah and many other African leaders of this era. Mazrui (2004: 22) summarises this contradiction by considering Nkrumah's legacy as one of 'positive Nkrumahism' – Nkrumah as one of the indisputable architects of pan-Africanism – and 'negative Nkrumahism' because of his introduction of the template of authoritarian rule via the one-party state.

But this Manichean dichotomisation of Nkrumah is simplistic. Like any other leader, Nkrumah needs to be understood as more than a two-dimensional figure, for as Marx states: 'Men make their own history. But they do not make it just as they please; they do not make it under circumstances chosen by themselves, but under given circumstances directly encountered, given and transmitted from the past' (1882: 15). Mazrui's dualism does not enable us to thoroughly interrogate the complexities, paradoxes and tensions in Nkrumah's thought and performance as a political leader in the context in which he acted. Intellectual nuances are not made possible in such cast-iron characterisations. For instance, in the context of Cold War animosities of the 1960s, countries such as Ghana, Tanzania, Guinea and many others embraced national unity against the threat of internal ethnic cleavages, in addition to having to economically 'develop' their societies. With populations that were barely literate and lacking infrastructure, the models of capitalism and socialism were the only models on offer to these emerging nation-states. There was an acute sense of urgency to catch up with the West in terms of economic development. It is in such competitive material circumstances – both global and national – that African leaders made ideological choices and in which they had very little choice *to make these choices work*. While Mazrui argues that Ghana established the template of authoritarian, single-party rule, other African countries, such as Guinea-Conakry, Mali, Côte d'Ivoire and many others were simultaneously grappling with similar problems of creating national cohesiveness from diverse ethnic groups, without dismantling the state structures they had inherited from the former colonial masters (Biney 2011). Consequently, it can be argued that these newly emerging states, out of necessity, found themselves reinforcing the authoritarian state structures they had inherited. The combination of systemically flawed postcolonial states and highly competitive geo-politics explains the top-down features of 'philosophical consciencism', the 'Arusha Declaration', 'African Socialism', 'Zambian humanism' and *négritude* as ideologies that buttressed an increasingly authoritarian state which, presenting itself as a reflection of the popular will, in reality had very little input, if any, from the popular masses.

Similarly, Mbeki's 2005 address on Heritage Day, in which he stated that South Africans should 'better effect the values and ethos of Ubuntu in our Moral Regeneration Campaign', was originally conceived in a similar top-down or ideological fashion before it became a movement that later sought to partner with civil society organisations, particularly faith-based organisations. How ordinary South Africans were to become actively involved in moral regeneration via the revival of the spirit of Ubuntu became a key problem of the campaign as crime, child rape and domestic violence against women increased. In the context of

South Africa, as elsewhere on the continent, state-led initiatives to promulgate the principles of African humanism, either ideologically or philosophically, proved difficult because a programme of action, principles and values are not clearly stated and there is a lack of implementation mechanisms. In other words, we can argue that similar to the South African state under Nelson Mandela and Mbeki, Nkrumah, Nyerere and Kaunda upheld the Platonic notion that the role of the state was to create the necessary environment for the cultivation of humanism and that the top-down approach of implementing pan-Africanism, humanism or socialism failed – and continues to fail – to decentralise democratically at a grassroots level, which then manifests as authoritarianism, rather than there being something intrinsically coercive about African humanism or socialism. Either way, the paradox of the uncaring neocolonial and neoliberal postcolonial state needs a closer look.

Humanising the postcolonial, neocolonial and neoliberal state?

For the ordinary people of Africa, both the colonial and post-independent experiences have been replete with brutalities that fly in the face of the philosophy and practice of African humanism/Ubuntu. For example, since formal independence, Sudan (before it divided into two separate countries in 2011), the Democratic Republic of Congo, Angola and Mozambique have been engaged in civil wars that have cost millions of lives and created millions of refugees living in dehumanising conditions; the Hutu-led government of Rwanda referred to Tutsis as 'cockroaches' in the climate of manufactured animosity that preceded and supposedly legitimated the 1994 genocide, which killed more than 800 000 people. The amputees of Liberia and Sierra Leone (and also the survivors of land-mines in Angola and Mozambique) are evidence of inflicted cruelties by fellow human beings; the president of Sudan, Omar al-Bashir threatened in mid-2012 to rescue the people of South Sudan from a government that he described as one comprising 'insects'. Of course, this dehumanisation of human beings by other human beings is not exclusive to Africa. Humanism, the principles and values of egalitarianism, co-operation, human dignity, respect and the well-being of the community, has coexisted with dehumanisation throughout history – from the British scalping of the heads of Native Americans under King George III, in order to physically occupy and dominate the New World of North America and European enslavement and colonialism, which subjugated three-quarters of non-European peoples around the world. 'Lesser' human beings have been defined as such by those with the power to define and subjugate others. Aimé Césaire famously argued that Hitler's crime was that 'he applied to Europe colonialist procedures which until then had been reserved exclusively for the Arabs of Algeria, the "coolies" of India, and the "niggers" of Africa' in the clinical and methodical gas chambers that killed almost 6 million Jews (1955: 36). Japanese colonialism in Asia was punctuated by the almost-forgotten rape of Nanking in December 1937, when more than 300 000 Chinese civilians and soldiers were systematically raped, murdered and tortured. The slaughter of the Khmer Rouge in Cambodia is yet another among the plentiful examples of human savagery across societies, time and space. What remains particular about the pernicious legacies of the experience of enslavement and colonialism, though, has been the insidious impact of continued racism in the dehumanisation and racialisation of African people and the prolonged conscious and unconscious treatment, perceptions and attitudes that allowed and continue to allow for Africans to be treated as semi-animals without historical agency.

The obvious violence of racism was one part of the legacy of colonialism. Another part of its legacy was the inheritance of the repressive structures of the colonial apparatus – a judiciary, police force, army and educational system that underwent 'Africanisation'. As European civil servants departed with generous pension schemes, Africans replaced them without a fundamental dismantling of these institutions or only half-hearted attempts to re-orientate them. Over time, the colonial state in Africa metamorphosed into the neocolonial state that 'has the outward trappings of international sovereignty', but 'in reality its economic system and thus its political policy is directed from outside' (Nkrumah 1965: ix). The neocolonial state in Africa has become the instrument through which avarice and corruption via what has invariably been characterised as neo-patrimonialism, clientalism and state patronage linked with nepotism in 'a dogfight for the spoils of political power' (Davidson 1992: 207). A minority has engorged themselves, while others die of hunger. Is it possible to humanise the existing neocolonial state and, if so, how? What social forces could contribute to such a project of rehumanising?

The decade of the 1980s saw structural adjustment programmes imposed on many African countries by the Bretton Woods institutions, accompanied in the late 1990s by an insistence on adhering to multiparty democracy and respect for human rights, as these new conditionalities were attached to aid and loans. Such policies led to many African states withdrawing the provision of health and education – services formerly provided by the post-independent states during the decades of the 1960s and 1970s.

Lack of access to health services and lack of money to purchase such services have prematurely taken the lives of many Africans in the last few decades. The commercialisation of these services – including electricity and water – continues to threaten the possibility of a humane existence for the vast majority of African people. The maximisation of profit and the allocation of all services and goods to the market prevails, while African farmers – the vast majority of Africa's people who cannot compete with the agricultural subsidies granted to farmers in the richer countries of the North – have their livelihoods destroyed by the invisible hand of the market. Alfred B. Zack-Williams argues that, 'for many rural Africans, the state has had little or no relevance, as it failed to provide security of any form of social citizenship' (2012: 2). As Tajudeen Abdul-Raheem graphically illustrates:

> Indeed, we should regard public officials and their private sector collaborators as mass murderers, killing millions of our peoples through inadequate public services compromised by corruption. Monies meant for drugs, roads, hospitals, schools and public security are siphoned away, making all of us vulnerable to premature death and our societies more unsafe and insecure for the masses (2010: 22).

Against this empirical materiality, African humanism will continue to be considered as a meaningless intellectual pastime, as long as it does not translate into improving the lives of ordinary people in a genuine quest for emancipation from poverty and oppression in various forms. In other words, the definitions of Ubuntu or African humanism remain on the normative level – that is, they concern what one would like to see in reality and not as reality actually operates in the lives of ordinary people, particularly not in relation to the state. The conceptual contributions of Amartya Sen on 'capability' and freedom are relevant here. For, if 'capability reflects a person's freedom to choose between different ways of living' (Sen 2006: 440), there is the reality that most Africans do not have such a freedom to choose and the government is often responsible for the lack of freedom in the lives of ordinary people. While African political parties often acquire their very mandate and legitimacy from the promise to improve the material living conditions of the poor, the reality is that they fail to deliver and consequently dehumanise the citizens who have voted for them by this failure to provide the conditions for a basic standard of living. Therefore in trying to understand and define African humanism, we must distinguish the abstract phenomenon – however defined – as what we would like to see from what actually exists in the lives of ordinary people subjected to their relationship with the African state and with each other.

This discrepancy between the assumed relevance of African humanism as a political and identity construct and its complete lack in political practice is clearly illustrated in two cases: the dumping of toxic waste in Côte d'Ivoire in 2006 and the response of the Mbeki government between 1999 and 2004 to the HIV and AIDs pandemic in South Africa. In both cases, the failure of the state to respond to human needs illustrates the abstract nature of African humanism/Ubuntu as it relates to the lived experiences of the African masses.

On 20 August 2006, the inhabitants of Abidjan awoke to a noxious smell from waste that had been dumped in locations around the city. Widespread panic emerged as people experienced acute breathing difficulties, headaches and nausea, among other symptoms. Local hospitals and health centres were quickly overstretched in dealing with the crisis and treated more than 100 000 people. Between fifteen and seventeen people died. A three-year investigation by Amnesty International and Greenpeace led to exposure of the cause of the tragedy: Trafigura (a multinational oil-trading company based in the United Kingdom) chartered a cargo ship, the *Probo Koalo*, to dump its toxic waste in Abidjan. Trafigura was aware that the waste should have been disposed of in city dumps or legally shipped out of the Netherlands. Instead, it illegally exported the waste from the Netherlands to Abidjan. According to Greenpeace and Amnesty International:

> On 13th February 2007 Trafigura and the government of Côte d'Ivoire reached a settlement, under which Trafigura agreed to pay the state of Côte d'Ivoire the sum of CFA95 billion (approximately US$195 million), and the government waived its right to prosecution or mount an action against the company. Neither Trafigura nor any of its executives were brought to trial in Côte d'Ivoire. Ultimately, only two individuals were convicted by a court in Abidjan: Salomon Ugborogbo, the head of Compagnie Tommy, and Essoin Kouao, a shipping agent from West African International Business Services (WAIBS).[3]

The amount that was finally agreed upon between the two parties on 23 September 2009 was US$45 million for 30 000 victims. However, to date only 6 000 victims have received some compensation and several thousand have not received any funds at all from the compensation fund set up by the Ivorian government. Furthermore:

Despite some action by the states involved to investigate and sanction those who were involved in the dumping of the toxic waste, the victims have not seen justice done. The central actor – Trafigura – has evaded all but a limited Dutch prosecution and the UK civil action. The truth about what happened has never fully come to light. Adequate compensation has not reached all of the victims. The circumstances that allowed more than 100,000 people to experience the horror of getting sick from an unknown toxic waste dumped where they live and work continue to exist.[4]

The second example of state indifference to the plight of vulnerable individuals is demonstrated by the position of President Mbeki's government on HIV and AIDS between 1999 and 2004 – an example that is all the more sinister given the central role Mbeki played in spearheading the so-called African Renaissance, with its promise of reviving an African ethics of care and shared humanity. Mbeki's position was that there was no direct causal link between HIV and AIDS – that HIV does not lead to AIDS. He was of the opinion that HIV and AIDS were simply diseases, in the same vein as tuberculosis and malaria; that condom use did not prevent AIDS and, critically, that poverty was at the centre of South Africa's health problems (Gumede 2007: 187–217). This position caused considerable uproar within South Africa among those suffering from HIV and AIDS, while the Treatment Action Campaign also mobilised for state provision of antiretroviral drugs for South Africans afflicted with the disease. Relevant for our purposes here is the callousness of the government, reflected in the statement by the minister of finance, Trevor Manuel, who stated at a meeting of the committee tasked with investigating the feasibility of a basic income grant: 'It does not make financial sense to spend money on people dying anyway, who are not even productive in the first place' (201). It appears Manuel's sentiments were shared by other elements within Mbeki's government, for

in June 2003, Mbeki's media spokesman, Parks Mankahlana, asked in an interview with *Science* magazine: 'Who is going to look after the orphans of AIDS mothers, the state?' The clear implication was that prevention of mother-to-child transmission of HIV would be counterproductive, since the children saved would end up as welfare cases in any event (Gumede 2007: 202).

The inhumane position of the Mbeki government continued at the same time that many died from lack of access to antiretroviral drugs. Meanwhile, it transpired in October 2001, during question time in Parliament, that several African National Congress (ANC) Members of Parliament were accessing antiretroviral drugs through their state medical aid (Gumede 2007: 207).

Economics finally forced Mbeki to shift his uncompromising position around March 2002. According to Gumede, 'members of his international investment council warned him at roughly the same time as the NEC meeting [of March 2002] that investors found the confusion over the government's approach to the disease unsettling, if not downright frightening' (2007: 210). A month later, when the Cabinet met, it was agreed that antiretroviral drugs would be made immediately available to pregnant women and rape survivors. Two weeks before the elections of April 2004, the drugs were rolled out to HIV and AIDS sufferers at state hospitals. While applauding the outcome, the Treatment Action Campaign and other AIDS activists also questioned the government's timing and motives.

In the present political and ideological climate of the African continent, a striking observation is that unlike the nationalist leaders who were swept into office by their promises of eliminating colonial rule, job creation via Africanisation programmes, eradication of disease and ignorance, building roads, schools and hospitals, Africa's contemporary leaders have capitulated to neoliberalism and neocolonialism in the wake of TINA ('there is no alternative'), while lacking the political will to adjust state policy along welfare-oriented lines, as is happening in Venezuela and Bolivia (which are seriously addressing mass poverty). What is now needed in most of these countries is a fundamental social (as opposed to political) revolution, the so-called second transition. The African state needs to be wholly reconfigured in a manner that it is controlled by its citizens towards an agenda that is genuinely people-centred and fundamentally anti-imperialist (Ake 1996: 132). This necessitates the establishment of a new relation between citizens and the state, in which the people exercise political agency and possess genuine decision-making power over economic issues in decentralised democratic structures (Fanon 1961). One way to conceive of this *real* revolution is to ask whether political rights or an induction into a global discourse on human rights has served Africa as well as the elite – who have benefited from the political transitions – like to say that they have. On face value, human rights discourse embraces a powerful and radical potential by asserting the innate dignity and equal worth of every human being and, as such, could be conceived as opening up the possibility of interrogating an emancipatory praxis of humanism. On the other hand, it is necessary to question the extent to which the discourse on human rights conceals beneath a mask of universalism and immutability a Trojan horse of imperialist hegemony that originates in the West and promotes its interests.

Can a Western notion of 'human rights' be reconciled with African humanism?
The human rights discourse and movement, with its genesis in the Western world, is far from non-ideological or non-political (Mutua 2002; Shivji 1989; Ake 1987). Underpinning the discourse are very specific concepts of the individual, the minimal state with its limited role and responsibilities and the functioning of society, politics and economics. The hegemonic capacity of the discourse lies in the fact that 'the establishment of hegemony requires the silencing or marginalizing not only of other ideas, but also of other ways and other processes of thinking' (Gibson 2011: 107). The paradox of the universalisation of human rights is evident in the grand narrative enshrined in the Universal Declaration of Human Rights of 1948 – embedded as it is in the historical specificities of European norms and jurisprudence – that conceals and perpetuates the 'savages, victims and saviors metaphor' as articulated by Makau Mutua (2002: 15) and elaborated on below. In essence, 'human rights ideology is an ideology of domination and part of the imperialist world outlook' (Shivji 1989: 5). Both Mutua and Issa Shivji provide salient critiques of the human rights discourse as it relates to Africa.

Mutua's critique of the ideological edifice of the prevailing human rights corpus unveils a language of domination and powerful interest groups (foreign-funded non-governmental organisations in Africa, international human rights organisations and local non-governmental organisations) who have vested interests in maintaining the 'Othering' of non-European cultures and peoples. According to Mutua, 'although the human rights movement arose in Europe, with the express purpose of containing European savagery, it is today a civilising crusade aimed primarily at the Third World' (2002: 19). He argues:

> Thus human rights rejects cross-fertilization of cultures and instead seeks the transformation of non-Western cultures by Western cultures. To the official guardians and custodians of human rights – the United Nations, Western governments, and senior Western scholars and human rights activists – calls by non-Westerners for the multicultural reconstruction of

human rights are blasphemous. Such calls are demonized as the hypocritical cries of cultural relativists, an evil species of humans who are apologists for savage cultures. What the guardians and custodians seek is the remaking of non-Europeans into little dark, brown, and yellow Europeans – in effect dumb copies of the original. This view of human rights re-entrenches and revitalizes the international hierarchy of race and color in which whites, who are privileged globally as a race, are the models and saviors of non-whites, who are the victims and savages (2002: 155).

In addition, there is the often-implicit assumption that the enforcement of human rights requires a particular form of democracy – liberal political democracy and its accompanying export of the theology of free market economics (Mutua 2002: 12). Such a perspective is devoid of any historical or cultural understanding of African realities and is mostly premised on advocating that liberal political and economic democracy can be grafted on to any society in the same way as the 'civilising mission' of the nineteenth century was premised on the unquestioning belief that the three 'Cs' of (Western) Christianity, Civilisation and Commerce would conquer savages.

The cultural precepts upon which traditional African society is centred, as noted above, are based on obligations to other members, rather than claims against them. They are constructed on collectivism and harmony as opposed to divergent interests, competition or conflict. As Ake points out:

> The idea of human rights, or legal rights in general, presupposes a society which is atomized and individualistic, a society of endemic conflict. It presupposes a society of people conscious of their separateness and their particular interests and anxious to realise them. The legal right is a claim which the individual may make against other members of the society, and simultaneously an obligation on the part of society to uphold this claim (1987: 5).

He contends that outside the urban areas of Africa, 'the phenomenon of the legal subject and human rights has not really developed, and those who are in a position to realise such rights are a minority' as they possess wealth and power (1987: 9–10). He further comments:

> The western notion of human rights stresses rights which are not very
> interesting in the context of African realities. There is much concern with
> the right to peaceful assembly, free speech and thought, fair trial, etc. The
> appeal of these rights is sociologically specific. They appeal to people with
> a full stomach who can now afford to pursue the more esoteric aspects of
> self-fulfilment. The vast majority of our people are not in this position.
> They are facing the struggle for existence in its brutal immediacy (1987: 5).

In essence, abstract legal rights associated with abstract individuals are likely to
make little sense to the consciousness of the woman or man in the Kenyan slums
of Kibera or to the young men scraping a living in the toxic computer dump
site of Agbogbloshie on the outskirts of Ghana's capital, Accra. The emphasis on
abstract political and civil rights in human rights scholarship and the human rights
movement tends to override other equally important rights, such as economic and
social rights. Ake argues that an African conception of human rights 'must include
among others, a right to work and to a living wage, a right to shelter, to health, to
education. That is the least we can strive for if we are ever going to have a society
which realises basic human needs' (1987: 10). In addition, there are the rights to
self-determination and development and the right to organise that have relevance
to a genuine emancipatory project for Africa (Shivji 1989: 81–7). 'The broad
masses have to regain and rebuild their organisational capacity mutilated by the
compradorial neo-colonial states,' argues Shivji (87). On a collective level, wholly
independent of the state, ordinary people must exercise the right to organise so
as to overturn the existing socio-economic and political order and construct a
state that serves their interests (84). These rights, identified by Ake and Shivji, are
essential to an anti-imperialist emancipatory praxis because human beings cannot
be free if they continue to be dominated by other human beings in new forms
of subordination and inferiorisation. Human beings must have the right to self-
definition. Yet, it appears that the prevailing construction of 'freedom' has been
turned into 'an instrument of oppression' (Monbiot 2011), in which people are
free to be poor; the rich have freedom to exploit the poor, while the banks are free
from regulation and the market is free to access the highest profits in the mythical
pursuit of 'trickle-down' growth. As David Harvey comments:

> It has been part of the genius of neoliberal theory to provide a benevolent
> mask full of wonderful-sounding words like freedom, liberty, choice, and

rights, to hide the grim realities of the restoration or reconstitution of naked class power, locally as well as trans-nationally, but most particularly in the main financial centres of global capitalism (2005: 119).

The way forward lies in genuine grassroots social movements, such as the shack-dwellers' movement of Abahlali baseMjondolo and others in South Africa, that are forging new definitions of humanism that demystify the language of both global capitalism and pseudo-Leftists (Gibson 2011: 201–2).

Some concluding questions

Timothy Kandeke contends: 'Humanism preserves selected values from the past, embodies convictions which grew up during the nationalist struggle, and adapts these principles to the problems of the present in order to give direction for the future' (1977: 212). If this is the case, we need to ask what these values are and how to adapt them to the problems of the present. Particularly, we need to consider how the forces of globalisation impact on African cultural expressions and values. If globalisation is a juggernaut of homogeneity at the levels of the political, economic, cultural and ideological, can it coexist with 'traditional Africa' or is 'traditional Africa' and its humanism obliterated by this juggernaut? To what extent will the hegemonic forces of globalisation deepen the divide between the 'haves' – who are considered human – and the dehumanised and invisible 'have-nots', who are expected to live on less than a dollar a day? African humanism or Ubuntu has been employed as part of a nation-building project not only during the post-independence era of Nkrumah, Nyerere, Kaunda and Senghor, but also in post-apartheid South Africa. In the context of Tanzania, Henry Bienen observes:

> Arusha, then, is not an excuse in ideology-making for its own sake or the acting out of one man's ideas. The function of the Arusha Declaration is to legitimize rule and to come to terms with conditions which are going to persist for some time. Arusha also provides a vision of a different and better future and it gives guidelines for achieving it (1972: 179).

Similarly, with the co-optation of Ubuntu by the South African state into, for example, the Truth and Reconciliation Commission, Ubuntu has become an intellectual philosophical discourse as well as part of South Africa's attempts to create a cohesive, unified society in the Christianised image of Archbishop Desmond

Tutu's 'rainbow nation of God'. But what role is there for Ubuntu, in South Africa and further afield, for driving a truly emancipatory politics?

To return to the point made at the beginning of this chapter with respect to the crisis confronting the African continent, which has both economic and political dimensions that are inextricably rooted in its colonial and postcolonial history, an equally important aspect of this crisis is the mental enslavement of African people and people of African descent. Addressing this mental disfigurement must surely be part of the project for human emancipation. In colluding in our subjugation, our ability to be ourselves and to fulfil our genuine potential is damaged and the status quo of deep-seated socio-economic and political inequalities remains intact. Steve Biko's point is pertinent here:

> The interrelationship between the consciousness of the self and the emancipatory programme is of paramount importance ... Liberation therefore is of paramount importance in the concept of Black Consciousness, for *we cannot be conscious of ourselves and yet remain in bondage*. We want to attain the envisioned self which is a free self (1978: 49, emphasis added).

Similarly, Paulo Freire (1996: 33) contends:

> One of the gravest obstacles to the achievement of liberation is that oppressive reality absorbs those within it and thereby acts to submerge human beings' consciousness. *Functionally, oppression is domesticating. To no longer be prey to its force, one must emerge from it and turn upon it. This can be done only by means of praxis: reflection and action upon the world in order to transform it* (1996: 33, emphasis added).

Africa requires a new type of emancipatory consciousness, which requires cultivating spaces (for example, in adult education in the community) in which people can think, question, exchange ideas, solve problems and continue to define what it means to be human in changing material and ideological circumstances. A critical humanism must involve a constant dialogue, reflection between theory and lived reality/practice, not only on the part of those inhabiting ivory towers, but also, surely, it must engage the 'wretched of the earth' in this empowering process? To cite Freire:

Attempting to liberate the oppressed without their reflective participation in the act of liberation is to treat them as objects which must be saved from a burning building; it is to lead them into the populist pitfall and transform them into masses which can be manipulated. *At all stages of liberation, the oppressed must see themselves as women and men engaged in the ontological and historical vocation of becoming more fully human.* Reflection and action become imperative when one does not erroneously attempt to dichotomize the content of humanity from its historical forms. *The insistence that the oppressed engage in reflection on their concrete situation is not a call to armchair revolution. On the contrary, reflection – true reflection – leads to action* (1996: 47, emphasis added).

Surely the starting point of any critical humanism must be to challenge, in order to end, 'the commodification of everything' (Harvey 2005: 165) – including human beings?

Notes

1. See http://www.goodreads.com/author/quotes/59710.Harriet_Tubman.
2. It is to be noted that much of the language of these three male nationalist leaders is submerged in the use of the patriarchal 'he' and the use of 'man' that was typical of the time.
3. See http://www.africafocus.org/docs12/tox1210.php.
4. See http://www.africafocus.org/docs12/tox1210.php.

References

Abdul-Raheem, T. 2010. 'Corrupt Leaders are Mass Murders'. In *Speaking Truth to Power Selected Pan-African Postcards*, compiled by A. Biney and A. Olukoshi, 20–22. Oxford: Pambazuka Press.

Ake, C. 1987. 'The African Context of Human Rights'. *Africa Today* 1st and 2nd Quarters: 5–12.

———. 1996. *Democracy and Development in Africa*. Washington, DC: Brookings Institution.

Amin, S. 1990. *Maldevelopment: An Anatomy of a Global Failure*. London: Zed Books.

Bienen, H. 1972. 'An Ideology for Africa'. In *Socialism in Tanzania, Vol. 1: Politics; An Interdisciplinary Reader*, ed. L. Cliffe and J. Saul, 178–9. Nairobi: East African Publishing House.

Biko, S. 1978. *Steve Biko, 1946–77: I Write What I Like*. London: Heinemann.

Biney, A. 2011. *The Political and Social Thought of Kwame Nkrumah*. New York: Palgrave Macmillan.

Césaire, A. 1955. *Discourse on Colonialism*. New York: Monthly Review Press.

Cooper, F. 2002. *Africa Since 1940: The Past of the Present*. Cambridge: Cambridge University Press.

Davidson, B. 1992. *The Black Man's Burden: Africa and the Curse of the Nation-State*. London: James Currey.

Dillon-Malone, C. 1989. *Zambian Humanism, Religion and Social Morality*. Ndola: Mission Press.

Fanon, F. 1961. *The Wretched of the Earth*. London: Penguin.

Freire, P. 1996. *Pedagogy of the Oppressed*. London: Penguin.

Gade, C. 2011. 'The Historical Development of the Written Discourses on *Ubuntu*'. *South African Journal of Philosophy* 30 (3): 303–29.

Gibson, N. 2011. *Fanonian Practices in South Africa: From Steve Biko to Abahlali baseMjondolo*. Pietermaritzburg: University of KwaZulu-Natal Press and New York: Palgrave Macmillan.

Gumede, W. 2007. *Thabo Mbeki and the Battle for the Soul of the ANC*. Cape Town: Zebra Press.

Harvey, D. 2005. *A Brief History of Neoliberalism*. Oxford: Oxford University Press.

Kandeke, T. 1977. *Fundamentals of Zambian Humanism*. Lusaka: National Educational Company of Zambia.

Kaunda, K. No date. *Humanism in Zambia and a Guide to its Implementation*. Lusaka: Zambia Information Services.

Marx, K. 1852. 'The Eighteenth Brumaire of Louis Bonaparte'. *Die Revolution*. Available at http://www.marxists.org/archive/marx/works/1852/18th-brumaire/.

Mazrui, A. 2004. *Nkrumah's Legacy and Africa's Triple Heritage: Between Globalization and Counter Terrorism*. Accra: Ghana University Press.

Mbeki, T. 2005. 'Address of the President of South Africa, Thabo Mbeki, on the Occasion of the Heritage Day Celebrations, Taung, North West Province on 24 September 2005'. Available at http://www.thepresidency.gov.za/pebble.asp?relid=3157.

Mbembe, A. 2001. *On the Postcolony*. Berkeley: University of California Press.

McDonald, D.A. 2010. 'Ubuntu Bashing: The Marketisation of "African Values" in South Africa'. *Review of African Political Economy* 37 (124): 139–52.

Metz, S. 1982. 'In Lieu of Orthodoxy: The Socialist Theories of Nkrumah and Nyerere'. *Journal of Modern African Studies* 20 (3): 377–92.

Monbiot, G. 2011. 'This Bastardised Libertarianism Makes "Freedom" an Instrument of Oppression'. *The Guardian*, 19 December. Available at http://www.guardian.co.uk/commentisfree/2011/dec/19/bastardised-libertarianism-makes-freedom-oppression.

Mutua, M. 2002. *Human Rights: A Political and Cultural Critique*. Philadelphia: University of Pennsylvania Press.

Nkrumah, K. 1964. *Consciencism: Philosophy and Ideology for Decolonization*. London: Panaf.

———. 1965. *Neo-Colonialism: The Last Stage of Imperialism*. London: Panaf.

———. 1972. 'African Socialism Revisited'. In *Revolutionary Path*, 438–45. London: Panaf.

Nyerere, J. 1968. *Freedom and Socialism: A Selection from Writings and Speeches 1965–1967*. Oxford: Oxford University Press.

Praeg, L. 2000. *African Philosophy and the Quest for Autonomy: A Philosophical Investigation*. Amsterdam: Rodopi.

Ramose, M.B. 1998. 'The Ethics of Ubuntu'. In *The African Philosophy Reader*, ed. P.H. Coetzee and A.P.J. Roux, 324–30. London: Routledge.

Sen, A. 2006. 'Development as Capability'. In *Capabilities, Freedom, and Equality: Amartya Sen's Work from a Gender Perspective*, ed. B. Agarwal, J. Humphries and I. Robeyns, 437–57. Oxford: Oxford University Press.

Shivji, I. 1989. *The Concept of Human Rights in Africa*. Dakar: CODESRIA.

Zack-Williams, A.B. 2012. 'Five Decades On: Some Reflections on 50 Years of Africa's Independence'. *Review of African Political Economy* 39 (131): 1–10.

CHAPTER 3

Ubuntu Versus the Core Values of the South African Constitution

Ilze Keevy

A version of this chapter first appeared in *Journal for Juridical Science* 2009 (2): 19–58 and is reprinted with permission.

In 1994, the Constitutional Court embarked, in classic Dworkinian style, on writing the first chapter of constitutional theory, according to Ronald Dworkin's metaphor of the chain novel.[1] As prescribed in Dworkin's *Law's Empire*, each chapter, though written by different judges, should fit into the next in such a way that it seems like the work of a single author (Van Blerk 2004: 92). In Chapter 1 of this imaginary chain novel, the Constitutional Court began to consider 'African law and legal thinking' and the values of ubuntu as part of the source of democratic values that section 35 of the 1993 Constitution (section 39 of the 1996 Constitution) required courts to promote.[2] Despite the fact that African jurisprudence was not researched for the deliberation on capital punishment in *S. v. Makwanyane and Another*, the promotion of African jurisprudence was part of the Constitutional Court's new democratic approach to jurisprudence.[3] The promotion of African jurisprudence was an essential step towards legitimising the Constitution for the new rainbow nation. In their new roles as 'social engineers and social and legal philosophers',[4] Constitutional Court judges introduced the jurisprudence of ubuntu in an effort 'for courts to develop the entrenched fundamental rights in terms of a cohesive set of values, ideal to an open and democratic society'.[5]

Chapter 1 of the Constitutional Court's chain novel reveals that '*ubuntu* is a shared value and ideal that runs like a golden thread across cultural lines' and that it has a 'universalistic ethos'.[6] Furthermore, '*ubuntu* is in consonance with the values of the Constitution in general and those of the Bill of Rights in particular' (Mokgoro 1998: 22).[7] If this is so, it implies a synergy between ubuntu and Western values (Bhengu 2006: 129), a synergy between values of one of the most progressive Constitutions in the world and ancient ubuntu values, which are not only 'central to age-old [African] custom and tradition' (128), but also inseparable from African religion (Ramose 2002: 93, 97).[8] Extralegal sources maintain that ubuntu constitutes the 'basis of African law' (Ramose 2002: 81; M'Baye 1974: 141); that ubuntu 'legal philosophy must be understood on the basis of the metaphysical' (Ramose 2002: 93) and that '*ubuntu* philosophy of law is the continuation of [African] religion' (97). Whereas ubuntu is said to be in consonance with the values of the Constitution in general and the Bill of Rights in particular, the Constitutional Court contends that African law is based on 'a deeply embedded patriarchy which reserved for women a position of subservience and subordination and in which they were regarded as perpetual minors under the tutelage of the fathers, husbands, or the head of the extended family'.[9]

While subsequent chapters of the chain novel have been consistent in producing 'a seamless text, one appearing to have been written by one author' (Van Blerk 2004: 92) on the 'prized value[s] of *ubuntu*' (Mokgoro 1998: 21), this chapter seriously questions the so-called synergy between the core values of the South African Constitution and ubuntu jurisprudence; it questions the humanitarian ideals of ubuntu (Bohler-Muller 2005: 278) and the statement that ubuntu is in consonance with the values of the Constitution generally and those of the Bill of Rights in particular. The aim of this chapter is to juxtapose ubuntu's shared beliefs and values with the core values of the South African Constitution, namely equality and human dignity.[10] In addition, it aims to show that individuals in ubuntu reality are not guaranteed equal rights and human dignity in its deeply embedded patriarchy.[11] As Sachs J. has pointed out, 'sexism and patriarchy are so ancient, all pervasive and incorporated into the practice of daily life as to appear socially and culturally normal and legally invisible'.[12] This chapter deconstructs ubuntu in the following terms: ubuntu as the basis of African law; ubuntu as ethnophilosophy; ubuntu and the oppression of women; ubuntu and the oppression of homosexuals, lesbians and witches; ubuntu, strangers and outsiders; ubuntu as African Constitution; and ubuntu and regional human rights mechanisms. This chapter concludes that ubuntu is *not* in consonance with the values of the Constitution in general and the Bill of Rights in particular.

Ubuntu as the basis of African law

Mogobe B. Ramose maintains that 'ubuntu is the basis of African law' (2002: 81; M'Baye 1974: 141). In order to assess whether ubuntu, as the basis of African law, is in line with the Constitution in general and the Bill of Rights in particular, this section deconstructs African law.

African law: A definition

African law is not codified customary law or official African customary law; it is uncodified living law, also known as living African customary law. Since precolonial times, African law has represented the oral tradition (Mutwa 1998).[13] As unwritten law, African law represents African oral culture, a meticulously preserved tradition, which is sacredly guarded and passed on by word of mouth from generation to generation. The fact that African law is unwritten does not mean that it is unknown or no longer practised (Ramose 2002: 97).

African law can be defined as unwritten 'rules of behaviour which are contained in the flow of life . . . the construction of communal life and resort to protection by supernatural forces as the basis of African law . . . [with] equilibrium, justice, harmony and peace the implicit aims of African law' (M'Baye 1974: 141). African law regulates the relationships between people in traditional African societies and consists of moral rules, which are handed down from generation to generation 'under the supervision of the initiated' or the ancestors (149).[14] The ancestors or living-dead are not only the authority behind African law, but also play a central role in preserving these male-dominated or patriarchal societies. Chukwuemeka Ebo states:

> The spirits of the ancestors also have their share of the stake and commitment
> in ensuring law is preserved intact against anything that would derogate
> from its plenitude of authority and control . . . the authority behind the
> law is so overwhelming as to make enforcement by means of a body of
> officials such as police unnecessary (1995: 39).

Ebo defines African law as a law not only for the living members of the clan or community, but a law also for its living-dead (1995: 145).[15] Furthermore, 'an act of rebellion against the legal status quo is regarded as odious and scandalous in the eyes of not only the living contemporaries but also of the ancestral spirits who perpetually hover around the edge of the community'. This inseparable symbiotic relationship between the living, the living-dead and African law illustrates why African law cannot be defined without incorporating the ancestors and African spirit world. Ramose describes this symbiotic relationship as follows:

Protection by supernatural forces constitutes the basis of African law . . . The constant communication between the living and the living dead (ancestors) speaks once again of the rheomodic character of African thought and law. In African thought, the triad of the living, the living dead and the yet-to-be born forms an unbroken and infinite chain of relations which are characteristically a one-ness and a wholeness at the same time . . . The authority of [African] law is justified by appeal to the living dead (2002: 94, 96).[16]

Jackton B. Ojwang defines African law as the unwritten law of tribal African societies, which reflects not only the social control systems and the cultural orientation of these societies, but also their shared values and beliefs (1995: 45). According to Ojwang, African law 'holds the seeds of local values and community morality' (56) and 'the laws of various [African] tribes have a considerable basis of uniformity' and rest upon face-to-face relations, mediation, conciliation and a common ideology shared by the people (44, 56). Like Ojwang, Ebo avers that certain principles of African law are common to all African societies, despite the fact that 'a panorama of indigenous law would appear as a kaleidoscope of shifting types' (1995: 139).[17] Credo Mutwa defines African law or the 'High Laws of the Bantu' as hundreds of commandments from the ancestors, which are 'common to all Bantu races in Southern, Central and East Africa' (1998: 624).[18] These sources confirm that certain principles, values and moral rules of African law are common throughout sub-Saharan Africa.

African law maintains the mystical and symbiotic relationship between the living and the living-dead and provides the theoretical support for the African belief in natural justice (Nduka 1995: 25).[19] Jack H. Driberg defines African law as follows:

African law is positive and not negative. It does not say 'Thou shalt not', but 'Thou shalt'. Law does not create offences, it does not create criminals; it directs how individuals in communities should behave towards each other. Its whole object is to maintain an equilibrium, and the penalties of African law are directed, not against specific infractions but to the restoration of this equilibrium (in Ramose 2002: 93).

African law maintains order, peace and equilibrium between communities and the spirit world (Tempels 1969: 123; Kamalu 1998: 89; Bhengu 2006: 13). As law for the living and the living-dead (Viljoen 2007: 304), African law maintains the inseparable relationship between the living and living-dead.[20] This law consists of moral rules, taboos, principles, values and beliefs, some of which are common to all traditional African societies throughout sub-Saharan Africa.

African law and legal thinking

In the imaginary chain novel, Sachs J. contends in *S. v. Makwanyane* that it is imperative to give 'long overdue recognition to African law and legal thinking as a source of legal ideas, values, and practices'. Justice Sachs did not clarify what he meant by 'African law and legal thinking', except that it had to be 'subject to the fundamental rights contained in the Constitution and the legislation dealing specifically therewith'.[21]

Various African sources distinguish between unwritten African law (also known as Bantu law, African customary law, African indigenous law, living customary law or unofficial customary law) and the codified version of African law, known as codified customary law or official customary law.[22] There is a clear distinction between 'indigenous law *for* indigenous people and indigenous law *of* indigenous people' (Bhengu 2006: 131). Indigenous law *for* the people signifies codified customary law, as documented since the era of colonialism, while indigenous law *of* the people represents African law or living customary law practised in traditional African societies.

The alienation of African law since the colonisation of Africa is a fact. The alienation and compartmentalisation of African law is highlighted in *Bhe v. Magistrate, Khayelitsha and Others*; *Shibi v. Sithole and Others* and *SA Human Rights Commission and Others v. President of the Republic of South Africa and Others*. In the *Bhe* case, the Court contended: 'Although customary law is supposed to develop spontaneously in a given rural community, during the colonial and apartheid era it became alienated from its community origins.'[23] The Court argued that the alienation of African law resulted in

> the term 'customary law' emerg[ing] with three quite different meanings:
> the official body of law employed in the courts and by the administration
> (which . . . diverges most markedly from actual social practice); the law
> used by academics for teaching purposes; and the law actually lived by the
> people.

In contrast with codified customary law used by the courts and academics, African law is the living law actually lived by Africans in traditional African societies throughout sub-Saharan Africa. African law is not a static or 'fixed body of classified rules . . . but a dynamic system of law which is continually evolving to meet the changing circumstances of the community in which it operates'.[24] The Court clearly distinguishes living African law from codified customary law used by the courts and academics for teaching purposes.

African law versus customary law
Prior to colonisation, Africa was not a lawless continent in a permanent state of anarchy. African jurisprudence has existed since time immemorial and regulated African societies long before the first colonisers appeared on the horizon. African jurisprudence, with '*ubuntu* [as] the basis of African law' (Ramose 2002: 81), ensured social control, unity and cosmic harmony in African societies. It differed profoundly from the laws of the European colonial powers.

In colonial Africa, a dual system of law lay at the heart of colonial rule: a European legal system and European-made customary law. This official, codified form of customary law was documented by Western anthropologists and academics, 'who lacked nuanced understanding of many of the rules and practices they were recording' (Roederer and Moellendorf 2004: 449).[25] Mahmood Mamdani argues that codified customary law was an 'administrative driven affair', which set Africans and their customs apart from the laws of civilised European society (1996: 2). Whereas colonial laws regulated civil society, the codified version of African law regulated traditional societies. Colonial laws regulated the private and public sphere and 'customary law regulated non-market relations in land; in personal (family) and in community affairs' (211). Not only was customary law perceived as 'primitive law ascribed to pre-literate peoples' (Ebo 1995: 139), but it also played an inferior role in relation to colonial laws in Africa, as it juxtaposed the individual and the group, civil society and the African community, rights and tradition (Mamdani 1996: 22).[26] Alexis Kagame describes the confusion created by this dual system of law among the African people:

First, there are juridical laws that the society controls through the judges and lawyers. They do not bind individual consciences, and whoever can escape them is considered intelligent. Second, there are taboo-laws, principally of a religious nature; these are generally negative and clearly specify what should be avoided. They contain in themselves an imminent power of sanction, and God is the sole judge. Therefore whatever the transgression, no human being – not even chief, priest, or king – can sanction or forgive the taboo sin. The problem and its resolution lie between the transgressor and God and also between his or her still existing family on earth and the departed ancestors (in Mudimbe 1988: 150).

The colonial custodians of the law eroded African jurisprudence with their codified versions of customary law. Because of the inferior role that customary law played during colonial rule (and later the apartheid regime), 'its development as a formal legal discipline has been stifled, and the official version thereof is said to have little in common with the way that cultural practice and ritual manifests itself in reality' (Roederer and Moellendorf 2004: 450). Christopher Roederer and Darren Moellendorf caution that codified or official customary law should be treated with suspicion if one attempts to ascertain the content of African jurisprudence, for it is 'both dysfunctional and distanced from the traditional values it is meant to represent'. The notion that codified customary law represents corrupted versions of African law and African jurisprudence was confirmed in the *Bhe* case. The Court contended that official customary law has failed to keep pace with changing social conditions; that it contrasts with living African law; that it is generally a poor reflection, if not a distortion of African law and that official customary law emphasises African law's patriarchal features, while minimising its communitarian features.[27] The fact is that codified customary law has become so distorted that it is perceived as out of step with the real values, cultural practices and ritual manifested in African law.

Sachs J. contended in *S. v. Makwanyane* that African law and legal thinking is 'a source of legal ideas, values, and practices'.[28] African sources, however, claim that *ubuntu* is the source of shared values and beliefs for all 'Bantu speaking peoples of Africa' (Ramose 2002: 8, 43; Abraham 1962; Mbiti 1991, 1992; Broodryk 1997, 2002; Bhengu 2006) and that these shared beliefs and values are grounded in African religion (Mbiti 1991: 179). Ramose posits that ubuntu is grounded in African religion since '*umuntu* cannot contain *ubuntu* without the intervention of the living dead' (2002: 51). As the basis of African law, ubuntu and African religion represent an inseparable oneness (Keevy 2009).

African law versus Western law

European colonial laws confronted urban African people with police, arrests, detentions, court procedures, imprisonment and capital punishment. Codified customary law confronted rural Africans with native courts, appeals and imprisonment. In African law, justice is not served by the prescription of penalties.[29] In contrast with Western law, a crime or dispute in rural Africa secured a process that involved the community of the living and the living-dead: 'The Bantu consider it utterly ridiculous for a judge or a state executioner to punish a person who had done them no wrong. Bantu execution is not merely punishment; it is a sacrifice to appease the ancestral spirits of a family, who cry out for revenge' (Mutwa 1996: 18).[30] Since not only the living, but also ancestral spirits punish an offender, African law has a spiritual dimension that has to be attended to before a matter can finally be set to rest.

In contrast with Western law, the primary aim of African law is not punishment, but the 'restoration of the balance upset by an unjust act' and to maintain equilibrium between the community and African spirit world (Ebo 1995: 34). As the aim of African law is not to create criminals, imprisonment is deemed senseless. Chinua Achebe, for example, narrates how African prisoners 'who had offended against the white man's law' in the colonial era had to clear government compounds, fetch firewood for the white commissioner or perform other menial tasks while serving prison sentences. According to Achebe: 'Some of the prisoners were men of title who should be above such occupation. They were grieved by the indignity and mourned their neglected farms' (1986: 125).

Western law and justice embrace individual rights, liberties and punishment, in contrast with African law and justice, which focus predominantly on group rights (Sebidi 1998: 63), duties, consensus, reconciliation (restorative justice) and the sense of shame instilled in the offender and his family.[31] Ali Mazrui argues that the emphasis in African law lies first, in the protection of the innocent; second, in compensation of the victim and third, in the sense of shame the community instils in offenders (1998: 256).

African justice ensures that the guilty person is shunned, ostracised and ridiculed or 'regarded as a non-person' or outcast. As an outcast, the offender loses not only his or her status in the community, but also his or her ability to participate in communal activities until the offence is purged and his or her status is restored (Ebo 1995: 39). Collective shame serves as an effective deterrent for potential offenders since it does not only affect the offender, but also shames his or her peer group and family who have to take collective responsibility for the offender.

In contrast with Western law, African law is inseparable from its patriarchal basis (Nhlapo 1995: 162), the ancestors and group solidarity or strong communitarianism.[32] Western law and justice do not follow these ancient African ideals and remain a foreign concept in traditional African societies.

African law and the ancestors

African law is an unwritten moral code, which is inseparable from African religion, the ancestors and the spirit world. According to Mutwa, the African 'High Law of Life' states: 'Man, know your life is not your own. You live merely to link your ancestors with your descendants. Your duty is to beget children even while you keep the Spirits of your Ancestors alive through regular sacrifices. When your ancestors command you to die, do so with no regrets' (1998: 625).

The elders and the living-dead or ancestors of the clan are respectively the creators and custodians of African law.[33] The ancestors play a central role in legislation, tribal courts, judgments and punishment in traditional African societies. Various African sources indicate that the ancestors are regarded as the legislators in traditional societies. The ancestors hand down moral rules, values and beliefs (M'Baye 1974: 141; Khapoya 1994: 49; Turaki 1997: 66; Mutwa 1998: 78; Somé 1999: 88; Head in Arndt 2002: 138). Community members have to carefully follow these rules, taboos, guidance and supervision of the ancestors in order to avoid punishment (Somé 1999: 88).[34] Ramose seems to disagree with these sources as he avers that the living (and not the living-dead) are the legislators who lay down norms and rules in these societies (Ramose 2002: 97). However, he does seem to agree with these sources that societal norms and rules can only come to force once the ancestors have authorised it, for 'the authority of [African] law is justified by appeal to the living dead (94, 96). Ramose maintains that all norms and rules have to be communicated to the ancestors for their approval since the ancestors are perceived as 'the basis for the authority of law in *ubuntu* philosophy . . . Because the living dead must always be honoured and obeyed, law justified in their name also deserves respect and obedience' (97). Whether African law is able to sustain peace and harmony between community members or communities depends solely on whether the ancestors gave their approval of the laws in question.[35]

Laws and taboos serve the purpose of keeping moral and religious order in African societies. The violation of African law 'is an offence against the departed members of the family and against god and the spirits, even if it is the people themselves who may suffer from such a breach and who may take action to punish the offender' (Mbiti 1991: 41). Whereas taboos 'strengthen the keeping of religious order', the violation of taboos disturbs the peace and harmony between the community and the spirit world. The violation of taboos results in punishment by both the community and the 'invisible world' or ancestors and may manifest in social ostracism, misfortune, death, sickness, poor harvest or poverty for the transgressor. Mutwa insists that African law and spirituality are inseparable and that matters of law and justice are only deemed settled after the spiritual dimension has been attended to (1998: 627). He explains that if a man seeks to divorce his wife, for example, he is compelled to confer with both his and his wife's ancestors on the reasons why he wants to dissolve the marriage. Only after consultation with the ancestors can the man take his problem to his family for advice.

The aim of justice in traditional African societies is to maintain equilibrium in the African 'flow of life' (Ramose 2002: 95).[36] In the case of minor offences that are 'not considered aggravation of the ancestral spirits of the family', judgment will be passed on behalf of the complainant to restore peace in the community (Mutwa 1998: 632).[37] In the case of more serious offences, the ancestors have to be invoked prior to the meeting or tribal court to affirm the infallibility of the elders and to serve as witnesses at the trial (Ephirim-Donkor 1998: 124).[38] After lengthy deliberation by all adult males present, the elders and chief have to reach consensus before judgment will be given (124–5).[39] Anthony Ephirim-Donkor emphasises the importance of not dismissing the ancestors before the court is adjourned as they serve as witnesses of the judgment. On their departure after the judgment, 'the ancestors take with them the verdicts of their earthly counterparts. This ensures that what is legal and binding on earth is also binding in the ancestral spirit world. When finally the deceased appear before the ancestors for accountability and judgment, there would be no room for error.' In contrast with Western jurisprudence, African jurisprudence is not isolated from the spirit world. African law and justice stand in relation to community, the ancestors and God, for 'to do wrong is to insult the spirit realm. Whoever does this is punished by the spirits' (Somé 1997: 50, 10, 53).[40]

African law and legal thinking is thus clearly based upon ubuntu; is inseperable from African religion; it has a patriarchal basis; it involves the living and the living-dead; it applies traditional African values; it aims at restoring equilibrium in the physical and spiritual realms by appeasing ancestral spirits; it propounds group rights and duties and utilises collective shame as deterrent for offenders.

African law and ubuntu

It is generally accepted that ubuntu is a very difficult concept to explain in a Western language. In *S. v. Makawanyane*, the Court contended that ubuntu 'envelops the key values of group solidarity, compassion, respect, human dignity, conformity to basic norms and collective unity, in its fundamental sense it denotes humanity and morality'.[41] Johann Broodryk (2002: 17) defines ubuntu as an ancient collective African world view that exists among all African cultures and African languages.[42] Broodryk suggests that despite the fact that different African languages have different names for ubuntu, its basic meaning and worth remains the same for all Africans. Various other sources (for example, Broodryk 1997, 2002; Mbiti 1991; Ramose 2002) concur that ubuntu is the ancient collective philosophy of traditional African people, which represents the African subcontinent's shared traditional value and belief system, or 'common spiritual ideal' (Khanyile in Broodryk 2005: 14) of all 'Bantu speaking peoples' (Ramose 2002: 43).[43]

Despite cultural differences, this ancient world view is 'fundamentally holistic' (Ramose 2002: 93) and engenders a spirit of community, mutual support, sharing, interconnectedness and respect for one another. As this world view is essentially spiritual, traditional African communities have a collective 'moral obligation to conform to traditions and conventions and override any desire for change or nonconformity. The conception is that the best in life lies in the past; the world of the ancestors and the origin' (Turaki 1997: 81, 49). This philosophy of collective solidarity or strong African communitarianism rejects Western atomistic individuality as it ultimately results in the disintegration of ubuntu and the spirit of African brotherhood (Bhengu 2006: 129).[44]

Ramose writes: 'Ubuntu philosophy of law is the continuation of [African] religion' (2002: 81, 97) and says that 'ubuntu is the basis of African law' (81; M'Baye 1974: 141). By applying the rhetoric of the Greek Sophists, the following syllogism can be deduced: because ubuntu is regarded as the continuation of African religion and the basis of African law, African law is also the continuation of African religion. Ramose, however, does not utilise the rhetoric of the Greek Sophists to come to a similar conclusion, namely that African law, like ubuntu, is inseparable from African religion and the metaphysics of ubuntu underlie the philosophy of African law (Ramose 2002: 92). African law is grounded in the shared values and beliefs of its basis, ubuntu, and the ancestors form 'the basis for the authority of law in *ubuntu* philosophy' (97).

Ubuntu

Ubuntu as ethnophilosophy

Léopold Sédar Senghor's 'Negritude and African Socialism' (1963: 13) and Placide Tempels's *Bantu Philosophy* (1969) introduced the unique collective world view of African societies to the West.[45] Kagame (1956), John S. Mbiti (1992), Willie E. Abraham (1962), Kwame Nkrumah (1964), Julius Nyerere (1968) and others all concur that all traditional African peoples of sub-Saharan Africa share a collective philosophy of shared values and beliefs.[46] As an ancient collective philosophy, ubuntu's shared traditional values and beliefs are regarded as sacred and unique. This unique collective world view is generally regarded as an 'African World View . . . [which] runs through the veins of all Africans' (Makudu 1993: 40).[47] What Tempels calls 'Bantu philosophy' (1969) and Henry Odera Oruka calls 'folk wisdom' (1990: 23), Paulin J. Hountondji calls 'ethnophilosophy'. He categorises the work of anthropologists, sociologists, ethnographers and philosophers based on the myths and folk wisdom of the collective world view of African peoples as ethnophilosophy (in Oruka 1990: 164).

The Kenyan Oruka identifies six trends in African philosophy: ethnophilosophy, sage philosophy, political philosophy, professional philosophy, the hermeneutical trend and the literary trend. He defines the collective philosophy of traditional African people or ethnophilosophy as 'a world outlook or thought system of a particular African community or the whole of Africa' (2002: 121). Ubuntu's 'indigenous, purely African, philosophy of life' (Dlomo in Broodryk 1997: 33) is not only regarded as the basis of African law and the 'root of African philosophy' (Ramose 2002: 40), but also 'the philosophical foundation of African practices among the Bantu speaking peoples of Africa' (8, 43). Broodryk maintains that ubuntu represents 'the recovery of the logic of brotherhood in ethnophilosophy' (1997: 33), for it represents the collective personhood and collective morality of the African people, best described by the Zulu proverb, '*umuntu, ngumuntu ngabantu*'; I am a person through other persons.

Ubuntu or ethnophilosophy is a collective or 'folk philosophy . . . [where] communality as opposed to individuality is brought forward as the essential attribute of African philosophy' (Oruka 2002: 121). Ethnophilosophy represents the ancient world view of traditional African societies, a collective philosophy that does not entertain individual philosophies or individual critique. Oruka argues that ethnophilosophy represents the group's mythical, uncritical and emotive part of African philosophy.[48] His critique of ethnophilosophy lies in the fact that he regards it as 'a communal consensus. It identifies with the totality of customs and common beliefs of a people. It is a folk philosophy . . . it is not identified with any particular individuals . . . It is at best a form of religion' (1990: 43).[49] It is said that this world view only exists in traditional African societies since 'that which is indigenous can only survive in a land that is indigenous' (Somé 1997: 57–8; Mutwa 1998: 691; Smit, Deacon and Schutte 1999: 32; Khumalo in Bhengu 2006: 58).[50] African feminists have argued that this 'folk philosophy' oppresses, marginalises and stereotypes African women:

> To uncritically accept those belief systems is to take an approach that ignores the experience of women in patriarchal and male dominated societies. In societies that have been dominated by men, dehumanising and oppressive customs, taboos and traditions are the 'normal' cultural elements. African women have suffered from these patriarchal structures (Imbo 1999: 68).

African feminists assert that because of this collective 'folk philosophy', traditional African women are not permitted to question or critique the status quo in their societies and that this 'folk philosophy' condones and sustains firmly entrenched sexism. African feminists (for example, Mercy A. Oduyoye, Dorothy Ramodibe and Rose Zoe-Obianga) state that it resulted in African men being regarded as superior to African women and that women are therefore kept in a state of submission, while oppressive gender stereotyping persists (Imbo 1999: 68). This collective world view has therefore been criticised for what is perceived as a general disregard for the human rights of African women, specifically, their rights to equality and human dignity.

Ubuntu, hierarchy and status

As a unique collective African world view, ubuntu sustains the deep-seated patriarchy in traditional African societies. Traditional African communities consist of patriarchal hierarchies, which assign rights 'on the basis of communal membership, family, status or achievement' (Bhengu 2006: 129).[51] Because status and hierarchy are justifiable in African law, the legal status of each person depends upon his or her position and status within the hierarchy.

Various sources confirm that rights in traditional societies are assigned 'on the basis of communal membership, family, status or achievement' (M'Baye 1974: 143–5; Broodryk 1997: 97). Within these hierarchies, 'everyone in the community has an assigned place and must do what he must do without any demands; everyone must obey the elders according to strict rules' (M'Baye 1974: 141). Any challenge to the hierarchy disturbs the balance, peace and harmony of the community. The concept of *uMona* (jealousy) functions to control individuals within the patriarchal hierarchy (Boon 2007: 124–5).[52]

Traditional African societies do not exist only in terms of the material or visible world, but also the invisible world. Therefore, the patriarchal hierarchies within these communities include the spiritual dimension, living people, animals, plants and material things.[53] According to Kéba M'Baye (1974: 143, 145), hierarchy and status within the community is maintained as follows, from top to bottom:

- At the top of the societal hierarchy is the African spirit world. Communities are represented and guided by God(s) and the ancestors. The king or chief holds all religious, political, judicial and military powers in the community.[54]
- Elders act as sages and judges of the community.
- Adult males are held in high esteem and have much higher status than younger males or women.
- Women are regarded as inferior to men. Gender equality does not exist in these societies.[55]
- Children under age are completely dependent on the chief of the group as he holds every right over them. The age of majority is not fixed. Should a girl marry, she finds herself under the authority of a new patriarch, the head of the husband's family. Notwithstanding a man's circumcision and initiation, he only reaches true majority once he either becomes the head of a family by succession, or sets up his own 'family house'.[56]
- Slaves and their descendants are not subjects of law.
- Mentally ill persons have no legal status.
- Strangers are rarely assimilated into the community and are situated at the outer edge of the village.

Yusufu Turaki confirms the existence of these patriarchal hierarchies, which have 'at the top, the ancestors, the aged [elders], [male] heads and leaders, men, women, children and the unborn' (1997: 57; Stewart 2005: 205; Morgan and Wieringa 2005: 261). Broodryk also acknowledges the existence of these hierarchies: 'A witchdoctor, *sangoma*, chief and elderly people [for example] are treated on different levels of status and in some cases it appears as if the families of these figures are also more respected and treated differently. The formation of classes is a known phenomenon in Africa societies' (1997: 97). Uninitiated persons, for example, are regarded as outcasts or 'its' and do not have the same status as the initiated in their age group (Somé 1997: 87; Ramose 2002: 65; Nyirongo 1997: 72, 101). Turaki explains: 'Every individual or group have their own destiny decreed for them by the Creator . . . Destiny is meant to be in gratitude. It is one's lot. Thus one's place in human society has been determined and fixed' (1997: 55). As all individuals are subordinate to the collective or community, the law of kinship specifies that

> the individual self does not exist in itself and has no social life of itself nor determines its course of life on its own. The individual takes his/her life and entire existence from the kinship foundations he/she belongs to in the community of kinships and of common ancestry. He/she is owned by his/her blood group (Turaki 1997: 61).

Turaki further argues: 'We do not only have a hierarchy of human beings but also that of people groups. Human beings at times assume themselves or their ethnic or racial or tribal group to be higher or superior to others' (1997: 45). This explains why ethnicity, racism and tribalism are deeply rooted in the community's beliefs, values, morals and ethics.

Like M'Baye, Broodryk and Turaki, Lenard Nyirongo (1997: 104) maintains that a person's status in these societies depends on his or her place within the patriarchal hierarchy, determined by gender, age and seniority in birth. Thus, circumcised males and females are more senior and privileged than their uninitiated peers; younger brothers have to carry the weapons of older brothers and a younger brother cannot marry before his older brother, for 'to do so is not only a sign of disrespect, but a sin against the community and ancestors, which will require an offer or sacrifice to appease them'. Children of the most senior wife of a polygamous marriage are regarded as more senior than those of junior wives; 'daughters are worth less than sons'; husbands are superior to their wives and African men who belong to secret societies are perceived to be closer to the ancestors and can therefore punish or reward ordinary community members (104–5).

Children in these societies have little or no life force and can, therefore, not become ancestors upon death:

> A child's worth is judged by his potential to live an adult life rather than by the mere fact that he too is a full person. In other words, because a man's

soul is worth much more when he qualifies as an ancestor, it follows that unless he grows up he is worth less than an adult (Nyirongo 1997: 103).[57]

While African patriarchal hierarchies are renowned for their brotherhood, little is said about the discrimination and human oppression associated with these patriarchies. Such 'opression is not always overt, physical violence . . . oppression is anything that limits the freedom or development of the individual or community' (Nyirongo 1997: 151).[58] As individuals in these societies are not equal, ubuntu's patriarchal hierarchy therefore diverges from the core values of the South African Constitution.

Ubuntu, justice, hierarchy and status

In ubuntu jurisprudence, restorative justice and consensus are paramount.[59] Because traditional African societies are based upon solidarity and consensus (not majority rule), reconciliation is paramount in restoring equilibrium. Group solidarity requires the restoration of peace and win-win situations between conflicting parties.[60]

Rights and justice are assigned on the basis of 'communal membership, family, status or achievement' (Bhengu 2006: 129). Whether or not damages will be awarded to an afflicted party depends largely upon the legal status of the person – the more influential the person against whom the injustice is committed, the more serious the injustice (Mbiti 1992: 208). Nyirongo makes it clear that an injustice is perceived as more serious when committed against a chief than against a man of lesser status; it is more severe to offend an elder than a child with less vital force; a teenager is expected to be less offended when antagonised by an elder than when affronted by another teenager and when 'a person of influence and status commits an offence against a poor man, it not as serious as when the poor man commits the same sin against him . . . This is because the older you get the more potent your words or dispositions are' (1997: 63).[61] In contrast with ubuntu jurisprudence, section 9 (1) of the South African Bill of Rights guarantees *every* person equality before the law.

The fact that ubuntu jurisprudence permits revenge in traditional African societies (Mutwa 1998: 630) juxtaposes African and Western notions of justice. In African societies, retribution is viewed as a collective right, which permits members to avenge offences or crimes committed against any member of their clan (M'Baye 1974: 146).[62]

Ubuntu and the oppression of women

In *Port Elizabeth Municipality v. Various Occupiers*, Sachs J. describes ubuntu as 'a unifying motif of the Bill Rights, which is nothing if not a structured, institutionalised and operational declaration in our evolving society of the need for human interdependence, respect and concern'.[63] In line with the court's 'social engineers and social and legal philosophers', who contend that ubuntu is 'a unifying motif of the Bill of Rights', Mfuniselwa J. Bhengu (2006: 38) maintains that if a nation lives by the principles of ubuntu, there is no discrimination.[64] African feminists and gender activists, however, oppose such utopian views and disclose that ubuntu represents an oppressive reality: it fosters a deep-seated patriarchy that entrenches gender inequality and disregard for the dignity of African women.[65] Though individual critiques against this ancient collective African world view are perceived as interference with age-old African practices and *not* tolerated (Mbiti 1991: 15; Turaki 1997: 61; Akatsa-Bukachi 2005: 11), African feminists and gender activists criticise its oppression of African women, its entrenched gender inequality and violation of women's human dignity (Mdluli 1987: 67).

Ubuntu's deep-seated patriarchy can be defined as the institutionalised social hierarchy in African societies, whereby the extended family grants males authority and power over women. Bessie Head criticises these patriarchal structures sharply and laments the fact that African women have to comply with and obey their rules, without thought or critique:

> When the laws of the ancestors are examined, they appear on the whole to be vast, external disciplines for the good of the society as a whole, with little attention given to individual preferences and needs. The ancestors made so many errors and one of the most bitter-making was that they relegated to men a superior position in the tribe, while women were regarded, in a congenital sense, as being an inferior form of human life. To this day, women still suffer from all the calamities that befall an inferior form of human life (in Arndt 2002: 138).

Volumes of texts by African feminists and gender activists speak out against this ancient oppressive collective world view, with its shared traditional values and beliefs in which women play a central but inferior role.[66] For African women, gender-based violence, including marital rape, wife-beating or 'correction', rape, polygamy, virginity testing, female genital mutilation (FGM), child marriages, abduction or forced marriages, widow inheritance and other forms of oppression are the order of the day (Aidoo 1991; Akatsa-Bukachi 2005: 11).[67] Despite the fact that the African Women's Protocol prohibits harmful traditional practices, FGM, 'virginity testing, dry sex, abduction or forced marriages, *ukungena*, and the burning and victimization of women called witches' persist in sub-Saharan African (Mukasa 2008: 147). African feminists argue that African traditionalists retain these patriarchal privileges to control women. The patriarchy maintains hegemonic masculinity and utilises violence to control female behaviour to ensure chastity, to promote abstinence, to control copulation and to deny the existence of sexual violence in Africa, 'as part of patriarchal power and socio-cultural norms reinforced by religious beliefs and injunctions to suppress, in particular, girls and women from the free expression of their sexuality' (Makinwa-Adebusoye and Tiemoko 2007: 7, 13). However, the struggle of African feminists and gender activists to reclaim the bodies of women 'from virginity-testers, rapists and abusers indicate that cracks in the structures of patriarchal femininity have begun to appear' (Rankhota 2004: 85).

Ubuntu's 'fundamental African value' of hospitality is well known and generally associated with reciprocity, openness and acceptance of others (Oduyuye 2001: 93). In ubuntu reality, it is considered a moral evil to deny relatives, friends and strangers hospitality (Mbiti 1991: 176).[68] This fundamental African value is regarded as a sacred duty and should ensure that guests are protected from harm during their stay in the community. African feminists, however, perceive this fundamental value as a form of oppression and state that it regulates female-male relationships, ignores the welfare of women and exploits their sexuality (Oduyoye 2001: 101). The fundamental value of hospitality also encompasses the following:

- Men who went to the same school of initiation can exchange wives.
- Absent husbands may be replaced by friends appointed by them.
- Brothers, especially twins, can share the duties of being husband and wife.
- Sterile husbands may appoint surrogates to have children.
- A healer may have sexual relations with his patient (Oduyoye 2001: 101–2).[69]

Oduyoye argues that this fundamental African value is 'incompatible with the dignity of women' (2001: 103–4). She accuses 'African male models of manhood' and 'leaders of public opinion in African societies' of being the guilty ones who erode the human dignity of women. Furthermore, African chiefs offer male visitors women of honour to keep them company for the duration of their visit or to be taken away as wives (Moyo in Oduyoye 2001: 102).[70] These and other sexual practices threaten women's reproductive rights and exacerbate their vulnerability and inability to negotiate and engage in safer sex (Malera 2007: 134). Oduyoye points out that the low social status and gender inequality of African women impact also on economic injustice against women (1989: 443).[71]

It has become popular to put great emphasis only on the positive traditional African values, conveniently ignoring the dark side of ubuntu, which erodes the human rights of women and others.[72] The collective philosophy's condoning of ancient 'harmful traditional practices in South Africa, and its resultant loss of life and/or abuse of women's human rights, is an area that urgently needs attention' (Mukasa 2008: 149).[73] Despite the fact that the South African Constitution guarantees human rights for all and that article 2 (b) of the African Women's Protocol prohibits all forms of discrimination against women, harmful traditional practices continue to endanger the health and general well-being of African women. For millions of women in South Africa (and elsewhere in Africa), ubuntu has been unable to liberate them or bring an improvement in their conditions into the private sphere or family.

Ubuntu and the oppression of homosexuals, lesbians and witches

Section 9 (3) of South Africa's Bill of Rights guarantees homosexuals and lesbians the right not to be unfairly discriminated against on the grounds of their sexual orientation. Africans in same-sex relationships, however, experience discrimination, gang rape, hate speech, harassment, stigmatisation and even murder because of their sexual orientation.[74] Throughout sub-Saharan Africa, homosexuality and lesbianism are regarded as 'unAfrican' and alien to African culture. Homosexuals are regarded as 'subhuman' and 'worse than dogs and pigs' (Nkabinde 2008: 131; Morgan and Wieringa 2005: 17).[75]

'This homophobia is based on the perception that same-sex relations are alien to African culture and an import from the depraved West' (Morgan and Wieringa 2005: 13).[76] African lesbians are regularly murdered and gang raped as 'punishment' for their 'deviant behaviour' and to reinforce male control over women: the 'rape of black lesbians is a weapon used to discipline our erotic and sexual autonomy' (Muholi 2004: 116–24).[77] Nkunzi Z. Nkabinde maintains that lesbians in South Africa are raped 'to teach them a lesson' and that this violation of female human dignity is called 'corrective rape' (2008: 145).[78] The fact that the shared values and beliefs of ubuntu declare same-sex relations taboo and 'unAfrican' makes 'lesbian women doubly oppressed' (Morgan and Wieringa 2005: 11). In these 'hierarchical and strongly patriarchal [societies] . . . particularly lesbians get the rawest deal' (Khumalo and Wieringa in Morgan and Wieringa 2005: 261).

Ubuntu's shared values and beliefs perceive witches as a reality in the African spirit world. Witches are among the most hated people in sub-Saharan Africa (Mutwa 1998; Holland 2001; Mbiti 1991). Witches are usually women and are frequently killed by their communities (Hallen and Sodipo 1997: 88).[79] Any person 'identified as a witch, is under intense pressure to accept responsibility. This is why ordinary people with no supernatural history and no guilt beyond ill-temper sometimes concede guilt when accused of witchcraft' and are killed (Holland 2001: 9).[80] The Provincial Commission of Inquiry of the Limpopo Province and a research team appointed by the Human Sciences Research Council found 'executions of witches without formal trials by members of the community increased dramatically over the past ten years'. The research team concluded that witchcraft and the killing (burning) of witches are factors that have to be reckoned with in all regions of South Africa (Teffo and Roux 2002: 169).[81]

In contrast with the equality clause of the South African Constitution, ubuntu jurisprudence ranks the status of homosexuals, lesbians and witches very low within its patriarchal hierarchy. Despite claims of equality in ubuntu, the violation of the human rights of individuals in same-sex relationships and witches throughout sub-Saharan Africa remains a reality that human rights and gender activists cannot conveniently ignore.[82] Although ubuntu is generally associated with African brotherhood and the spirit of 'sharing, caring, kindness, forgiveness, sympathy, tolerance, respect, love, appreciation [and] consideration' (Broodryk 2002: 33) within the clan, Nyirongo is unequivocal:

> They have said nothing at all about the violence that goes on within the tribe because of its faulty view of office, authority, power and irresponsibility. This in my view is an illusion . . . the caring and sharing atmosphere we see is not as innocent as it appears (1997: 149)![83]

Little is ever said about this violence or dark side of ubuntu – for the collective 'folk philosophy' has cultivated a cult of silence, which does not tolerate individual critique (Mbiti 1991: 15; Turaki 1997: 61; Akatsa-Bukachi 2005: 11).[84]

Silence also surrounds the fact that ubuntu's shared beliefs and values accommodate sangomas, some of whom are infamous for *muti* murders.[85]

Sangomas are spiritual leaders in traditional Africa who maintain a unique relationship with the ancestors (Mutwa 2003: 27). They can cure spirit-possessed persons and can interact with the ancestors who assist them in their work (Mutwa 1996: xv; Nkabinde 2008: 11; Broodryk 2007: 127–8).[86] Despite the South African Constitution being hailed as one of the most advanced in the world, guaranteeing human rights for all, *muti* murders have not ceased since the dawn of South Africa's new democracy. This ancient practice, where animal and human body parts are taken to make *muti* or medicine, 'remain[s] disturbingly common' and continues year after year (Van der Zalm 2008: 909).[87]

Ubuntu, strangers and outsiders

African societies are founded on shared traditional African values, beliefs, rules, taboos, customs, elders, ancestors and the African spirit world (Wiredu 1980: 4). The 'universal brotherhood for all Africans' embraces a spirit of group solidarity, conformity, sharing, caring, respect and hospitality within these societies (Mdluli 1987: 64). But neither the African brotherhood nor African law guarantees strangers or outsiders the right to equality, for African law (like African religion) applies only to the community or clan and not to strangers or outsiders.[88]

A stranger in African societies is defined as 'one who comes in from outside; another continent, another race, another civilisation, another worldview. Strangers are people with other values, other perspectives, other objectives, other principles of life' (Oduyoye 2001: 95). The fundamental African value of hospitality entails that 'as long as you [the stranger] stay in the village you are cared for as a spirit envoy and respected. This is the law' (Somé 1999: 88). Strangers are entitled to hospitality and respect for as long as they stay in these communities, but are perceived as 'a form of second-class citizen. They are seen as outsiders, as "other", since they have a different culture and a language which are different from the "norm"' (Mnyaka and Motlhabi 2005: 123).

Turaki avers that the law of kinship in traditional African societies is the most powerful and pervasive of all African laws and that it creates two types of morality and ethics: one for the community and one for strangers and outsiders (1997: 61). Turaki describes the 'law of kinship', which regulates African societies, as follows:

> The law of kinship defines in unequivocal terms those who are 'insiders' and 'outsiders'. Outsiders and strangers do not belong, for this reason they are not entitled to (1) equal treatment; (2) ownership; (3) affinity, loyalty

and obligation; (4) community rights and protection and (5) they are not people, they are outside of the commonwealth, they are strangers . . . Those who belong are to be treated equally and preferentially as against outsiders and strangers (1997: 61).

In contrast with ubuntu's loving and caring atmosphere that prevails in the brotherhood, 'anything outside the kinship system is labelled "outside world" . . . In this sort of place, kinship or tribal rules do not apply. In fact there is no set of rules to govern its operation or control.' Furthermore, 'in such a place "might is right"; "the end justifies the means"; "it is a war zone"' (Turaki 1997: 63). Nyirongo (1997: 139) confirms this attitude towards outsiders and maintains that outsiders are not looked upon as equals or brothers: African law permits differential treatment of outsiders and the discrimination and the oppression of outsiders. The attitudes of traditional African societies towards outsiders are closely related to the value systems of closed societies (Popper in Broodryk 1997: 88).[89] In closed societies, all people who are not community members are perceived as outsiders. Not only do traditional African values or ubuntu values 'enhance ethnic or group harmony [but] traditional African values [also] promote ethnic or group superiority over others, parochialism, dominance, subordination, prejudice and discrimination' (Turaki 1991: 173).

In contrast with Western jurisprudence, which guarantees individual rights and liberties, ubuntu jurisprudence guarantees group rights and duties. Ubuntu does not guarantee fundamental human rights for individual members, strangers or outsiders (Turaki 1997: 68), as the concern for societal survival is greater than the concern for individual rights.[90] Thus, what is perceived as equality in ubuntu reality is fundamentally different from the right to equality as understood in Western jurisprudence (Nyirongo 1997: 139).[91] It can therefore clearly be argued that human rights law is fundamentally at odds with traditional African values (Viljoen 2007: 305).

Ubuntu as African Constitution

African sources confirm that the laws that regulate traditional societies in sub-Saharan Africa are 'unquestionably similar to one another' (Ramose 2002: 81; Mutwa 1998: 624; Ebo 1995: 40; Ojwang 1995: 56; M'Baye 1974: 139); that ubuntu constitutes the basis of African law and that '*ubuntu* philosophy of law is the continuation of religion' (Ramose 2002: 81, 97). Ubuntu is generally perceived as the ancient collective philosophy of sub-Saharan African traditional societies that regulates the flow of life.

Ubuntu jurisprudence is well known throughout sub-Saharan Africa. Though ubuntu is perceived as the basis of African law, Jordan K. Ngubane (1979: 78), Ramose (2002: 97) and Bhengu (2006: 33) maintain that ubuntu's collective philosophy is more than a mere ancient collective African world view. They argue that ubuntu functions as the highest law or African Constitution in traditional African societies. As highest law, the African Constitution structures societies by means of shared traditional values, beliefs, customs, laws, taboos and traditions (Bhengu 2006: 33). According to Ramose, ubuntu functions as 'constitutional law' in African societies – it commands obedience from the people and protects all traditional African communities (2002: 97). Bhengu makes it clear: 'The function of the [African] Constitution is to create, regulate and perpetuate a social order in which the person could realise the promise of being human' (2006: 33).

Ngubane, Ramose and Bhengu divulge very little about the African Constitution, leaving much open to speculation. There is no written evidence that such an ancient African Constitution exists. This chapter postulates the following about the African Constitution: As ubuntu, the African Constitution consists of uncodified moral rules, passed on orally from generation to generation. As highest law, the African Constitution (like African law) functions as private law. Its function is to regulate interpersonal relationships by way of shared customs, rules, taboos, values, beliefs and traditions. The African Constitution or ubuntu constitutes the basis of African law and is inseparable from African religion, the ancestors and the African spirit world.[92] The ancestors play a central role as legislative and executive authorities that make and enforce law. Whereas the African Constitution is group-orientated and gives preference to group rights and duties, the South African Constitution is codified; individualistically orientated; guarantees fundamental human rights; regulates state power, relationships between citizens and the state and relationships between individuals. The South African Constitution is based upon a jurisprudence of equality and its legislative, judicial and executive authorities are independent of the African spirit world.

As the basis of African law, the African Constitution assigns rights on the basis of 'communal membership, family, status or achievement'. It sustains patriarchal hierarchies and does not guarantee the rights of equality, human dignity and life to women, homosexuals, lesbians, witches and others. While the African Constitution does not guarantee individuals equality before the law, the South

African Constitution guarantees *everyone* fundamental human rights: equality before the law and their rights to life, equality and human dignity. It has to be seriously questioned whether ubuntu is 'a unifying motif of the Bill Rights' as contended in *Port Elizabeth Municipality v. Various Occupiers.*[93]

Ubuntu versus regional human rights mechanisms

In 2007, South Africa and other Southern African Development Community (SADC) member states signed the draft SADC Protocol on Gender and Development (GAD). Not only did member states commit themselves to enshrine gender equality in their Constitutions by 2015, but they also agreed in article 4 (1) that gender equality would take precedence over customary, religious and other laws. In article 4 (2), member states undertook to eliminate all practices that negatively affect the rights of women, men, girls and boys in SADC. Therefore, further discourse on ubuntu is essential in order to align ubuntu with international and regional human rights mechanisms.

Conclusion

Section 39 (1) of the Constitution imposes the duty on South African courts to promote values that underlie a democratic society, based on human dignity, equality and freedom.[94] Section 39 (3) of the Constitution implies that more than one system of law operates in South Africa and that African law, customary law and religious laws may at times conflict with the democratic values of the Constitution. It is imperative, as emphasised by the Constitutional Court in *S. v. Makwanyane*, that recognition be given to African law and legal thinking as part of the source of values that section 39 of the 1996 Constitution requires courts to promote. As in the case of religious and customary laws, African law has to be considered in consonance with the Constitution, the draft SADC Protocol on GAD, the Protocol to the African Charter on the Rights of Women and international human rights mechanisms.

It is argued that ubuntu is an ancient collective world view of shared traditional values and beliefs, which constitutes not only the root of African philosophy, but also the basis of African law. As a moral philosophy, ubuntu is inseparable from African religion and is regulated by the interplay of spiritual forces of the African spirit world. As a form of religion (Oruka 1990: 43), ubuntu constitutes the core of African law and sustains the deep-seated patriarchy throughout sub-Saharan Africa. Although ubuntu values and beliefs have sustained traditional

African societies since time immemorial, the fact that they entrench discrimination and erode the non-derogable rights of South Africa's Bill of Rights has been conveniently ignored by the court. As a collective philosophy, ubuntu sustains not only communities, extended families, values, beliefs, tradition, morals, law and justice in these societies, but also the patriarchal hierarchy, discrimination, inequality and stereotyping of women, children, homosexuals, lesbians, witches, strangers and others (Osei-Hwedie in Jacques and Lesetedi 2005: 154; Ngubane 1979: 78; Bhengu 2006: 33).

'Social engineers and social and legal philosophers' have equated the 'prized value[s] of *ubuntu*' with 'the values of the Constitution generally and the Bill of Rights in particular' (Mokgoro 1998: 21–2), ignoring the fact that 'sexism and patriarchy are so ancient, all pervasive and incorporated into the practice of daily life as to appear socially and culturally normal and legally invisible'.[95] In their effort to legitimise the South African Constitution, judges have equated ubuntu with the constitutional values in section 1 of the 1996 Constitution: 'human dignity, the achievement of equality and the advancement of human rights and freedoms . . . and non-sexism'. The 'seamless text' of constitutional theory on ubuntu jurisprudence obscures the fact that ubuntu is inseparable from African religion and that it sustains a deep-seated patriarchy, discrimination, inequality and the violation of human dignity (Van Blerk 2004: 92). Neither African law and legal thinking nor its basis, ubuntu, is in compliance with international human rights notions of equality and human dignity or the African Women's Protocol.[96] In order to meet the SADC goals for gender equality by 2015, 'social engineers and social and legal philosophers' need to break the cult of silence and start asking probing questions regarding ubuntu. For the fact is that ubuntu is *not* in consonance with the values of the Constitution in general and the Bill of Rights in particular.

Notes

1. The use of 'ubuntu' here should be interpreted independently of the distinction made between 'ubuntu' (praxis) and 'Ubuntu' (retrodicted, postcolonial philosophy) used elsewhere in this volume.
2. *S. v. Makwanyane and Another* 1995 (3) SA 391 (CC), para. 365, per Sachs J. It was also argued that 'recognition should be given also to African law and legal thinking as part of the source of values which sec. 35 of the Constitution required Courts to promote' (para. 373).
3. *S. v. Makwanyane*, paras 252, 258, 371–2.
4. In *Baloro and Others v. University of Bophuthatswana and Others* 1995 (940) SA 197 (B): 235, E–F, Friedman J.P. contended that courts and specifically judges have the additional

role of 'social engineers and social and legal philosophers' to promote values referred to in section 35 of the Constitution. According to Théophile Obenga (2004: 35), the ancient Egyptian definition of the word 'philosopher' was found in the *Inscription of Antef* in the twelfth dynasty, 1991–1782 BC. The *Inscription of Antef* states that a philosopher is a person 'whose heart is informed about these things which would be otherwise ignored, the one who is clear-sighted when he is deep into a problem, the one who is moderate in his actions, who penetrates ancient writings, whose advice is sought to unravel complications, who is really wise, who instructed his own heart, who stays awake at night as he looks for the right paths, who surpasses what he accomplished yesterday, who is wiser than a sage, who brought himself to wisdom, who asks for advice and sees to it that he is asked advice.'

5. *S. v. Makwanyane*, para. 302, per Mokgoro J.

6. Ibid., para. 307, per Sachs J.; *City of Johannesburg v. Rand Properties (Pty) Ltd and Others*, 2006 JOL 16852 W, para. 62, per Jajbhay J. In *Wormald N.O. and Others v. Kambule* 2006 (3) SA 562 (SCA), paras 36–7, Maya A.J. contended that the spirit of ubuntu combines individual rights with a communitarian philosophy and serves as a unifying motif of the Bill of Rights.

7. *S. v. Makwanyane*, para. 237, per Madala J.

8. Bhengu posits that 'the concept of human rights as natural, inherent, inalienable rights held by virtue of the fact that one is born a human being, remains a creation of Western civilisation and is foreign to [African] indigenous law. In indigenous society rights are assigned on the basis of communal membership, family, status or achievement. Ubuntu philosophy comes in here' (2006: 129). Bhengu argues that the Bill of Rights was framed from a distinct Western perspective and that this foreign Western culture has been thrust upon indigenous African cultures through the process of colonisation.

9. *Bhe v. Magistrate, Khayelitsha and Others* 2005 (1) BCLR 1 (CC), para. 87; see also *Shibi v. Sithole and Others*; *SA Human Rights Commission and Others v. President of the Republic of South Africa and Others*. Patriarchy is the institutionalised social hierarchy in traditional African societies, whereby the extended family grants males authority and power over women. Akatsa-Bukachi defines patriarchy as 'the organisation of social life and institutional structures in which men have ultimate control over most aspects of women's lives and actions' (2005: 6).

10. The preamble of the 1996 Constitution states that the Constitution is based on democratic values, social justice and fundamental human rights. Section 7 of the Bill of Rights refers to the 'democratic values of human dignity, equality and freedom'. In *Minister of Home Affairs v. Fourie (Doctors for Life International and Others, Amici Curiae); Lesbian and Gay Equality Project and Others v. Minister of Home Affairs* 2006 10 SA 254 (CC), para. 48, Sachs J. referred in the majority judgment to 'the concepts and values of human dignity, equality and freedom'.

11. Section 9 (4) of the 1996 Constitution guarantees *all* people the right not to be unfairly discriminated against.

12. *Volks N.O. v. Robinson* 2005 (5) BCLR 466 (CC), para. 163. In *Du Plessis v. De Klerk* 1996 (3) SA 850 (CC): 930, Mokgoro J. refers to the 'delicate and complex' task of accommodating customary laws to the values embodied in the South African Bill of Rights and notes that 'this harmonization exercise will demand a great deal of judicious care and sensitivity'.

13. According to Mutwa (1998), certain aspects of the oral tradition are kept secret by traditional African societies. South Africa's most well-known Zulu High *Sanusi*, sangoma and sage, Mutwa discloses that the 'Great Knowledge' or the total of all African knowledge of history, legends, mythology, philosophy, psychology and spiritualism, 'with a strong leaning to the occult', are controlled by the 'Chosen Ones' or 'High Custodians' of traditional Africa (654). Only certain knowledge is passed on from the Chosen Ones to the High Ones of the tribe and only if their duties require such knowledge; little knowledge is passed on to the ordinary or 'common people' of the tribe and *no* knowledge is ever revealed to 'strangers' or outsiders (555–6). Mamdani cites Governor Cameron who explains how difficult it was for a judge during the colonial era to find out what customary law entailed because African assessors 'knew perfectly well, but for one reason or the other, they may not tell you' (1996: 112).

14. Kagame maintains that African law is 'primarily of a religious nature' (in Mudimbe 1988: 150).

15. The dead implies the living-dead or ancestors. M'Baye (1974) defines the ancestors as 'those corporally dead but still living' who keep watch over the living and keep things the way they are.

16. According to Ramose, this oneness or extended family involves 'three interrelated dimensions' (2002: 47) or the 'inseparable trinity' (50–1, 94), which consists of not only persons who are alive, but also those who have passed away and others yet to be born. Mbigi (1997: 52) points out that the belief in reincarnation is a very significant pillar of African religion. When a man dies, he continues to live among his relatives as an ancestral spirit who protects them from danger and attends to their daily needs. In return, spiritual sacrifices are made in honour of the spirit. People who were influential before their deaths may choose a suitable host or medium to possess regularly during appropriate ceremonies and rituals. In African religion, reincarnation is viewed as an important opportunity for the spirit to return to its people, tribe and family.

17. Mamdani (1996: 22) argues there was not one set of living customary rules for all Africans, but as many laws as there were tribes and that while colonial authorities selected certain forms of customary law, they suppressed others.

18. According to Mutwa, the High Laws include the following commandments: 'The killing of one woman is so great a crime that it needs a thousand men to die in battle of vengeance . . . The separation of a man from his wife by an external influence is listed as one of the Three High Crimes and calls for a war of vengeance and punishment . . . if you touch a man's wife, mother, sister, or daughter, call them names or refer insultingly to their womanhood, he is bound by law to kill you. If he fails he will make his children's children take oaths to kill your children's children . . . There are only three grounds for divorce: frigidity (a refusal to carry on the ancestral name); adultery (excreting in the spirit hut); and sexual perversity (the madness to let outsider bulls graze in the green pastures of our ancestors) . . . if one man of another race killed a member of your race, tribe or family, do not rest until you, or a descendant of yours, have killed a member of his race, tribe or family . . . The African motto is "an eye for an eye" and the Zulus have a saying; "once you poke me in the eye, I must not rest until I have gouged out one of yours" . . . a wizard shall die that particular kind of death set aside for wizards . . . adulterers, perverts and rapists were given the ant death . . .

In the land of the Xhosa all witches were thrown from a high cliff and in Central Africa all adulteresses were fed to the crocodiles. Adulterers were castrated. In Lesotho and also in Zululand, witches were imprisoned in their own huts and burnt to death. Witchdoctors who broke the law were killed . . . A thief caught stealing oxen was given an appropriate death . . . when a man commits rape he is arrested and executed; a man must keep away [sexually] from his wife for at least a year whilst she is breast-feeding', etc. (1998: 621–35). These laws are, according to Mutwa, currently not 'in full force' in South Africa.

19. Achebe states that judgment would only be given after 'we have heard both sides of the case' (1986: 67). Tempels (1969: 123), Kamalu (1998: 89), Bhengu (2006: 13) and others state that African law is founded on natural law principles. Mbiti maintains that 'these laws of nature are regarded as being controlled by God directly or through his servants' (1991: 41). Natural law implies that law has a moral dimension. The characteristic feature of natural law is that a moral code exists, irrespective of human interaction or positive law. Natural law contrasts with positive law, which is perceived as law separated from morality and laid down in statutes, rules and court decisions.

20. Viljoen (2007) maintains that African jurisprudence concerns itself with living human beings, the ancestors and inanimate objects.

21. *S. v. Makwanyane*, paras 365 and 366.

22. *Bhe v. Magistrate, Khayelitsha*, para. 109 distinguishes between living and official customary law. Bekker, Rautenbach and Goolam (2006: 8) differentiate between unofficial and official customary law.

23. *Bhe v. Magistrate, Khayelitsha*, para. 151.

24. Ibid., para. 153.

25. In the *Bhe* case (para. 43), the Court maintains that 'this approach led in part to the fossilisation and codification of customary law which in turn led to its marginalisation. This consequently denied it of its opportunity to grow in its own right and to adapt itself to changing circumstances.'

26. Hlope states that 'Africans had no choice but to obey the white man. This meant that their own systems of life, including their laws, were regarded as backward and irreconcilable with civilisation' (in Bhengu 2006: 129). Whites could not tolerate any moral values in conflict with what they perceived to be right or wrong, according to their standards. Mamdani is of the opinion that the compartmentalisation of customary law and civil law institutionalised racism in Africa and perceives apartheid as 'the upgrading of indirect rule authority in rural areas to an autonomous status combined with police control over "native" movement between the rural and urban areas' (1996: 211, 29).

27. *Bhe v. Magistrate, Khayelitsha*, paras 84, 86, 87 and 89.

28. *S. v. Makwanyane*, para. 365.

29. Driberg (1934: 232) argues that African law is always constructive and palliative.

30. According to Mazrui, 'the substitution of the cage for the villain to replace compensation for the victim, the insistence on objective guilt as against subjective shame, the focus on personal individual accountability as against collective responsibility have all resulted not only in escalating violence, and criminality, especially in African cities, but also in the relentless decay of the police, judiciary, legal system and prison structures' (1998: 257).

31. Sebidi states: '*Ubuntu* is more than just an attribute of individual human acts that builds a community. It is a basic humanistic orientation towards one's fellow human beings . . . one's humanity; one's personhood is dependent upon one's relationship with others. Therefore *ubuntu*, however inchoate in terms of strict philosophical formulation, certainly rejects the rugged individualism that seems to be encouraged by some philosophical systems and ideological persuasions. *Ubuntu* is anti-individualism and pro-communalism' (1998: 63). Article 27 (1) of the African (Banjul) Charter on Human and Peoples' Rights provides that every individual shall have duties towards his family and society. Article 29 (1) stipulates that individuals have the duty to preserve the harmonious development of the family and to work for the cohesion and respect of the family, to respect their parents at all times and to maintain them in cases of need.

    Restorative justice is a characteristic of African law. Tutu states: 'Ubuntu-botho did not allow perpetrators to escape the necessity of confessing and making restitution to survivors since it placed the needs of society – the restoration of relationships – at the heart of reconciliation' (in Allen 2006: 347).

32. See *Bhe v. Magistrate, Khayelitsha*, para. 89. Strong communitarianism is the cornerstone of ubuntu. African communitarianism is portrayed in the Zulu proverb '*umuntu, ngumuntu ngabantu*', affirming that 'I am because we are, and since we are, therefore I am.' Biko describes the African community as a 'true man-centred society whose sacred tradition is that of sharing. We must reject, as we have been doing, the individualistic, cold approach to life that is the cornerstone of the Anglo-Boer culture' (2007: 113).

33. According to M'Baye, African 'Gods, Genii [spirits] and Ancestors' act as African legislators; they lay down the laws and guide man to survival (1974: 141–2). M'Baye describes genii as spirits superior to men: 'They have rights which must be scrupulously respected . . . Genii intervene continually in daily life, and wisdom dictates a sacrifice to them either before or after every event in life of however little importance.'

34. Somé states: 'In Africa people's welfare and rights are safeguarded by the Ancestors. It is the ancestors who ultimately punish wrongdoing, by sending trouble or illness, even death to the transgressors' (1999: 89).

35. According to Ngubane, 'the person was created according to the Law; he was conceived according to the Law; he was born, fed and clothed according to the Law; all he did; all his thinking and behaviour; all his hopes, victories, fears and defeats translated the Law into action. He could not violate the Law because he incarnated it. Nothing could oppose the Law because everything in the cosmic order conformed to the Law. Conflict itself was a translation into action of the Law. The person grew up and thrived in terms of the Law; he matured, aged and died according to it; he evolved perpetually into eternity according to Law' (in Bhengu 2006: 24).

36. Ramose says the '*ubuntu* legal philosophical principle seek[s] the restoration of disturbed equilibrium regardless of the time when the disturbance occurred'. According to Driberg: 'A debt or feud is never extinguished till the equilibrium has been restored, even if several generations lapse' (in Ramose 2002: 95).

37. Bekker, Rautenbach and Goolam (2006: 118) say that all adult men are members of the court council, but only the chief and elders of the patrilineage fulfil court duties.

38. According to Ephirim-Donkor (1998: 126), elders have already attained immortality and ancestorhood in the flesh and are awaiting the final transformation through death: 'Elders take their responsibilities seriously, for they are being watched by the omniscient ancestors before whom they must appear and be judges upon their deaths.' Should elders fail in their duties, they are removed from their duties – first, for having been rejected by the ancestors and second, for failing the community.

39. Ephirim-Donkor (1998) argues that freedom of expression is paramount during court deliberations.

40. According to Mangena, the community knows the various forms of punishment for different forms of misbehaviour. 'This in itself shows that there is no separation between the theory and practice in these systems. Sex groups consulted with each other when one of their lot had to be judged and punished for misconduct. For instance, a young man could be punished by being ostracised by his group for a defined period. The young women of that particular age group would be consulted in the judgment of the case and they would participate in carrying out the punishment against the culprit. The young man would therefore be ostracised also by the women of his age group' (1996: 59).

    Somé maintains that African villages have no police as the ancestors of these villages protect all homes. He accentuates the dire need for communities to invoke the spirits of the ancestors to create safety for themselves.

41. *S. v. Makwanyane*, para. 308, per Mokgoro J.

42. Broodryk (2002: 27) states that the Zulu refers to the philosophy of African collective unity or brotherhood as *ubuntu*; *ubuntu* or *umuntu* in Xhosa; *botho* in Sesotho; *bunhu* in Tsonga; *vhuthu* in Venda; *numunhu* in Shangaan; *nunhu* in Shona; *utu* in Swahili and *abantu* in Ugandan. According to Kamwangamalu (1999: 25), ubuntu is known in Kenya as *umundu* in Kikuyu; as *ununtu* in Kimeru; in Tanzania it is known as *bumuntu* in kiSukuma and kiHaya; in Mozambique it is known as *vumuntu* in shiTsonga and shiTswa; in the Democratic Republic of Congo ubuntu is called *gimuntu* in kiKongo and in Angola it is known as *gimuntu* in giKwese.

43. Gyekye agrees: 'The moral values of various African societies are the same across the board; that most values can be said to be shared in their essentials by all African societies . . . and derived from African religion' (1996: 55–6).

44. Bhengu argues that the concept of human rights is a creation of Western civilisation that it is foreign to African law. See also Broodryk (1997: 97) and M'Baye (1974: 143–5).

45. Senghor defines Negritude as 'the sum total of African cultural values', which emphasise the uniqueness of African racial and cultural consciousness: 'Negritude is the whole complex of civilized values, economic, social and political – which characterize the black peoples, or more precisely, the Negro-African world. All these values are essentially informed by intuitive reason. Because this sentient reason, the reason which comes to grips, expresses itself emotionally, through the self-surrender, that coalescence of subject and object, through myths, by which I mean the archetypal images of the collective soul' (1963: 13).

    Tempels describes the most fundamental and basic concept in Bantu thought as a 'vital force' or African spirituality, saying that 'mythological *Bantu philosophy*, namely the wisdom of the Bantu based on the philosophy of vital force is accepted by everyone; is not subjected to criticism, for it is taken by the whole community as the imperishable truth' (1969: 75). Tempels maintains that ethnophilosophy is based on African religion.

According to Oruka (1990: 9), the works of Tempels, Kgame, Senghor, Mbiti, Horton, Ruch, Onyewuenyi and Anyanwu are perceived as ethnophilosophy.

46. According to Carel and Gamez, Nkrumah and Nyerere 'developed ethnophilosophical observations about the communal character of African societies into African socialism which they used to solve concrete political problems in Ghana and Tanzania' (2004: 101).

47. Broodryk describes ubuntu as 'a worldview transferred verbally through generations' (1997: 198–9).

48. Oruka describes ethnophilosophy as 'emotive, mystical and unlogical' and juxtaposes it with philosophy in the strict sense, which exhibits 'the method of critical, reflective and logical enquiry' (2002: 121, 120). Hallen suggests that the sources of ethnophilosophy are 'authentic traditional culture of the pre-colonial variety of Africa prior to modernity' (2002: 50). Kapagawani (1990: 182) cites ethnophilosophy's sources as traditional wisdom, institutions, myths, folktales, beliefs and proverbs of Africa.

49. Tempels maintains that ethnophilosophy is based on African religion. According to Tempels, everything in Baluba reality interacts with the metaphysical (1969: 55). Bantu wisdom or knowledge consists of the 'Bantu's discernment of the nature of beings, of forces; true wisdom lies in ontological knowledge' (71). Tempels sees Bantu knowledge as metaphysical in nature and Bantu moral standards dependent 'on things ontologically understood' (73, 121).

50. Bhengu states that 'the majority of the population of Southern Africa today cannot be properly said to know and live Ubuntu by virtue of any continuity with village life' (2006: 101–2).

51. Khumalo and Wieringa argue that these societies 'are hierarchical and strongly patriarchal. Those at the bottom, women and particularly lesbians, get the rawest deal' (in Morgan and Wieringa 2005: 261).

52. Boon states: 'Personal accountability works directly against the African concept of *uMona*, or tallest poppy syndrome. If you stick your head out or raise it above the group, it is seen as exposing the group, and pressure will be brought to bear on the individual to retreat. This can extend to threats of violence, witchcraft and even death, and needs to be taken very seriously . . . Leaders must be aware of the enormous courage it takes for any individual to stand against uMona' (2007: 124–5). According to Boon, *uMona* implies that if an individual suddenly acquires material wealth, it is deemed to be the result of magic and dealt with accordingly. Vilakazi considers a person who suddenly acquires wealth as a danger to society and comments that the Zulu, for example, regard such a person as a sorcerer (in Broodryk 1997: 11). Somé contends that abundance among the Dagara people 'insulted the entire setup of the tribe. People waited for the inevitable. It [death] occurred quickly' (1997: 15). Broodryk (1997: 42) states that what Western culture perceives as a lack of initiative by Africans is in fact a result of the latter's view that a person should not aspire to more status or power than that accorded to him by the specific position of seniority he occupies. Ambition is traditionally not viewed as a virtue.

53. Thus, according to M'Baye (1974: 144), women, strangers, children, sick men and slaves have very low legal status, if any, in traditional African societies.

54. According to Mbigi (1997: 53, 56–9), the African spirit world consists of God, the ancestors, nature spirits and evil spirits. The hierarchy within the African spirit world, from top to bottom, constitutes rainmaker spirits (regarded as representatives of God on earth), hunter spirits, clan spirits, spirits of divination, war spirits, wandering spirits, avenging spirits and witches, who have the lowest status in the African spirit world.

Nyirongo (1997: 104) posits that the souls of women and daughters do not qualify as ancestors, except in a few matrilineal tribes where inheritance falls in female lines. This explains why the elders are men.

55. Broodryk states: 'Traditionally, the husband is the head of the household and the wife realises that she is not equal to the husband. She addresses the husband as "father" and by doing this the children are given an example of how to behave. A woman does not cross words with a man and should she do this it reflects a bad image of her – a poor development sense of Ubuntu' (1997: 24). Idowu explains: 'Where she [a woman] behaves herself according to prescription and accepts an inferior position, benevolence, which becomes her "poverty", is assured, and for this she shows herself deeply and humbly grateful. If for any reason she takes it into her head to be self-assertive and claims footing of equality, then she brings upon herself a frown; she is called names; she is persecuted openly or by indirect means; she is helped to be divided against herself . . . a victim who somehow is developing unexpected power and resilience which might be a threat to the erstwhile strong' (1975: 77). African feminist Nawal El Sawaadi makes it very clear: 'Women are at the rock bottom of society, of the family unit, of the home, the connective tissue of society, the mainstay of economic life, the producers and reproducers. They shoulder 90% of all work but own only 10% of what is owned' (in Stewart 2005: 205).

56. Menkiti argues that 'the absence of ritualised grief over the death of a child in African societies contrasts with the elaborate burial ceremony and ritualised grief of deceased older persons', who have attained personhood and status (in Gyekye 2002: 302).

57. Mutwa explains that a child is born without a soul or *ena*, which only 'builds up slowly of the memories and thoughts and the experiences as it grows up into a man or woman'. A child who dies without an *ena* cannot therefore become an ancestor (1998: 568–9).

58. 'Africa has a repressed memory. Why is there so much silence in Africa? If African women started remembering all of the violence that they experienced, well, it would be an explosion. Is this really a good thing? I believe that they succeed in killing the event by silence, and perhaps in our case it is for the better' (Liking in Stewart 2005: 196).

59. In *Dikoko v. Mokhatla* 2006 (6) SA 235 (CC), Mokgoro and Sachs J.J. link ubuntu to reconciliation and restoration. Tutu (1999: 51–2) describes restorative justice as a strong point of indigenous African culture. Naudé (2006: 101) points out that restorative justice is not unique to ubuntu as it can be linked to both African and Western jurisprudence. Naudé claims that restorative justice is known in indigenous communities in Canada, Australia, New Zealand and countries in Africa, as well as in the ancient Greek, Roman and Arab civilisations. Naudé also suggests that reconciliation is not always sought where disputes involve strangers or outsiders in traditional African societies (102).

60. Mangena states: 'This [consensus] was the African form of democracy. According to Kenyatta, among the Gikuyu there was a "spirit of collectivity" in the council's meetings. No one spoke in terms of the personal pronoun "I". Instead each individual reverted to

the "WE". The "we" stood also for the members of the lineage represented by the elders because it was the voice of the people or public that ruled the country. Individualism and self-seeking were ruled out, for every respective elder spoke in the name of his particular group' (1996: 58). According to Mbigi, 'traditional African political systems and values treasured democracy, freedom of expression, consensus, grass-roots participation, consultation and institutionalization to preserve the collective solidarity of ubuntu above confrontation, foreign ideologies and personal cults; this ensured political stability and unity. These elements remain crucial and relevant to the task of nation building in modern Africa' (1997: 28). Mandela describes consensus democracy as follows: 'Everyone who wants to speak is entitled to do so and everyone is heard whether it is chief or subject, warrior or medicine man, shopkeeper or farmer, landowner or labourer. In the African environment, people spoke without interruption and meetings lasted for hours since all men were free to voice their opinions and were equal in their value as citizens. Such meetings would continue until consensus was reached. They ended in unanimity or not at all. Democracy meant all men were to be heard and a decision was taken together as a people. Majority rule was a foreign notion' (1994: 21). Mangena explains that according to the oral tradition, women are not necessarily refused attendance at communal gatherings. They are however expected to listen and not talk (1996: 56).

61. 'This is so because the greater a person is; the closer he is to the ancestors' (Nyirongo 1997: 63).
62. According to Mutwa, 'Bantu execution is not merely punishment; it is a sacrifice to appease the ancestral spirits of the family, who cry out for revenge' (1998: 632). He also maintains that 'the black man is the most ardent of grudge bearers and revenge-lovers . . . the black man of Africa has not learnt the meaning of the word forgiveness. His mind cannot fathom that there are other races that can fight today and be friends tomorrow' (630).
63. *Port Elizabeth Municipality v. Various Occupiers* 2005 (1) SA 217 (CC), para. 37. See also *Union of Refugee Women and Others* 2007 (4) SA 395 (CC), para. 145.
64. The Moral Regeneration Movement, Ubuntu Pledge, Heartlines Project, the Ubuntu Project and African Renaissance aspire to rekindle ancient ubuntu values.
65. Kunene avers: '*Ubuntu* is the very quality that guarantees not only separation between men, women and the beast, but the very fluctuating gradations that determine the relative quality of that essence. It is for that reason that we prefer to call it the potential of being human' (in Mokgoro 1997: 2).
66. Tsitsi Dangarembga says: 'The victimization I saw was universal. It didn't depend on poverty, on lack of education or on tradition. It didn't depend on any of the things I had thought it depended on. Men took it everywhere with them . . . femaleness as opposed and inferior to maleness' (in Stewart 2005: 173).
67. Violence against women is endemic in Africa. The United Nations defines violence against women broadly as 'any act of gender-based violence that results in, or is likely to result in, physical, sexual or psychological harm or suffering to women, including threats of such acts, coercion or arbitrary deprivation of liberty, whether occurring in public or private life'. It includes female genital mutilation and rape (see http:// www.un.org/womenwatch/daw/beijing/platform/violence.htm). The United Nations (International) Children's (Emergency) Fund (UNICEF) describes violence against women as 'one of the most pervasive of human rights violations, denying women and girls equality, security, dignity, self-worth and their

right to enjoy fundamental freedoms' (see http://www.unicef-irc.org/publications/pdf/digest6e.pdf). There is a strong connection between violence and the spread of HIV and AIDS, dubbed the dual epidemics in women's lives (Banda 2005: 170; Terry 2007: 137). Women infected with HIV and AIDS 'face new forms of violence – accusations, battery, being made homeless, being poisoned and killed – the list goes on' (Otive-Igbuzor 2007: 210).

Suzanne Leclerc-Madlala (in Stein 2000) and Rankhotha (2004: 87) both see virginity testing as a weapon that men use to enforce patriarchal masculinity over women. According to Rankhotha, patriarchal masculinity is forced on women through physical violence and rape. Virginity testing of girls younger than sixteen continues in the Eastern Cape, Limpopo, KwaZulu-Natal and other regions in South Africa. This violation of their human rights denies them their rights to autonomy and human dignity (Mukasa 2008: 149). Though section 12 (4) of the Children's Act 38 of 2005 prohibits virginity testing of children younger than sixteen, the Bill of Rights has been unable to guarantee human dignity to girls who are still subjected to the violation of their human rights through virginity testing. Moodley states that virginity testing 'merely serves to promote patriarchal interests by keeping women inferior, marginalised and subservient' (2008: 70).

Female genital mutilation (FGM) is currently practised in 28 African countries and constitutes a rite of passage that imparts the future roles and positions of young girls in the patriarchal hierarchy as wives and mothers. FGM's additional role is to curb the sexual desires of women. Most girls are circumcised between the ages of four and twelve to alleviate the trauma associated with the surgery and to circumvent governmental intrusion (Moodley 2008: 67–9). Despite the fact that article 5 of the African Women's Protocol prohibits FGM, it is widespread in sub-Saharan Africa (Terry 2007: 48–50). Section 12 (3) of the Children's Act 38 of 2005 prohibits FGM in South Africa.

In spite of South Africa's constitutional guarantees of gender equality; prescriptions in the Sexual Offences Amendment Act 32 of 2007, which deems sex with children younger than sixteen as statutory rape; provisions in the Children's Amendment Act 38 of 2005; CEDAW (United Nation's Convention on the Elimination of all Forms of Discrimination Against Women) and the African Women's Protocol, which outlaw marriage to girls younger than eighteen, the ancient cultural practice of *ukuthwalwa* still prevails in traditional societies in South Africa. Thirty-one African girls between fourteen and sixteen years old were recently abducted from their houses in the Eastern Cape under the pretext of age-old custom. These girls were traded by their families 'for as little as three sheep apiece' to men 'between 55 and 70 years old, widowed and HIV positive'. While twenty of the thirty-one girls were fortunate enough to manage to flee, eleven of these girls 'were raped and forced into domestic chattelhood by their new husbands' (*Sunday Times*, 31 May 2009).

Section 5 of the Prevention of Family Violence Act 113 of 1993 provides that a man can be found guilty of raping his spouse. South Africa is one of the few countries in the world that has criminalised marital rape.

68. Mnyaka and Motlhabi contend that hospitality was 'a public duty where the honor of the community was at stake and reciprocity was more likely to be communal than individual . . . hospitality was a sacred duty' (2005: 230).

69. Oduyoye states that in many villages there is a *femme du village*, a collective wife of a known group of men. This practice is called polyandry and not prostitution. 'The men are not clients and do not remain anonymous. They are known and the relationship is approved. Lala maintains prostitution and celibacy as modes of expressing sexuality were unknown in Africa' (in Oduyoye 2001: 103).
70. Wamue reports that 'among the Agikuyu this practice is euphemistically associated with making a bed for a guest . . . the women, wife or daughter can refuse to make the bed and the guest can also decline the honour' (in Oduyoye 2001: 102).
71. Osei-Hwedie argues that 'gender inequality is one of the most pressing problems in contemporary Africa, because it is one of the major causes of the low status of women and the poverty characteristic of the majority of women . . . patriarchy remains the overarching obstacle to women's advancement and equality with males' (in Jacques and Lesetedi 2005: 154, 155).
72. Ebeku states: 'African women have for too long suffered a great deal of human rights abuses' (2004: 1).
73. Rankhotha argues that the current reintroduction of 'outdated cultural practices is not only unfounded, but that traditionalists want to cling to patriarchal privileges in the context of the new culture of human rights and gender equality seems tilted against them and self interest' (2004: 80).
74. Nineteen-year-old Zoliswa Nkonyane was stoned to death by twenty males of a Khayelitsha gang because of her sexual orientation (*Mail & Guardian*, 30 October – 5 November 2009).
75. See also *The Economist*, April 2007: 46.
76. Reddy asserts that most African states are homophobic, criminalise homosexuality and withdraw rights of citizenship to gays and lesbians: 'This is, in part, fuelled by the notion of the "un-Africanness" of homosexuality, despite the overwhelming evidence of its existence' (2004: 7). Kenya's President Moi verbally attacked homosexuals and lesbians on various occasions, saying 'Kenya has no room or time for homosexuals and lesbians. Homosexuality is against African norms and traditions, and even in religion it is considered a great sin' (Baraka et al. in Morgan and Wieringa 2005: 25). The International Lesbian and Gay Association (ILGA), based in Brussels, estimates that Africa has more than 24 million active homosexuals (*The Economist*, April 2007: 46) and says that 38 African countries still criminalise consensual same-sex activity between adults (*Mail & Guardian*, 16–22 May 2008).
77. See Muholi (2004: 116–24) for an account of hate crimes against African lesbians.
78. *Die Burger, By* (August 2009: 11–12) quotes an African lesbian who says that 99 per cent of African lesbians who come out of the closet in South Africa are either raped or sexually assaulted.
79. Hallen and Sodipo see witchcraft as an explanation that is used when no othe explanations are forthcoming. Witchcraft becomes a type of explanation 'that provides for the victims doing something concrete about their misfortunes' (1997: 88).
80. Holland explains that where witchcraft is suspected, strict procedures for accusation must be adhered to. The family first has to consult a traditional healer who has to confirm a witch's involvement. 'But once the healer names a witch, invariably someone living in the same village as the victim, the family declares its accusation by leaving a small heap of ash

or some other token in the doorway of the accused's house during the night. When the suspect awakes and acknowledges the accusation, often amid strenuous protests, he or she goes to see the headman who arranges a trial by order' (2001: 18–20). If the accused is found guilty after various tests, she can either confess and be spared or protest and be killed in a ceremony at sunrise, or be beaten and driven away like a wild animal. Oduyoye says that exile is deemed worse than judicial execution (2001: 26). Many accused as witches are burned alive in their huts.

81. According to Mutwa, 'it is believed that burning a person to death not only destroys the body but also the *ena* and the soul – fire itself being a "spirit" capable of dissolving other kinds of spirits' (1998: 629, 632).

The executive council of the Northern Province (currently Limpopo) appointed the Commission into Witchcraft Violence and Ritual Murders in March 1995 (Mukasa 2008: 148). Police statistics revealed that 445 cases of witchcraft were reported between 1990 and 1995 in this province and that between 1 April 1994 and 16 February 1995, 97 women and 46 men were killed as a result of accusations of witchcraft. Currently the killing of witches prevails in South Africa. The reality of the belief in witchcraft was recently highlighted when the South African Defence Force's first black female judge, Colonel Nomoyi, allegedly doused herself in petrol and set herself alight. Her defence was that she was bewitched when she attempted to kill herself. Despite the fact that attempted suicide is deemed a serious offence in the South African military, the judge escaped prosecution because 'some of the SA National Defence Force's top brass allegedly believed her claim that she was bewitched' (*Sunday Times*, 9 November 2008: 9).

82. The notion of equality in traditional African societies differs profoundly from the Western notion of equality. Muendane describes ubuntu equality as follows: 'Everyone in the group complies with the dictates and standards set by the particular group; everyone in the group is simply expected to do that. When an individual belonging to the group deviates from the cultural standard or norm, everyone else becomes disturbed and that can result in isolation, ostracism, condemnation, criticism or censure of the deviating individual. At any rate, that individual will forfeit something of benefit, as members of the group with whom the particular cultural behaviour is associated, withdraw different forms of cooperation and other benefits from him or her. This response to the deviating person by the group is normal within all groups as it is intended to protect group cohesion. Group cultural practices have the function of helping members of the group to easily identify one another because individuals in any group use the properties of the custom or culture as *reference* for action within the group to ensure cooperation and harmony. Without the cooperation of others, one can never accomplish anything in life. The groups we belong to are the first port of call in our endeavour to seek cooperation to achieve our goals. This is as things should be, and is applicable universally' throughout sub-Saharan Africa (2006: 91).

83. Violence is also evident during male initiations. Despite the fact that section 12 of the Children's Act prohibits circumcision of boys under the age of sixteen, the traditional ritual in preparation for manhood continues. Van der Zalm says that 'problems arise when circumcisers are blunt . . . and when punishments for such lapses as forgetting words of a chant become too severe – some boys are literally beaten to death' (2008: 907). Nyirongo explains that 'throughout the training the members [male initiates] are forbidden to see

women and to stray out of the camp. Anyone who disobeys the rule is instantly killed within the camp' (1997: 132).

84. Mutwa (1996: 9, 2003: xv) maintains that Africans who disclose secrets of traditional African societies to outsiders are despised by their people.

85. Mutwa (2003: xxii–iv) distinguishes between inyangas and sangomas: the former (also known as herbalists) inherit their profession from their relatives, but sangomas receive 'a call from the spirits'. The sangoma understands and controls the same occult forces as the sorcerer and can cure persons affected by the magic spells of the sorcerer. The sangoma's power, however, transcends that of the sorcerer. Broodryk writes that sangomas 'are more often than not the murderers of people and young children, or the instigators of such murders, in order to obtain human parts for *muti* (medicine)' (2005: 123).

86. Mutwa says: 'An African can lie with great ease to any missionary, chief, magistrate or judge. He can lie without winking an eye. But no African will dare to lie to a witchdoctor' or sangoma (1998: 627).

87. 'South Africa has the only specialized investigation force in the world dealing specifically with muti murders . . . [and] up to 300 muti killings occur each year' (Dynes in Van der Zalm 2008: 911). During *muti* murders, the body parts of victims are harvested for use in traditional healing practices. Body parts will usually be removed while the victim is still alive as the victim's screams invoke the ancestors and make the *muti* or traditional medicine more powerful. Mbiti (1992: 68–70), Mbigi (1997: 56–9), Mutwa (2003: xxii) and Broodryk (2007: 127–8) all agree that sangomas are seen as intermediaries of God and regarded as scientists, psychologists, parapsychologists, clairvoyants, artists, diviners, doctors, purifiers of age sets; predictors and solicitors of rain; curers of spirit-possessed persons and communicators with the dead in African societies. According to Mutwa (2003: xxii), sangomas fulfil the same role as priests and psychiatrists in Western societies.

88. Mbiti (1992: 5), Turaki (1997: 63) and Mbigi (1997: 56) confirm that African religion is inaccessible to outsiders. M'Baye (1974: 142) and Turaki (1997: 61, 139) show that African law does not apply to outsiders. Naudé (2006: 102) states that African justice does not apply to outsiders. Mutwa (1998: 555–6) avers that sacred knowledge is never revealed to outsiders.

89. A closed society is defined as a society characterised by belief in magical taboos and superstitions. Open societies give preference to reason. Turaki says that because the ubuntu world view is 'essentially spiritual', the community has a 'moral obligation to conform to traditions, and conventions override any desire for change or nonconformity. The conception is that the best in life lies in the past; the world of the ancestors and the origin' (1997: 49). Biakolo says that the model of traditional African thought 'is a closed system because unlike the open scientific culture neither understands nor tolerates alternative thought . . . In the event, traditional African thought turns out to be lacking in logic' (2002: 17). Biakolo also explains that 'all traditional African thought [is] based on religion'.

90. 'What is right and wrong can only be committed against a member of the own ethnic group, race or tribe, but not against a stranger or an outsider. An outsider has no rights or protection and anything done to him has no moral or ethical value. It is an insider who has rights, privileges and protection under racial and tribal laws. Thus killing or discriminating against an outsider is not a crime' (Turaki 1997: 68).

91. Nyirongo (1997), M'Baye (1974: 141) and Turaki (1997: 61) argue that the right to equality does not exist in traditional African societies because every person fits into a social hierarchy (see also Mqeke 1996: 365).
92. According to Ramose, '*ubuntu* philosophy of law is the continuation of religion' (2002: 97).
93. *Port Elizabeth Municipality v. Various Occupiers*, para. 37.
94. Osei-Hwedie insists that equality (and specifically gender equality) and human dignity are the most pressing humanitarian problems in sub-Saharan Africa (in Jacques and Lesetedi 2005: 154).
95. 'Social engineers and social and legal philosophers' is from *Baloro v. University of Bophuthatswana*: 235, E–F, per Friedman J.P.

     Bhengu argues that ubuntu is 'Africa's key to freedom and equality for all . . . [embodying] the spirit of human dignity, justice and equality' (2006: 8, 206).

     'Sexism and patriarchy are so ancient, all pervasive and incorporated into the practice of daily life as to appear socially and culturally normal and legally invisible' is from *Volks N.O. v. Robinson*, para. 163, per Sachs J.
96. *S. v. Makwanyane*, para. 366.

References

Abraham, W.E. 1962. *The Mind of Africa*. London: Weidenfeld & Nicolson.

Achebe, C. 1986. *Things Fall Apart*. Oxford: Heinemann.

Aidoo, A.A. 1991. *Changes: A Love Story*. New York: Feminist Press.

Akatsa-Bukachi, M. 2005. 'African Feminism: Does it Exist?' Presentation made at the Tanzania Gender Networking Programme Gender Festival, 6–9 September.

Allen, J. 2006. *Rabble-Rouser for Peace: The Authorized Biography of Desmond Tutu*. London: Rider.

Arndt, S. 2002. *The Dynamics of African Feminism*. Trenton: Africa World Press.

Banda, F. 2005. *Women, Law and Human Rights: An African Perspective*. Oxford: Hart Publishing.

Bekker, J.C., C. Rautenbach and N.M.I. Goolam. 2006. *Introduction to Legal Pluralism in South Africa*. Durban: Butterworths.

Bhengu, M.J. 2006. *Ubuntu: The Global Philosophy for Humankind*. Cape Town: Lotsha Publications.

Biakolo, E. 2002. 'Categories of Cross-Cultural Cognition and the African Condition'. In *Philosophy from Africa: A Text with Readings*, ed. P.H. Coetzee and A.P.J. Roux, 9–19. Cape Town: Oxford University Press.

Biko, S. 2007. *Steve Biko: No Fears Expressed*. Johannesburg: Mutloatse Arts Heritage Trust.

Bohler-Muller, N. 2005. 'The Story of an African Value'. *SA Public Law* 20 (2): 266–80.

Boon, M. 2007. *The African Way: The Power of Interactive Leadership*. Cape Town: Zebra Press.

Broodryk, J. 1997. 'Ubuntuism as a Worldview to Order Society'. Ph.D. diss. Pretoria: Unisa.

———. 2002. *Ubuntu: Life Lessons from Africa*. Pretoria: Ubuntu School of Philosophy.

————. 2005. *Ubuntu Management Philosophy*. Randburg: Knowledge Resources Publishing.

————. 2007. *Understanding South Africa: The Ubuntu Way of Living*. Pretoria: Ubuntu School of Philosophy.

Carel, H. and D. Gamez (eds). 2004. *What Philosophy Is: Contemporary Philosophy in Action*. London: Continuum.

Driberg, J.H. 1934. 'The African Conception of Law'. *Journal of Comparative Legislation and International Law* 3 (XVI): 230–46.

Ebeku, K.S.A. 2004. 'A New Hope for African Women: Overview of African Women's Protocol on Women's Rights'. *Nordic Journal of African Studies* 13 (3): 264–74.

Ebo, C. 1995. 'Indigenous Law and Justice'. In *African Law and Legal Theory*, ed. G.R. Woodman and A.O Obilade, 33–42. Aldershot: Dartmouth Publishing.

Ephirim-Donkor, A. 1998. *African Spirituality: On Becoming Ancestors*. Trenton: African World Press.

Gyekye, K. 1996. *African Cultural Values: An Introduction*. Philadelphia: Skofana Publishing.

————. 2002. 'Person and Community in African Thought'. In *Philosophy from Africa: A Text with Readings*, ed. P.H. Coetzee and A.P.J. Roux, 297–312. Cape Town: Oxford University Press.

Hallen, B. 2002. *A Short History of African Philosophy*. Bloomington: Indiana University Press.

Hallen, B. and J.O. Sodipo. 1997. *Knowledge, Belief and Witchcraft: Analytic Experiments in African Philosophy*. Stanford: Stanford University Press.

Holland, H. 2001. *African Magic: Traditional Ideas That Heal a Continent*. Johannesburg: Penguin.

Idowu, E.B. 1975. *Traditional African Religion: A Definition*. New York: Oribis.

Imbo, S.O. 1999. *An Introduction to African Philosophy*. Maryland: Rowman & Littlefield.

Jacques, G. and G.N. Lesetedi (eds). 2005. *The New Partnership for Africa's Development: Debates, Opportunities and Challenges*. Pretoria: Africa Institute of South Africa.

Kagame, A. 1956. *La philosophie Bantu-Rwandaise de l' être*. Brussels: Académie Royale des Sciences.

Kamalu, C. 1998. *Person, Divinity and Nature: A Modern View of the Person and the Cosmos in African Thought*. London: Karnak House.

Kamwangamalu, M.N. 1999. 'Ubuntu in South Africa: A Sociolinguistic Perspective to a Pan African Concept'. *Critical Arts* 13: 25.

Kapagawani, D.N.A. 1990. 'Bantu Nomenclature and African Philosophy'. In *Sage Philosophy: Indigenous Thinkers and Modern Debate on African Philosophy*, ed. H.O. Oruka, 181–204. New York: E.J. Brill.

Keevy, I. 2009. 'The Constitutional Court and Ubuntu's Inseparable Trinity'. *Journal for Juridical Science* 34 (1): 61–88.

Khapoya, V.B. 1994. *The African Experience: An Introduction*. Upper Saddle River: Prentice Hall.

Makinwa-Adebusoye, P. and R. Tiemoko. 2007. 'Healthy Sexuality: Discourses in East, West, North and Southern Africa'. In *Human Sexuality in Africa*, ed. E. Maticka-Tyndale, R. Tiemoko and P. Makinwa-Adebusoye, 1–18. Johannesburg: Jacana Media.

Makudu, N. 1993. 'Cultivating a Climate of Co-Operation through Ubuntu'. *Enterprise Magazine*, August.

Malera, G.T. 2007. 'Women, Reproductive Rights and HIV/AIDS: The Value of the African Charter Protocol'. *Agenda* 72: 127–37.

Mamdani, M. 1996. *Citizen and Subject: Contemporary Africa and the Legacy of Late Colonialism*. Princeton: Princeton University Press.

Mandela, N. 1994. *Long Walk to Freedom: The Autobiography of Nelson Mandela*. Boston: Little, Brown.

Mangena, J.M.O. 1996. 'Eurocentric Development and the Imperative of Women's Emancipation in Sub-Sahara Africa'. Ph.D. diss. Amsterdam: University of Amsterdam.

Mazrui, A.A. 1998. 'Post-Colonial Society and Africa's Triple Inheritance of Law: Indigenous, Islamic and Western Inheritance of Law'. In *Enlightenment, Rights and Revolution: Essays in Legal and Social Philosophy*, ed. N. Maccormack and Z. Bankowski, 252–63. Aberdeen: Aberdeen University Press.

M'Baye, K. 1974. 'The African Conception of Law'. *International Encyclopedia of Comparative Law* 1: 138–58.

Mbigi, L. 1997. *Ubuntu: The African Dream in Management*. Pretoria: Sigma Press.

Mbiti, J.S. 1991. *Introduction to African Religion*. London: Heinemann.

———. 1992. *African Religions and Philosophy*. London: Heinemann.

Mdluli, P. 1987. 'Ubunto-Botho: Inkatha's People Education'. *Transformation* 5: 60–77.

Mnyaka M. and M. Motlhabi. 2005. *The African Concept of Ubuntu/Botho and its Social-Moral Significance in Black Theology*. London: Equinox Publishing.

Mokgoro, Y. 1997. 'Ubuntu and the Law in South Africa'. Paper delivered at the first Colloquium on Constitution and Law, Potchefstroom, 31 October.

———. 1998. 'Ubuntu and the Law in South Africa'. *Buffalo Human Rights Law Review* 4: 15–24.

Moodley, I. 2008. 'Customary Initiation Rites and the Children's Act 38 of 2005'. *SA Public Law* 23: 65–86.

Morgan, R. and S. Wieringa. 2005. *Tommy Boys, Lesbian Men and Ancestral Wives: Female Same-Sex Practices in Africa*. Johannesburg: Jacana Media.

Mqeke, R.B. 1996. 'Customary Law and Human Rights'. *South African Law Journal* 113: 365–9.

Mudimbe, V-Y. 1988. *The Invention of Africa: Gnosis, Philosophy, and the Order of Knowledge*. London: James Currey.

Muendane, N.M. 2006. *I Am an African*. Pretoria: Jakaranda.

Muholi, Z. 2004. 'Thinking through Lesbian Rape'. *Agenda* 61: 116–24.

Mukasa, R.S. 2008. *The African Women's Protocol*. Johannesburg: Jacana Media.

Mutwa, V.C. 1996. *Isilwane, the Animal: Tales and Fables of Africa*. Cape Town: Struik.

———. 1998. *Indaba, My Children*. Edinburgh: Payback Press.

———. 2003. *Zulu Shaman: Dreams, Prophesies and Mysteries*. Rochester: Destiny Books.

Naudé, B. 2006. 'An International Perspective of Restorative Justice Practices and Research Outcomes'. *Journal of Juridical Science* 31 (1): 101–20.

Nduka, O. 1995. 'Traditional Concepts of Justice among the Ibo of South-Eastern Nigeria'. In *African Law and Legal Theory*, ed. G.R. Woodman and A.O. Obilade, 19–31. Aldershot: Dartmouth Publishing.

Ngubane, J.K. 1979. *Conflict of Minds: Changing Power Dispositions in South Africa*. New York: Books in Focus.

Nhlapo, T. 1995. 'African Customary Law in the Interim Constitution'. In *The Constitution of South Africa from a Gender Perspective*, ed. S. Liebenberg, 157–69. Cape Town: Community Law Centre, University of the Western Cape, in association with David Philip.

Nkabinde, N.Z. 2008. *Black Bull, Ancestors and Me: My Life As a Lesbian Sangoma*. Johannesburg: Fanele.

Nkrumah, K. 1964. *Consciencism: Philosophy and Ideology for Decolonisation*. London: Panaf.

Nyerere, J. 1968. *Ujamaa: Essays on Socialism*. Oxford: Oxford University Press.

Nyirongo, L. 1997. *The Gods of Africa and the God of the Bible: The Snares of African Traditional Religion*. Potchefstroom: Institute for Reformational Studies.

Obenga, T. 2004. 'Egypt: Ancient History of African Philosophy'. In *A Companion to African Philosophy*, ed. K. Wiredu, 31–49. Oxford: Blackwell.

Oduyoye, M.A. 1989. 'Christian Feminism and African Culture: The "Hearth" of the Matter'. In *The Future of Liberation Theology: Essays in Honour of Gustavo Guttierez*, ed. M.H. Ellis and O. Maduro, 441–8. New York: Orbis.

———. 2001. *Introducing African Women's Theology*. Sheffield: Sheffield Academic Press.

Ojwang, J.B. 1995. 'The Meaning, Content and Significance of Tribal Law in an Emergent Nation: The Kenyan Case'. In *African Law and Legal Theory*, ed. G.R. Woodman and A.O. Obilade, 43–58. Aldershot: Dartmouth Publishing.

Oruka, H.O. 2002. 'Four Trends in Current African Philosophy'. In *Philosophy from Africa: A Text with Readings*, ed. P.H. Coetzee and A.P.J. Roux, 120–6. Cape Town: Oxford University Press.

Oruka, H.O. (ed.). 1990. *Sage Philosophy: Indigenous Thinkers and Modern Debate on African Philosophy*. New York: E.J. Brill.

Otive-Igbuzor, E. 2007. 'Sexuality, Violence and HIV/Aids in Nigeria'. In *Human Sexuality in Africa*, ed. E. Maticka-Tyndale, R. Tiemoko and P. Makinwa-Adebusoye, 199–218. Johannesburg: Jacana Media.

Ramose, M.B. 2002. *African Philosophy through Ubuntu*. Harare: Mond Books.

Rankhotha, C.S. 2004. 'Do Traditional Values Entrench Male Supremacy?' *Agenda* 59: 80–9.

Reddy, V. 2004. 'Sexuality in Africa: Some Trends, Transgressions and Tirades'. *Agenda* 62: 7.

Roederer, C. and D. Moellendorf (eds). 2004. *Jurisprudence*. Cape Town: Juta.

Sebidi, L.J. 1998. 'Toward a Definition of Ubuntu as African Humanism'. In *Perspectives on Ubuntu*, ed. M.G. Khabela and Z.C. Mzoneli, 61–70. Alice: Lovedale Press.

Senghor, L.S. 1963. 'Negritude and African Socialism'. *African Affairs* 2: 13.

Smit, J., M. Deacon and A. Schutte. 1999. *Ubuntu in a Christian Perspective*. Potchefstroom: Potchefstroom University Press.

Somé, M.P. 1997. *Ritual: Power, Healing and Community*. New York: Penguin/Arkana.

———. 1999. *The Healing Wisdom of Africa: Finding Life Purpose through Nature, Ritual, and Community*. New York: J.P. Tarcher/Putnam.

Stein, J. 2000. 'Virginity Tests in an AIDS War'. *City Press*, 3 September. Available at http://152.111.1.87/argief/berigte/citypress/2000/09/03/3/13.html.

Stewart, J. 2005. *Quotable Africa*. Cape Town: Penguin.

Teffo, L.J. and A.P.J. Roux. 2002. 'Themes in African Metaphysics'. In *Philosophy from Africa: A Text with Readings*, ed. P.H. Coetzee and A.P.J. Roux, 161–74. Cape Town: Oxford University Press.

Tempels, P. 1969. *Bantu Philosophy*. Paris: Présence Africaine.

Terry, G. 2007. *Women's Rights*. Johannesburg: Jacana Media.

Turaki, Y. 1991. 'Toward a Conception of Christian Social Ethics in Africa: A Methodological Approach'. In *Cultural Diversity in Africa: Embarrassment or Opportunity?*, ed. B.J. van der Walt, 162–210. Potchefstroom: Potchefstroom University for Christian Higher Education.

———. 1997. *Tribal Gods of Africa: Ethnicity, Racism, Tribalism, and the Gospel of Christ*. Nigeria: Crossroads Media Services.

Tutu, D. 1999. *No Future Without Forgiveness*. London: Rider.

Van Blerk, A.E. 2004. *Jurisprudence: An Introduction*. Durban: Butterworths.

Van der Zalm, C.T. 2008. 'Protecting the Innocent: Children's Act 38 of 2005 and Customary Law in South Africa; Conflicts, Consequences, and Possible Solutions'. *Emory International Law Review* 22: 891–926.

Viljoen, F. 2007. *International Human Rights Law in Africa*. Oxford: Oxford University Press.

Wiredu, K. 1980. *Philosophy and an African Culture*. Cambridge: Cambridge University Press.

CHAPTER 4

From ubuntu to Ubuntu
Four Historic a Prioris

Leonhard Praeg

This is an extract from Chapter 1 of *A Report on Ubuntu* (University of KwaZulu-Natal Press, 2014). Text inserted or omitted here is not indicated.

To understand the relationship between *being* and *belonging* in what Patrick Chabal (2009) refers to as a precolonial political economy of obligation, it may be useful to start by disentangling *association* and *obligation*. In terms of association, Chabal basically offers a communitarian description of the dictum, which, as Christian Gade (2011) rightly points out, only very recently appeared as an accepted synecdoche of Ubuntu, 'I am because we are.' One's existence is recognised as a function of the existence of others or, in terms of Chabal's analysis of *being*:

> Since the attributes of the person are inherently linked to the identity of the locality, one is only 'human' in so far as one is part of a kin network. It is for this reason that those who break from that bond or are cast away become non-persons, socially 'dead' as it were (2009: 47).

The 'because' is the lynchpin of existence in the dictum 'I exist *because* of others'. Where the understanding of 'us' is ontologically or metaphysically grounded with reference to a meaning of locality that includes the reality of the sacred (in the form of the living-dead), a violation of the 'because' motivated by the pursuit of self-interest would not only be considered an act of disloyalty, but indeed present as an all-destroying act of ontological betrayal, a threat to existence as such – a logic which, given the extension of the political economy of obligation as living praxis into postcolonial politics, often manifests as a politics fraught with the understanding of difference as violence: too much of a difference always threatens the assumption of interdependence (the priority of 'unity') so that difference is always more than simply a difference of opinion.

In order to sustain the existence of the 'we' and to give reality to what it means, one needs to recognise and honour certain obligations. This effectively means that 'one's responsibilities as an individual are . . . the mirror image of those features that contribute to one's identity as a human being' (Chabal 2009: 47). Alternatively, obligations are the currency of associations (48); they make the association real, visible, manifest:

> To have no obligation is not to belong; it is not to be fully and socially human. Obligations therefore, are not seen – as the western concept seems to imply – as impositions, claims on one's otherwise better used time and energy, but as a means of sustaining one's place in a network of belonging: that most vital attribute of humanity, sociability and, ultimately, being-in-the-world (48).

From this ontological understanding of association as a form of strong or deep communitarianism and its manifestation in reciprocal obligations follow a clear understanding of what constitutes morally good and bad behaviour. In a world where 'morality is indistinguishable from the rest of African social life' (Richardson 2009: 131) or where 'the life of the community, with its conscientious observance of rituals and traditions, is its own ethic' (135), in a world where 'religious beliefs were fused with moral values to form a single whole' (Prozesky 2009: 5), those actions will be considered good that sustain the association and those that threaten it will be considered bad. In the memorable formulation of Placide Tempels, we have to imagine a world in which '[morality] depends on things ontologically understood' (1969: 121). Recognising this reciprocity and honouring its implicit obligations is a condition for being referred to as someone who 'has ubuntu' since it 'refers to one's diligence as a member of society to accept the duties the community imposes on its members' (Coertze 2001: 113).

Naturally this understanding of belonging is not simply something of the past. In fact, the continuation of this political economy of obligation into modern or post-apartheid South Africa defines its postcoloniality and issues the politician with the specific challenge 'to fashion political space above and beyond such worlds of kinship' (Chabal 2009: 50). But therein lies the rub. At its simplest, postcoloniality presents as the tension between a national domain of politics, imagined in terms of a *contractual* understanding of association – which views obligation mostly in terms of negative restraints on the autonomy of the individual – and a local domain of politics that, spilling over and overlapping with the national, expresses being and belonging visibly and tangibly in terms of kinship, reciprocity and a political economy of obligation. The *contractual* understanding of association is the *imaginaire* of a 'post-industrial revolution South Africa' (Bayart 1993: 35), its self-conception as a modern, constitutional state in which the basic axiom or a priori is that entities are prior to relations. The master trope here is *difference*: how to conceive it, manage it, encourage it and institutionalise it, in order to facilitate, guarantee and promote it, but also to contain it. In the political economy of obligation, on the other hand, the axiom or a priori is that relations are prior to entities. The master trope here is *unity*: how to sustain it, protect it, reimagine or reconstitute it in political as opposed to sacred terms, how to negotiate the fragmentation of kinship-based unity, conceived in terms of origin and locality, into quasi-deontologised versions of it as a kind of 'network society', pivoting around shared political and economical interests.

The problem here is how to square the logic of *unity* with a neoliberal modernity that promotes the relentless pursuit of interests conceived in terms of its *individualist* a priori, while criminalising, delegitimising or struggling to reduce to mere *difference* any pursuit of interests articulated, formally or informally, as attempts to honour, recognise and sustain the value of *unity*. Of course, these domains do not overlap with any geographical demarcation (rural/urban); neither are they reducible to race or even the binary Western/African. Better to think of them as two *imaginaires* that mark the outer or most extreme logic of each set of assumptions, with membership fluid in the sense that individuals may, under various circumstances, participate in or encourage either logic, with varying degrees of commitment and permanence, in order to obtain rewards associated with one *imaginaire*, but not encouraged or more difficult to obtain or even simply not available in the logic of the other (see Kemahlioglu 2011).

The task of tracing the fluidity and overlapping nature of these *imaginaires* is perhaps better left to political sociologists. My aim here has been twofold: first, through a description of the political economy of obligation to raise as a formal principle of that political economy what I shall be referring to as a 'logic of interdependence'. This phrase will enable us, where and whenever necessary, temporarily to suspend the normative evaluation of the recognition of our interdependence as either good, useful or desirable, or bad, treacherous and problematic. Of course, in precolonial Africa, this question seems to have been relatively (not absolutely) straightforward: recognising and adhering to the logic of interdependence was not only good, but good *because* constitutive of the meaning of *being* and *belonging*. In fact, so constitutive of their meaning was it that the very logic of interdependence must be recognised to describe, first and foremost, the relationship between the concepts of *being* and *belonging* themselves. My second aim here was to introduce, however obliquely, the question of values: historically, what it meant for someone to recognise and adhere to the logic of interdependence, what it meant for someone *to be recognised* as one 'who has ubuntu' was inescapably constituted as a value-laden or normative recognition. Two things are at work in this description: first, that the recognition of me as one 'who has ubuntu' was a function of, or presupposed as a condition of sorts, *my prior recognition* of the logic of interdependence, of the fact that I lived being *as* belonging, that *my* being is *our* belonging and so on; second, that this prior recognition was never a recognition of interdependence in the abstract, as idea or philosophy or even as principle, but in *praxis* or in the *act* of living the reality and actuality of that interdependence. The recognition of 'having ubuntu' meant not only the actualisation of our interdependence, but also the actualisation of that interdependence in terms of the values that gave interdependence content and made it meaningful. In other words, to become the embodiment of ubuntu meant to have become the embodiment of the values presupposed by it. Combined, these two dimensions (prior recognition and the affirmation of values) suggest that the condition for recognising me as one who 'has ubuntu' resulted from my prior re-en*act*ment of (my) being as belonging, of the self (*being*) recognising being as a function of *belonging*, understood or decoded in terms of the values that make *belonging* meaningful. This further suggests that ubuntu cannot meaningfully be construed as either adjective or predicate. One cannot have ubuntu, firstly and obviously because it is not something one can *have*, but secondly and more importantly, because it is not something *one* can have. The statement is directed at 'one' who has demonstrated that s/he is primarily not one. To say, then, that 'you have ubuntu' is not to recognise a personal attribute, but rather, already the *return* of recognition, the return of a compliment (as response to your prior recognition, in praxis, of the fact that I exist, that I matter and so on). Strictly speaking, then, the statement 'you have ubuntu' is really a logic of interdependence reflecting itself, articulating itself, naming itself – not 'self' as in auto-nomination (from the Greek *autos*, 'self'), but the mutuality of self, a mutual-nomination – the cultural iteration of praxis as speech or an isomorphic doubling up of culture and speech, perhaps even the tautological reiteration of praxis *as* speech.

We get a good sense of the constellation of values that are articulated as the re-enactment of ubuntu in their historical context from Chabal's analysis of the political economy of obligation. Much else has been written on the tension between this historic constellation of 'phallo-primocentric values' (Praeg 2007: 141) and the postcolonial, liberal, democratic constellation of equality and rights (see, for instance, Keevy 2009a, 2009b, 2009c). The question I want to keep circumscribing is a narrower and more focused question about the relationship between historical values and contemporary philosophical practices, between ubuntu as cultural praxis and Ubuntu as philosophical practice. Crudely put, I am intrigued by the question of whether or not a contemporary Ubuntu, shorn of its phallo-primocentric values, still constitutes a meaningful political, social and/or philosophical practice. What difference does it make? What difference *can* it make?

It seems to me there are at least two ways of approaching this question and the distinction between them is premised on a dangerously arbitrary distinction between local and global, between thinking from the 'inside' and thinking from the 'outside'. First, we can take as point of departure the global or the exterior – Western ideologies and philosophies, such as humanism, communitarianism, virtue ethics, socialism and so on – and effectively sidestep the question of values by allowing these pre-existing ideologies and philosophies to filter in and out certain aspects of ubuntu praxis, in order to leave us with an *African* humanism, *African* communitarianism, *African* socialism and so on. But this route is fraught with contradictions and circularities, in addition to which, it is fundamentally premised on the dead end of a politics of recognition and the violence of sovereignty associated with it (*we* also have communitarian traditions, *ours* is the original socialism, *our* humanism is more extreme and profound).[1] Alternatively, we can start on the 'inside' – and this is a very loose and fuzzy notion of the 'inside' that perhaps denotes more of an intention than a location – and proceed by way of a critique that will trace in the broadest and most abstract of outlines the historical processes, the interplay between local aspirations and global expectations, which will explain how ubuntu praxis became reconstituted as decontextualised and abstract Ubuntu. While the first route is predominantly epistemological (what is the difference between socialism and African socialism?), the second is predominantly political (how did we come to talk about Ubuntu the way we do?). The reason I am opting for the second route is because I think it will better equip us to ask the kind of questions that are likely to get sidelined by the first approach, such as: What are the Western, modernist assumptions at play in this quest for an authentically African

Ubuntu? How does the politics of recognition predetermine the thinking through which we try to describe the nature and emancipatory potential of Ubuntu? What forms of racism and exoticism are at work in the gaze that so eagerly appropriates Ubuntu as 'exceptional' (as a *form of* humanism, exceptional *to* Africa) and so on.

Migrant thinking: Four a prioris

> The majority of the population of Southern Africa today cannot be properly said to know and to live *ubuntu* by virtue of any continuity with village life. They have to be educated to pursue (under the name of *ubuntu* [Ubuntu]) a global and urban reformulation of village values.
> — Wim van Binsbergen, '*Ubuntu* and the Globalisation
> of Southern African Thought and Society'

The political economy of obligation and its constitutive formal principle, the logic of interdependence, would be shattered by a number of events and outcomes that can be considered historical conditions of the possibility of talking about Ubuntu in the manner that we have come to do. Certain things happened that effectively removed or, in the words of Gilles Deleuze and Félix Guattari (2004), *de-territorialised* ubuntu from the domain or territory of cultural praxis and reinserted or *re-territorialised* it in a different context as a trope or philosophy, an abstract idea or perhaps a set of ideas, in a way that sometimes (under certain conditions and in specific contexts) allows Ubuntu to function as legitimate sign for 'us all'. That Ubuntu can signify or speak to 'all South Africans'; that is, beyond the territory of a political economy of obligation, is the basic assumption of every Ubuntu theorist who believes not only in the recovery or reappropriation of ubuntu as a unifying sign for an African image of thought and a mode of being, but also in the possibility of formalising it as, say, African humanism in such a way that other people, far removed from its originating territory may benefit from it or learn from it or, at the very least, use it as a point of entry to understanding 'the African mind'. There are two assumptions at work in this belief: one, that Ubuntu can be abstracted from the values implicit in ubuntu praxis and two, that this abstracted Ubuntu will remain at once specific enough to be African *and* general enough to be understood and applied outside the context of its originating values.

I think four historical conditions – two global and two local – have made it possible to think about Ubuntu in this way. These conditions are only analytically distinct and to present them as subtle and complex interfaces between global and local conditions or a prioris, one ideally needs a three-dimensional text or any representation with spatial depth in which to posit the two global conditions as vast background determinants over which, and interacting with which, we find the local conditions or a prioris. Without such a medium at hand, we can proceed with the next best alternative and that is to splice the global and local a prioris into an elliptical unity of sorts. And that is what I do below, to splice – which literally means to join or connect ropes by interweaving strands – these two global and two local a prioris that have made postcolonial Ubuntu possible.

First global a priori: Colonialism

Historically, the different normative evaluations of the logic of interdependence that came to be associated with Africa(ns) were a function of two different a prioris. By historic a priori I mean, following Michel Foucault, that which

> in a given period, delimits in the totality of experience a field of knowledge, defines the mode of being of the objects that appear in that field, provides man's everyday perception with theoretical powers, and defines the condition in which he can sustain a discourse about things that is recognized to be true (1982: 158).

To simplify, we can also think of this a priori as a historic predisposition to fragment reality in a way that would render it digestible by the disciplinary subjects (anthropology, philosophy, etc.) invented for the study of reality, while keeping in mind the manner in which those very disciplinary structures in turn determine how we see reality, what they allow us to consider as serious objects of study and what procedures are considered legitimate for the analysis and discussion of the objects of study so defined. The two main historic a prioris that, over the last 300 years, would give normative content to the logic of interdependence were, first, a *historicist* and, second, a *relativist* a priori.

The *historicist* a priori – of which the whole colonialist project was a function – considered the logic of interdependence as a mere reminder or 'symbol of Western prehistorical experience' (Mudimbe 1991: 11). By historicist I mean the assumption, embedded in disciplines of the time, that there is but one path of social evolution or development, that the West was further down this road of development than Africa and that the pre-eminence of a logic of interdependence in Africa was proof of the underdeveloped nature of African societies. From the perspective of this historicist a priori, the logic of interdependence was considered both necessary and potentially negative: *necessary* because it was a stage of development that all societies have to go through, *potentially negative* because undue adherence to it would become a stumbling block to future development (modernity). This negativity was reflected in the terms used to describe it: tribe, ethnicity, collectivism, clan and so on. The legitimation of the colonialist project derived entirely from this historicist a priori and amounted to an attempt to transform Africa in the image of a West considered further down the path of development (see Praeg 2008: 369; Mudimbe 1991).

Informing the very logic of colonialism was the desire to transform African nature (in the dual sense of the word) to reflect the more advanced, Western nature. On the one hand, colonialists transformed physical nature into a reflection of European spaces by recreating the West in African cities, landscapes and nation-states. On the other hand, they set out, through 'civilisation', education and Christianisation, to transform the very nature of colonised people into a reflection of the Western self. The *implicit legitimacy* of this transformation (implicit, for the West did not need to explicitly legitimise itself) derived from the racialised belief that primitive societies (much like children) are in the process of re-enacting or recapitulating stages of development that the more civilised West (*qua* adults) had already gone through.

However, 'by the 1940s, a new *a priori* detached itself from the very experience of the normative language, and it became accepted that all languages, all civilizations, are arbitrary' (Mudimbe 1991: 11). This *relativist* a priori was the historic condition for the political processes that, over the next twenty years, would culminate in the independence of African states from colonial rule. The resulting discourse on African self-determination was a function of this relativist a priori. Through the struggle for liberation and post-independence attempts to give content to what liberty meant, a different normative evaluation of the logic of interdependence emerged, premised on a rejection of the historicism of the colonialist project. The logic of interdependence was hence celebrated, not merely as passing stage of development, but as a mark of cultural authenticity, of what is most unique about Africans and the African state and that should therefore be saved and appropriated as a sine qua non of the future development of these states. Of this desire to found the African state on a reappropriation of the logic of interdependence as an authentic mode of being, the African socialism project was probably the most coherent and ambitious example. Closer to home, the suggestion by Drucilla Cornell and others that Ubuntu should be considered foundational to the Constitution, the Law of law or meta-purpose that should inform our interpretation of the law, is another example.

First local a priori: Urbanisation

R.D. Coertze (2001) distinguishes between '*Ubuntu/botho* the original concept' and two semantic shifts that the concept has undergone in the process of becoming what we now refer to as Ubuntu or the 'philosophy of *ubuntu*'. Of the original concept, he notes the following:

- the terms *ubuntu/botho* referred to the essence of being human, but this 'theoretically included both the positive and negative qualities found in [humanity]' (113);
- in the Nguni languages, derogatory terms such as *abelungu* or *makgowa* were used to refer to white people, suggesting that '*ubuntu* and *botho* refer only to the essence of humankind from Africa';
- the logic of interdependence was actualised in kinship-based cultural practices and rituals, which meant that reciprocal duties and obligations were perpetuated or sustained through a 'process of enculturation within the extended family [which] ensured that the members of a new generation accept the preferred conduct and the duties expected of them' (114);
- in this very enculturation, we find at work a certain constitutive violence, the ambivalent interplay of solidarity and coercion we have come to recognise in all forms of communitarianism: 'Within . . . peer groups the individual could not only call on support but was through the pressure of co-members compelled to conform and perform according to the example and expectation of the majority';
- for this very reason, 'it becomes very difficult for the individual to subscribe to absolute standards of kindness, morality or goodwill that are not endorsed by specific examples of such sentiments within the societal framework of every-day existence';
- and lastly, his research suggests:

> There are no proverbs or sayings . . . in which either *ubuntu* or *botho* were explained or praised as abstract concepts [but the] observance of the abstract qualities of kindness, goodwill and high moral standards . . . were all extolled in concrete situations between relatives, friends or persons having common interests or speaking the same language (115).

Wim van Binsbergen concurs: 'I have never witnessed the technical terms *ubuntu* (or local morphological equivalents) or *Zambian humanism* to be used as a matter of course, of accepted parlance, in these concrete situations of the village and the family' (2001: 69). I do not interpret these authors to mean that there was no abstract recognition of our interdependence, such as suggested by the Venda proverb, '*Muthu u bebelwa munwe*' (a person is born for the other) (Murove 2009a: 30) or in the recognition that 'so-and-so has ubuntu', but rather that in these situational invocations, 'utterances invoking principles of sociability . . . are set in a context of elaborate rhetorical acts . . . [and] that the socio-ritual events in which they feature produce *implied* meaning . . . much more than that they articulate *explicit and codifiable* meaning' (Van Binsbergen 2001: 68) and that this implied meaning was understood, historically, as the actualisation of culturally specific values. The idea that ubuntu could make sense beyond the immediate context of values 'belongs to a later stage than the original or traditional life style' (Coertze 2001: 115). In fact, as I argue below, this codification would come about first as a result of colonialism and, second, through resistance to colonialism.

Colonialism and the processes of industrialisation and urbanisation that produced South Africa's industrial revolution brought about a sustained reorganisation of the socio-economic substratum of people's lives (Munyaka and Motlhabi 2009: 79–83). In the townships and cities of industrialising South Africa, Africans encountered the solitariness of life associated with modernity in a context where it is expected of individuals not always to rely on community networks, but to learn to 'fend for themselves amidst strangers in a strange and hostile environment' (Coertze 2001: 115). The impact of these socio-economic changes on a traditional political economy of obligation was far-reaching because, as Ncedile Saule comments, not only were the 'traditional religious forms of worship and customs of which kings and chiefs were custodians . . . destroyed [but by implication also] the very roots of *ubuntu*' (in Munyaka and Motlhabi 2009: 79) – to the extent that Jacobus Hendrik Smit, Moya Deacon and Augustine Shutte can claim that ubuntu currently exists 'mainly in South African rural areas, it being a value [that was] lost through the process of urbanisation' (80).

But I think we should be careful here. What colonialism and urbanisation brought about was the destruction of a coherent ubuntu praxis. Carried forth alongside emerging forms of individualism was a very political version of that praxis – and by political I mean a political strategy centred on the master trope of 'solidarity' deployed, sometimes consciously and sometimes unconsciously, to great effect in the struggle for liberation. To put this somewhat bluntly, with urbanisation and the anti-apartheid struggle came the expansion or secularisation of the formal principle of ubuntu praxis, so that it no longer referred to local, kinship-based and visible communities of metaphysical locality, but rather to larger, imagined communities of political practice. This expansion into secular, modern politics of a principle historically associated with an ontological praxis was merely symptomatic of a greater widening or expansion. In this regard, Coertze notes that 'the reciprocity inherent in the [practice of] *ubuntu* or *botho* was under these circumstances understandably extended to include those working together or to include those living in the same neighbourhood of a specific urban township' (2001: 115).[2] Beyond this, 'contact with others than one's relatives or tribe-members [*sic*] or those having the same life style eventually necessitated the extension of *ubuntu* or *botho* to include the entire amorphous total of humanity'.

The importance of this shift derives from the fact that Ubuntu became an abstract concept, the meaning no longer simply derived from an implicit agreement about what was meant or understood by one's diligence as a member of society to accept the duties imposed by the community on its members. Rather, as an idea or a concept abstracted from historical praxes, the meaning of Ubuntu increasingly became articulated in confluence with the very discourses through which Western modernity articulated its imposition on Africa, namely Christianity and a liberal discourse on individual human rights. Ubuntu, once severed from the historical praxes of a visible community, had to speak a language that would be understood by everyone who derived a sense of purpose from acknowledging their imagined shared humanity and who, through such acknowledgement, came to constitute the *we* of the 'I am because we are' in the imaginary terms of various political communities – the local, struggle/township community, 'Africans' as opposed to Westerners, and later the 'nation' itself.[3] This process explains Van Binsbergen's comment that Ubuntu, once decoupled from the ubuntu praxis, came to have 'a very wide and internally richly textured semantic field, a vast area of possibilities and implications, out of which in concrete contexts a specific selection is being made, triggered by the juxtapositions which accompany the root –*ntu* . . . in that context' (2001: 54).

Context and circumstances so favoured Christianity and human rights as the two discourses most suitable to retrodict a meaning of Ubuntu that it was now assumed ubuntu had always already been their articulation (much like Julius Nyerere, for whom traditional African societies were socialist long before

106

the invention of socialism). In this regard, Coertze notes: 'From the demands of Christianity as well as the precepts of Western philosophy the African individual was now called upon to profess a personal commitment to abstract standards of morality, kindness, charity and even benevolence as well as mercifulness' (2001: 115). But here a paradox emerges as a result of a clash between the identity-based claim (Ubuntu is unique) and the circularity through which a meaning is derived from the present, only to be retrodicted as a voice of the past. In both cases – Christianity and human rights – the borrowing of an abstract language is accompanied by the paradoxical claim, on the one hand, that ubuntu always already articulated or represented the insights contained in these discourses and, on the other hand, a conflation of its meaning with that of Christianity and human rights so that they become virtually indistinct.[4] In other words, a paradox emerges as a result of asserting that these external influences tell us nothing we do not already know and, on the other hand, only ever being able to articulate what it is that we already knew in and through these discourses. This paradox registers a tension between identity politics and dogmatism that plays out in claims that are either strange: 'No one who does not have Ubuntu should be called a Christian' (Mqhayi in Bonn 2007: 865), perplexing:

It is this very principle [of sharing] whose spirit as well as application is similar to the message of Christ. Accordingly, while Jesus Christ might have been necessary for those segments of humanity who have readily accepted Christianity, it may not be inferred that he was therefore necessary for most traditional societies in Africa (Ramose 1999: 34).

or problematically identitarian: 'It also outlines the five stages of the peacemaking process found among ubuntu societies: acknowledging guilt; showing remorse and repenting; asking for and giving forgiveness; and paying compensation or reparations as a prelude to reconciliation' (Murithi 2009: 221).

This simple equivalence of Ubuntu with a regime of rights is particularly glib, not because the concept of Ubuntu is heterogenous to the concept of law – on the contrary, it is the very embodiment of a specific *nomos* or spirit of Law (as per Montesquieu) – but because Ubuntu is, in very useful ways, the complete antithesis of the law as represented by the a priori of constitutionalism – from which the status of Ubuntu as both a function and a critique of Western modernity derives. To present Ubuntu as a representation of such rights *avant la lettre* is to forget that ubuntu does not substantiate notions of individual or even collective rights as much as it does duties and obligations. As Coertze reminds us: 'Neither the traditional nor the acculturative formulation of *ubuntu* or *botho* imbued the individual with specific rights as a human being. To be human, as of old, meant to shoulder the concomitant duties and thus to be judged an example to others' (2001: 115). In this regard, Bede Onuoha notes that the traditional African 'thought more of his duties to his community than of his rights' (1965: 41) and Coertze concludes that the shift towards human rights discourse 'ended with a concept granting inherent rights to all human beings without a concomitant stress on duties. This is completely different from the emphasis placed in the past on the necessity to accept the duties entailed by the membership of various societal cohesions' (2001: 117).

It is possible that the putative tension between a regime of obligations and a regime of rights, evident in much of Ubuntu discourse, merely reproduces the basic binary of African communitarianism versus Western individualism. In this case, it would be as problematic to read Ubuntu as an exemplification of the former regime as it would be to appropriate it as an expansion of the latter. Ubuntu *qua* glocal, retrodicted phenomenon can illuminate and enrich our understanding of both regimes exactly because it can be interpreted to represent an 'interplay between rights and obligations' (Wiredu 2008: 333), premised on the contemporaneity of the individual and the social (Eze 2008). This said, much of the relevance and potential power of Ubuntu lies in the idea that membership of imagined communities entails duties and obligations. Whether or not it would be useful to think of citizenship along the lines of membership suggested here and what the implications of doing so would be for a political system premised on the priority of individual rights is another question.[5]

Second global a priori: The dialectic of recognition

The struggle against colonialism presented in two registers that Paget Henry (in Gordon 2008) has called the historicists and the poeticists.[6] Lewis Gordon summarises the difference between these two traditions as follows: 'The former [the historicists] are primarily concerned with problems of social change and political economy. The latter [the poeticists] celebrate the imagination with a focus on the conceptions of the self as represented by literature and poetry' (175). Historicists respond to colonialism by disputing the historicism of colonialism, while poeticists are concerned with restoring the dignity of the African self through an analysis of the inner life, past, present and future. The difference can be illustrated with reference to two forms of secular humanism that emerged in twentieth-century Africa. The work of Cheikh Anta Diop (1923–86) represents the historicist dimension, in as much as he was concerned with showing not only that Africa indeed had a history, but also that its history was foundational to human civilisation as such. Léopold Sédar Senghor (1906–2001) is the father of Africa's poeticist tradition (191). He wanted to demonstrate that Africans had their own distinct ways of knowing and being. He argued that whereas the West valorized being rational and analytic, the African's emotional and passionate nature was not only equally valuable, but also an equally valid way of being in and knowing the world. Senghor forms part of a tradition of African philosophy known as ethnophilosophy, of which the three main principles – the temporal, existential and epistemological – remain relevant for the contemporary discourse on Ubuntu.

In terms of its temporal dimension, ethnophilosophers consider colonialism as a fundamental rupture pivoting around the binary opposition of pre- and postcolonial. This binary, in turn, produces two radically different and incompatible conceptions of a Western way of being (individualist) and an African way of being (communalist) that typically are taken to represent two irreconcilable ideas about the nature of human existence (ontologies). The temporal and existential beliefs are closely related in the sense that the radically different time of precolonial Africa corresponds to a radically different way of being. And this is where the third principle – the epistemological – comes in. Ethnophilosophers believe in the possibility of recovering the logic of interdependence as the cornerstone of a politics of identity that will confirm the essential authenticity of Africans, while also serving as the ideological foundation for the sovereign, postcolonial state. Historically this project – essentially one of liberation as self-recognition – replicated the historicism at the root of colonialism in a number of problematic ways. Suffice it here to delimit some of the most obvious consequences of appropriating the logic of interdependence in this way. These become visible the moment we remember that, just as Africans did not know they were black before Westerners told them they were not white, Africans did not celebrate their 'communalism' before colonialists told them they lacked a sense of individualism. The categories of 'being back' and 'having communalist traditions' are functions of a global a priori, first of colonialism (their negative denotation) and subsequently of postcoloniality and self-determination (their positive denotation). Succinctly placing this in historical context, V-Y Mudimbe writes:

> Eboussi-Boulaga aptly wrote that *at least for Africans*, the emergence of an African 'We-Subject' was the major human phenomenon of the second half of [the last] century . . . [Thus] emerged . . . a strong emphasis on history and a new anthropology as a means for better understanding of both African tradition and identity (1988: 60).

This has obvious resonance with the notion of double consciousness as theorised in critical race theory as far back as W.E.B. Du Bois and which found some of its most poignant expressions in the work of Frantz Fanon. According to Gordon, when Fanon stated that blackness is 'a white construction', he meant that

> the people who have become known as black people are descendants of people who had no reason to have regarded themselves as such. As a consequence, the history of black people has the constant motif of such people encountering their blackness from the 'outside,' as it were, and then developing, in dialectical fashion, a form of blackness that transcends the initial, negative series of events (2008: 158).

Fanon famously summarised this insight in 'Algeria Unveiled' when he stated: 'It is the white man who creates the Negro. But it is the Negro who creates negritude' (1980: 25). The creation of Negritude (or Black Consciousness, for that matter) 'originates in the need to respond to the negations of blackness embedded in Western philosophical discourse . . . [It] becomes a means of overloading the denominating structure with precisely that which the latter names as negative' (Quayson 2002: 586). In other words, a system that nominates the fact of blackness as negative will engender in the various forms of resistance to it, dialectical oppositions aimed at 'overloading the denominating structure with precisely that which the latter names as negative'.

The reinvention of Ubuntu was never going to escape the logic of double consciousness and the power struggle implicit in offering counter-representations of Africa's 'primitive communalism' that would 'overload the denominating structure' of colonialism with precisely that which the latter always named as negative (by re-presenting Ubuntu as a messianic, even salvific humanism, for instance). Following the logic of double consciousness, African communalism in general and Ubuntu in particular is a 'white construction' in the precise sense meant by Fanon, namely that Africans encounter it from the outside as a result of being told that they lack not only whiteness, but also a concept of the individual. Just as black people have set out in dialectical fashion to develop a meaning of blackness that would overcome its initial postulate as lack, so they/we have set out in dialectical fashion to develop a meaning of communalism aimed at transcending the initial colonialist insistence that a lack of individualism equates with a lack of humanity.

The problem here is the dialectic itself, for to conceive of the self in the binary logic presented by it, to accept the idea that the most significant fact about the African self is its communal (as opposed to its individualist) nature, is to affirm the very violence of Western thought through the act of contesting it *on its own terms*. Whether it is indeed possible to proceed in a non-dialectical manner is, of course, another question, one that Fanon grappled with all his life. All I am pointing out here is that to accept Ubuntu as a signifying fact of blackness or Africanness is already to constitute its relevance and meaning in predetermined ways and to commit oneself to proceeding in a binary fashion that will necessarily conflate 'Western' with 'individualist' – thereby rendering impossible any rigorous comparison of Ubuntu with, say, a feminist ethics of care (see, for instance, Friedman 1989) – while in the process denying the reality of ascendant forms of individualism in Africa that *pre-dated* colonialism. A non-dialectical response to racist modernity may be difficult to imagine, but the very least we can do is to remain conscious of the violence we perpetuate as part of the liberating performativity of dialectic opposition – in this instance, the violence necessarily inflicted both on the Western Other and African Self as a prerequisite for talking about Ubuntu as exceptional or as a 'solution to Western individualism' and so on.

Second local a priori: Constitutionalism as 'liberation'

> Whenever a phenomenological concept is drawn from primordial sources, there is a possibility that it may degenerate if communicated in the form of an assertion. It gets understood in an empty way and is thus passed on, losing its indigenous character, and becoming a free-floating thesis.
>
> — Martin Heidegger, *Being and Time*

In 'Person and Community in African Traditional Thought', Ifeanyi Menkiti stirred up a controversy when he suggested three features of the traditional African world view that distinguish it from 'most Western views' of humanity (1984: 171).

Two of these – that 'the reality of the communal world takes precedence over the reality of individual life' and that the moral community includes the living-dead – will for the moment be accepted as unproblematic facts of being and belonging in a political economy of obligation. The third feature has had a more complicated reception and is related to the notion of 'processual personhood' or the idea that in precolonial African societies, 'full personhood is not perceived as simply given at the very beginning of one's life, but is attained after one is well along in society' (173). There is ample evidence in contemporary literature of what such a processual understanding of personhood would mean in practical terms. In Thando Mgqolozana's *A Man Who is Not a Man*, the male narrator speaks about his depraved youth in Cape Town and how the soccer coach reprimanded him and his friends for wasting their lives:

> That is why Ta-Diski, the coach, called us into his kamer and treated us to a long belting session when he heard of our wayward actions outside the kasi. He was the first to suggest that what we needed was uKwaluswa – to be circumcised. Among traditional people, uKwaluswa is commonly held to be the remedy for mischievous behaviour like ours (2009: 16–17).

The reason for this remedy is explained a little later in the novel:

> According to the elders, if a boy reached a stage where he was problematic in society, there was only one way to curb this, and that was 'the obvious'. The boy's mischief was considered to be an indication of wanting a rite of passage into manhood. The things that were done at the mountain were held to be so powerful that they could root out any foolish notions from a boy's stubborn head, sending him back with a clear sense of right and wrong (29).

But initiation is not only about morality; it is about morality embedded in a greater, genderised conception of personhood and humanness. In addition, non-participation or failed participation in such rituals leaves the individual a non-person, inhuman, 'ostracised from humanity' (182). The narrator's friend warns him before he leaves to undergo his initiation:

> Finally, he told me the things I was to avoid. Above all the cautions, Mc-squared emphasised that I should avoid landing up in hospital at all

costs. 'It is better to die than to go to hospital. It would be the end of you anyway,' he warned me. 'There's no living space for failed men in our society. Either you become a man the expected way, or you are not one at all' (65).

This is no empty threat because the warning prefigures exactly how the narrator is treated by one of the nurses when he eventually ends up in hospital as a result of a botched circumcision:

> She was openly insulting us for having landed up at the hospital – we cowards! She was bringing home to us the disgrace of our being survived by our empty huts at the mountain, impressing on us our invalidity, the manhood rejects that we had become by fleeing to the hospital and the sub-human status that we were about to assume in society as a result. Her reaction might seem extreme, but it was typical of the mockery and censure that we could expect to encounter outside (122).

The fate of the narrator's girlfriend articulates the connection between ritualised becoming and personhood even more clearly:

> She started doing sex with strangers she met at the beachfront. She'd disappear from home for days and come back looking like the fifteen-year-old junkie she'd become. It was after the incident when she and Tracey were caught by the police in possession of drugs that her mother decided to send her to the villages to learn humanness anew (55).[7]

The point here is that this processual dimension of ubuntu may be a function or epiphenomenon of ubuntu *praxis*, but it will for obvious reasons generate complex tensions in a context of equality and inalienable rights – as scholars such as Ezra Chitando (2008: 45) have indeed argued. One way out of this dilemma is to argue, along with Kwasi Wiredu (2002), that what is at stake in the process of becoming is not personhood, but social status – an interpretation I find unconvincing because it underestimates the fact that in a political economy of obligation to have no social status (in terms of gender, to not be reckoned a 'man') is, for all intents and purposes, indistinct from not being recognised as person or human being. This follows from the fact that in the philosophical anthropology outlined by Chabal

(2009), the category 'man' – both in the sense of hu*man* and the gendered man – is a functional concept which, as Alasdair MacIntyre argues in *After Virtue*, is rooted in the form of social life in which 'to be a man is to fill a set of roles each of which has its own point and purpose: member of a family, citizen, soldier' and so on (1982: 16–17). In a world where there is such an inextricable link between morality and function, between being and purpose, to accuse a man of not being able to fulfil his function *as a man*, is per (functional) definition to suggest that he is subhu*man*. The debate on this issue of processual personhood remains open.[8] What interests me is not whether or not this conclusion is justified or correct, but rather what is at stake in the debate. For it seems to me that in order for ubuntu praxis to be reappropriated as Ubuntu, a certain circumcision is called for, one through which the *ontic* orientation of ubuntu, the fact that 'having ubuntu' is a function of ritualised becoming-through-other-people, will need to be deontologised or reinvented in order to retain its relevance in a postfunctionalist context, where our humanity or personhood as rights-bearing individuals is accepted as an existential and ontological bottom-line, not subject to the vagaries of communitarian consensus or ritualised processes of belonging. I spent some time on the example from Mgqolozana's novel in order to demonstrate something of the arrow of time at work in the process that saw, first, the adoption of the 1996 Constitution as a culmination of the struggle for liberation and, second, the formalising, through the Constitution, of the principle that tradition will be actively and passively developed in line with constitutional values.

Colonialism was in many ways the beginning of the end of the political economy of obligation as a sustained and coherent praxis. The struggle for liberation conceived in terms of a Western a priori – that entities precede relations and, hence, that individual rights are more fundamental than social obligations – continued this movement away from that praxis and is sustained in the idea that tradition and custom should be actively and passively developed in line with constitutional values. The meaning of Ubuntu reproduced in and through this interface with constitutionalism is neither one in which Ubuntu is simply reducible to human rights discourse nor one that can simply be dismissed as a traditional form of communitarianism at odds with a constitutional regime of rights. Instead, Ubuntu should be considered a *glocal* phenomenon that must be understood both as a product *of* and a critical response *to* Western modernity.

What I am interested in outlining in this second local a priori is the role of constitutionalism in the reproduction of such a *glocal* Ubuntu. To start delimiting this role, we have to bear two things in mind: (1) The movement from ubuntu praxis to Ubuntu philosophy always involves a process or movement of *translation* or *codification* and (2) the formal principle distilled from Chabal's analysis, namely the logic of interdependence, by virtue of its normative neutrality, allows us to bring into sharper focus the politics involved in every such act of translation or codification. In this specific case, it will allow us to understand how an ubuntu praxis is refracted through constitutionalism in order to produce a rather shallow, because very carefully delimited and circumscribed, glocal meaning of Ubuntu.

We can retrace this refraction by making two moves that seem relatively unproblematic to me: one, by positing the logic of interdependence as a conceptual or formal a priori of the political economy of obligation; two, by recognising the adoption of the 1996 Constitution as a pivotal moment of modernity, which, through the very logic it represents (a Western-modern axiomatic of the individual as conceptual and, now, historical a priori of the political), stands as a clear separation between a now *historical* praxis or political economy of obligation and a *contemporary* or *future* political economy of individual freedom or republican constitutionalism (Kant 1970: 99), premised on three principles: the *freedom* of the members of a society (as human beings), the *dependence* of all on a single, common legislation (as subjects) and the law as guarantor of the *equality* of all (as *citizens of the state*).

These two moves allow us to imagine the Constitution as a point of refraction through which the post-apartheid political domain is reconstituted. Much like a prism refracts a beam of light, the Constitution refracts the logic of interdependence into various forms or manifestations of that interdependence in a political order at odds with the totality of its expression. What used to be a singular and unified or coherent whole – an ubuntu praxis of interdependence – is refracted into a multiplicity or manifold manifestations of interdependence, each of which, from this pivotal point of refraction onwards, cannot but appear prejudged in a constellation of philosophical and political traditions of thought peculiar to the domain in which it manifests (law, economics, culture, etc.). In each of these domains, a whole matrix unified around the assumption of an individualist a priori is brought to bear on any particular manifestation of the logic of interdependence in that domain, which renders it either as subversive of that a priori or as a salvific alternative to it: *juridically* (restorative justice can subvert the rule of law *and* appear as a salvific alternative to retribution); *economically* (the destructive pursuit of individual interest is good, tenderpreneurship is not) and *politically* (ruthless personal ambition is good, nepotism is not). In most constellations, the logic of interdependence creates a certain undesirable 'white noise' that needs to be named, condemned and filtered out, eliminated in order for these domains to retain their chosen (although always contested) (neo)liberal integrity. In the economic constellation, for instance, nepotism is prejudged as an unacceptable economic manifestation of that interdependence, while economic activities that represent the logic of interdependence within the confines of the capitalist system (for example, the *stokvel*) are encouraged, even legitimised.[9]

But the refraction of the logic of interdependence does not always give us the equivalence of separate colours suggested by the refraction metaphor. We also find judgements that bleed across the colour bar, for instance those that are both normative and juridical (depending on the context, restorative justice is sometimes *better* than retributive justice) or *moral-economic* (at the macro-level of ideology, socialism is problematic in a way that the micro-level, economic, quasi-socialist praxis of the *stokvel* is not) and so on. Relevant to our purposes is how the process of refraction seemed to have managed to carefully hedge Ubuntu – formerly epiphenomenon of the totality of a praxis of interdependence – into the constellation of 'culture' in a manner that leaves it impotent to challenge or contest two discursive and materialist conditionalities of neoliberalism: one, shared humanity is not to be confused with shared resources, much less should the materialist dimension of sharing be considered an inextricable condition for shared humanity; two, even this dematerialised Ubuntu should be interpreted solely as a unifying sign of everything positive about these refractions. In a sense, this second condition is a function of the first: Ubuntu becomes associated with forgiveness, reconciliation, restorative justice and the *stokvel* in a way that dissociates it from any implication in vengeance, tenderpreneurship, nepotism, socialism and so on. In God's rainbow nation, cultural entrepreneurs and the proxies of constitutionalism have successfully colluded in the production of a conception of Ubuntu that is mostly vacuous because it really functions as shorthand for 'being nice', a kitsch Afro-chic artefact that in many ways resembles the sort of thing late capitalism exists to produce.

Be that as it may and, considered as a totality, all these judgements of the manifestation of the logic of interdependence within and against the neoliberal order pivot around an emotive distinction between *empathetic* and *antipathetic* manifestations of the logic of interdependence in post-apartheid South Africa. And while there appears to be no *über*-sign or master trope that unifies all antipathetic manifestations, other than predictable neo-racist liberal tropes such as 'banana republic', 'return of the state of nature', 'traditionalism' and 'culture', it seems that Ubuntu does function as *über*-sign for the unification of all the empathetic manifestations of the logic of interdependence across the various constellations – be they juridical, economic, social or cultural.

The empathetic nature of Ubuntu as master sign derives from the fact that it taps into what we may think of as the unthought of neoliberalism – which is more than simply its opposite (although it often appears as that). Rather, under the notion of 'unthought', I mean to gather everything that a system premised on the axiomatic that 'entities are prior to relations' necessarily needs to repress and forget in order to construct itself as viable *imaginaire*. In such an order, Ubuntu becomes not only a glocal sign that unifies elements of endogenous praxis with global discourses on law, the political and the spiritual, but also an uncanny sign of the very relationality that needed to be suspended, destroyed or repressed in each of these domains in order for Western modernity to violently reinvent itself as the postcolony *qua* politico-juridico-economic system or Constellation of constellations. Those manifestations of the logic of interdependence will be empathetic; that is, celebrated as manifestations of Ubuntu, which either deliver a profound and necessary critique of this violence or concretely and practically manifest a world-disclosing humility as an alternative to it through a praxis that resurfaces forgotten relations (the Truth and Reconciliation Commission, the *stokvel* and so on). It seems, then, that the logic of interdependence is refracted to produce a figure or sign, 'Ubuntu', through a process of reification that proscribes, through a logic resembling that of the ban, a range of elements that historically were a condition for the very possibility of ubuntu, but which now appear as troublesome or destructive within a liberal democratic order.

Notes

1. This amounts to what Paulin Hountondji calls a form of 'cultural exhibitionism which compels the "Third World" intellectual to "defend and illustrate" the peculiarities of his tradition for the benefit of a Western public' (1983: 67).
2. There is evidence that this change in the socio-economic base from rural to urban or even semi-urban also reflects shifts in the understood meaning of ubuntu. In her study, Marta Bonn reports that ubuntu 'meant "cooperation, sharing and interdependence" to the rural children much more often (30%) than to the urban children (6%), or to the semi-urban children (17%)' (2007: 871).

3. There is some resonance here with Kwasi Wiredu's (2008: 335) distinction between communalism (the kinship-based social formation) and communitarianism (the representation of that communalism as theory).
4. For example, 'Kaunda's Humanism stems from the Christian concept of the brotherhood of mankind' (Babu 1981: 65).
5. For a critical exploration of this question, see Enslin and Horsthemke (2004) and, for a response, see Letseka (2012).
6. For a detailed discussion, see Gordon (2008).
7. On this, see also Van Binsbergen (2001: 63).
8. See Bewaji (2003: 395), Murove (2009b: 71–2, 260, 323) and Shutte (2009: 92). This debate is, for obvious reasons, highly charged. What seems indisputable to me is that in a precolonial African cosmology, the failure 'to become a proper member of a community of persons [as] a processual, evolutionary, developmental, intellectual maturation kind of thing' (Bewaji 2003: 395) will carry ontological implications very different and far more serious from those faced by an individual living in a society understood as the reciprocal recognition of inalienable human rights. Further, as argued here, this functionalism can be a useful way of framing or bringing into focus the implications of adhering to a processual understanding of personhood in the context of contractual modernity.
9. 'A *stokvel* is a very popular example of informal social security. This where, for instance, a group of five friends make monthly contributions to a *stokvel* or pool. Each member will have a turn (every fifth month) to use the total of the pool, enabling them to buy goods such as furniture and school clothes' (Tshoose 2009: 15).

References

Babu, A.R.M. 1981. *African Socialism or Socialist Africa?* London: Zed Books.

Bayart, J-F. 1993. *The State in Africa: The Politics of the Belly*. London: Longman.

Bewaji, J.A.I. 2003. 'Beyond Ethno-Philosophical Myopia: Critical Comments on Mogobe B. Ramose's *African Philosophy through Ubuntu*'. *South African Journal of Philosophy* 22 (4): 378–415.

Bonn, M. 2007. 'Children's Understanding of "Ubuntu"'. *Early Child Development and Care* 177 (8): 863–73.

Chabal, P. 2009. *Africa: The Politics of Suffering and Smiling*. London: Zed Books.

Chitando, E. 2008. 'Religious Ethics, HIV and AIDS and Masculinities in Southern Africa'. In *Persons in Community: African Ethics in a Global Culture*, ed. R. Nicolson, 45–65. Pietermaritzburg: University of KwaZulu-Natal Press.

Coertze, R.D. 2001. 'Ubuntu and Nation Building in South Africa'. *South African Journal of Ethnology* 24 (4): 113–18.

Deleuze, G. and F. Guattari. 1994. *What is Philosophy?* London: Verso.

Enslin, P. and K. Horsthemke. 2004. 'Can Ubuntu Provide a Model for Citizenship Education African Democracies?' *Comparative Education* 40 (4): 545–58.

Eze, M.O. 2008. 'What is African Communitarianism? Against Consensus as a Regulative Ideal'. *South African Journal of Philosophy* 27 (4): 386–99.

Fanon, F. 1980. 'Algeria Unveiled'. In *A Dying Colonialism*, 13–42. London: Writers and Readers Cooperation.

Foucault, M. 1982. *The Archaeology of Knowledge*. New York: Pantheon.

Friedman, M. 1989. 'Feminism and Modern Friendship: Dislocating the Community'. *Ethics* 99 (2): 275–90.

Gade, C.B.N. 2011. 'The Historical Development of the Written Discourses on Ubuntu'. *South African Journal of Philosophy* 30 (3): 303–29.

Gordon, L.R. 2008. *An Introduction to Africana Philosophy*. Cambridge: Cambridge University Press.

Heidegger, M. 2008. *Being and Time*. Trans. John Macquarrie and Edward Robinson. New York: HarperPerennial.

Hountondji, P.J. 1983. *African Philosophy: Myth and Reality*. Trans. H. Evans, with collaboration of J. Ree. London: Hutchinson University Library for Africa.

Kant, I. 1970. 'Perpetual Peace: A Philosophical Sketch'. In *Kant's Political Writings*, ed. H. Reiss, 93–131. Cambridge: Cambridge University Press.

Keevy, I. 2009a. 'The Constitutional Court and Ubuntu's Inseparable Trinity'. *Journal for Juridical Science* 1: 61–88.

———. 2009b. 'Ubuntu: Ethnophilosophy and Core Consitutional Values'. In *Ubuntu, Good Faith and Equity: Flexible Legal Principles in Developing a Contemporary Jurisprudence*, ed. F. Diedrich, 24–49. Cape Town: Juta.

———. 2009c. 'Ubuntu Versus the Core Values of the South African Constitution'. *Journal for Juridical Science* 2: 19–58.

Kemahlioglu, O. 2011. 'Jobs in Politicians' Backyards: Party Leadership Competition and Patronage'. *Journal of Theoretical Politics* 23 (4): 480–509.

MacIntyre, A. 1982. *After Virtue: A Study in Moral Theory*. London: Duckworth.

Menkiti, I.F. 1984. 'Person and Community in African Traditional Thought'. In *African Philosophy: An Introduction*, ed. R.A Wright, 171–80. Lanham: University Press of America.

Mgqolozana, T. 2009. *A Man Who is Not a Man*. Pietermaritzburg: University of KwaZulu-Natal Press.

Mudimbe, V-Y. 1988. *The Invention of Africa: Gnosis, Philosophy, and the Order of Knowledge*. Indiana: Indiana University Press.

———. 1991. 'Revelation as a Political Performance'. In *Parables and Fables: Exegesis, Textuality, and Politics in Central Africa*, 3–32. Madison: University of Wisconsin Press.

Munyaka, M. and M. Motlhabi. 2009. 'Ubuntu and its Socio-Moral Significance'. In *African Ethics: An Anthology of Comparative and Applied Ethics*, ed. M.F. Murove, 63–85. Pietermaritzburg: University of KwaZulu-Natal Press.

Murithi, T. 2009. 'An African Perspective on Peace Education: Ubuntu Lessons in Reconciliation'. *International Review of Education* 55: 221–33.

Murove, M.F. 2009a. 'Beyond the Savage Evidence Ethic'. In *African Ethics: An Anthology of Comparative and Applied Ethics*, ed. M.F Murove, 14–33. Pietermaritzburg: University of KwaZulu-Natal Press.

———. (ed.) 2009b. *African Ethics: An Anthology of Comparative and Applied Ethics*. Pietermaritzburg: University of KwaZulu-Natal Press.

Onuoha, B. 1965. *The Elements of African Socialism*. London: Deutsch.

Praeg, L. 2007. *The Geometry of Violence: Girard, Africa, Modernity*. Stellenbosch: SUN Press.

———. 2008. 'An Answer to the Question: "What is [Ubuntu]?"' *South African Journal of Philosophy* 27 (4): 367–85. Reprinted in *Au-delà des lignes: Fabien Eboussi Boulaga, une pratique philosophique*, ed. L. Procesi and K. Kavwahirehi, 347–74. Munich: LINCOM Europa, 2012.

Prozesky, M.H. 2009. 'Cinderella, Survivor and Saviour: African Ethics and the Quest for a Global Ethic'. In *African Ethics: An Anthology of Comparative and Applied Ethics*, ed. M.F. Murove, 3–14. Pietermaritzburg: University of KwaZulu-Natal Press.

Quayson, A. 2002. 'Obverse Denominations: Africa?' *Public Culture* 14 (3): 585–8.

Ramose, M.B. 1999. *African Philosophy through Ubuntu*. Harare: Mond Press.

Richardson, N. 2009. 'Can Christian Ethics Find its Way and Itself in Africa?' In *African Ethics: An Anthology of Comparative and Applied Ethics*, ed. M.F Murove, 129–55. Pietermaritzburg: University of KwaZulu-Natal Press.

Tempels, P. 1969. *Bantu Philosophy*. Paris: Présence Africaine.

Tshoose, C.I. 2009. 'The Emerging Role of the Constitutional Value of *Ubuntu* for Informal Social Security in South Africa'. *African Journal of Legal Studies* 3: 12–19.

Van Binsbergen, W. 2001. '*Ubuntu* and the Globalisation of Southern African Thought and Society'. *Quest* 15 (1–2): 54–89.

Wiredu, K. 2002. 'The Moral Foundations of an African Culture'. In *Philosophy from Africa: A Text with Readings*, ed. P.H. Coetzee and A.P.J. Roux, 287–97. Oxford: Oxford University Press.

———. 2008. 'Social Philosophy in Postcolonial Africa: Some Preliminaries Concerning Communalism and Communitarianism'. *South African Journal of Philosophy* 27 (4): 332–8.

CHAPTER 5

Ubuntu
Affirming a Right and Seeking Remedies in South Africa

Mogobe B. Ramose

The main point of discussion in this chapter is the experience and concept of Ubuntu.[1] Ubuntu is not only a word or a concept. It is not a philosophical abstraction in the fashion of Plato's Ideas or Forms. On the contrary, Ubuntu is a lived and living philosophy of the Bantu-speaking peoples of Africa. It is a philosophy with a past, a present and a project in the future. For these reasons, it is questionable to treat Ubuntu as an ahistorical philosophy that may be turned into a thought experiment – by which I mean something like John Rawls's *A Theory of Justice*, which has nothing to say about the condition of the Native American Indian and the problem of race in the United States of America (Mills 2009: 163). That Ubuntu philosophy is the lived and living experience of human beings means that the human dignity of the Bantu-speaking peoples demands recognition, protection, promotion and respect on the basis of equality with all other human beings, wherever they may be on planet Earth. Whereas the fact of being a human being is contingent, the right to be a human being is inherent to everyone, which places all people on an equal plane. The principle of equality means that a right is a trump demanding mutual recognition in both substance and form. In practice, this means the protection, promotion and respect of the right to be a human being. The ramifications of this fundamental right to life, such as the right to development and a liveable environment, are all included in my use of the term 'right'. In light of this understanding, I have chosen to focus on Ubuntu not in the abstract, but as a question of a right demanding affirmation in view of the experience of the transition from the old to the 'new' South Africa, formally inaugurated in 1994. The experience at issue here pertains to two specific factors, namely the meaning of political-economic change and the decision to opt for constitutional supremacy in the 'new' South Africa.

The problem

The placement of Ubuntu as an 'endnote' in the interim Constitution of 1993 and its subsequent exclusion from the 1996 Constitution amounts to the exclusion of certain peoples – for historical reasons, the Khoi and San peoples, together with the 'Coloureds' and Indians are included here – and their Ubuntu philosophy from substantive political and economic engagement and consequently violates their right to life, despite the formal conferment of rights upon them through the questionable legal dispensation of constitutional supremacy.

A Constitution does not by itself guarantee and deliver justice. It is a vulnerable and fragile means for the actual realisation of justice. The same is true of democracy. Proceeding mainly from the standpoint of political economy, Sampie Terreblanche states the above problem, without the legal dimension, in the following terms:

> It is really a pity that the work of the Truth and Reconciliation Commission was not complemented by a *justice* and *reconciliation commission* tasked to uncover the systemic enrichment and the systemic exploitation and deprivation (or impoverishment) that were brought about by the politico-economic systems that were in place in South Africa from 1894 until 1994, institutionalised by the British empire and supported by Western governments and Western corporations on behalf of two white (or European) settler groups in Africa until the late twentieth century. Why was a justice and reconciliation commission not appointed by the ANC? ... The elite compromise (or the elite conspiracy) which was agreed upon between the corporate sector and a leadership core of the ANC before 1994 exonerated the white corporations and the white citizens from the part they played in the exploitation and deprivation of blacks, and it also enabled whites to transfer almost all their accumulated wealth, their social and physical wealth – and also the part that was accumulated *undeservedly* – almost intact to the new South Africa ... The ANC leadership core was, admittedly, able to implement a policy of black elite formation, but it was deprived of the power to hold white corporations and white citizens accountable for the systemic exploitation and deprivation that was committed by them during the 'century of injustice: 1894–1994' towards black people (2012: 109).

Texts such as Allister Sparks's *Tomorrow is Another Country* (1996), Patrick Bond's *Elite Transition* (2005) and John Pilger's *Freedom Next Time* (2006) confirm that meetings took place between the South African mineral-energy complex (MEC), transnational corporations, United States and British pressure groups and the African National Congress (ANC) 'leadership core'. Terreblanche characterises the meetings as 'secret' and says, 'that rather close interaction (or consultations) took place between the two versions of the negotiations is beyond dispute' (2012: 69).

The problem of justice for the indigenous peoples of South Africa, who were conquered in the unjust wars of colonisation, occupied the minds of the architects of the 'new' South Africa. But as the citation from Terreblanche elucidates, justice for these peoples was compromised even before the birth of the 'new' nation. Historical injustice was metamorphosed into legal justice and then transferred into the 'new' South Africa under the robust protection of the new legal dispensation of constitutional supremacy. In these circumstances, it is an ethical exigency to affirm the right to life of Ubuntu, as clarified and qualified in this context, and to seek remedies to the constitutionalised injustice. This is the the meaning of the title of this chapter.

Scope

My focus is limited to South Africa. However, this does not mean indifference to 'postcolonial' Africa, which undoubtedly was, prior to the conferring of 'independence', treated in the same manner as the 'new' South Africa (Makonnen 1983). I am also conscious of how, throughout the history of slavery and colonisation, the peoples of Africa were forcibly uprooted from the continent and implanted in various regions of the world. The result was an epistemological disturbance that continues to occupy the peoples of African origin in the diaspora. It is therefore necessary to recognise this history as the foundation of cultural bonding – however disturbed – and the matrix for the exchange of experiences between the continental African peoples and those in the diaspora.

It is necessary to state that the concept of a 'right' in the title of this chapter also refers to 'Africa' as a manifestation of the major theme of this chapter, namely, the exclusion, indifference and marginalisation of the peoples of this continent in the invention and imposition of the very name 'Africa'. The crucial point here is the invention and imposition of the name, as if the peoples of the continent lacked, or still lack, the linguistic resources to arrive at the name 'Africa' or that they could actually confer such a name upon themselves as a voluntary act (Khan 2007). I will not discuss this issue here, though its relevance should not be underestimated.

Instead, I want to identify a certain number of themes relating to the 'place' of Ubuntu in post-apartheid South Africa.

Major themes

The ethical and political affirmation of the right of excluded peoples to Ubuntu is an imperative for the redefinition of the political discourse in South Africa. Here I briefly focus on the right to education, not merely as an imperative to the access of education but, equally important, as vehicle for the ethical and political obligation to insert and inscribe Ubuntu philosophy – its ramifications, especially epistemology, ethics, religion and law – in post-apartheid political discourse. In so doing, the concepts Ubuntu, Africanness, Afrocentricity, Afrocentrism, Africanity, humanness and wholeness are discussed, with particular reference to epistemology and ethics. Afrocentricity as 'a consciousness, quality of thought, mode of analysis, and an actionable perspective where Africans seek, from agency, to assert subject place within the context of African history' (Asante 2007: 16) can be contrasted with Afrocentrism, defined as 'a negation of the idea of Afrocentricity as a positive and progressive paradigm' (17). These in turn can be brought into a critical conversation with the Africanity and philosophicality of African philosophy, understood as a 'historical essay' by African philosophers:

> In conducting their historical essay, African philosophers want to rectify the historical prejudices of negation, indifference, severance and oblivion that have plagued African philosophy in the hands of European devil's advocates and their African accomplices. African historical investigations go beyond defense, confrontations and corrections. They are also authentic projects and exercises in genuine scientific construction of African philosophy concerning the diverse matters of its identity and difference, problem and project, its objectives, discoveries, development, achievements and defects or failures (Osuagwu 1999: 25).

Such a consideration must include the epistemological dimension. In this regard, the significance of the suffix -ness in 'humanness' is critically explored towards the end of this chapter in the exposition of Ubuntu as a philosophical concept that conceptually links concepts of humanness and wholeness. I argue that since epistemology is empty without practice, ethics and morality are the next step to give practical content to epistemology. The question of fundamental and natural justice is crucial here and particular reference is made to the historical justice arising from the conquest of the indigenous peoples of Africa in the unjust wars of colonisation, together with the forcible uprooting of African peoples during the slave trade. Law based on 'the right of conquest' and the implications of this in the light of the 'new' South Africa through the 1996 Constitution are critically considered. These things combined become a conduit in the search for an appropriate pedagogy for the examination of issues pertaining to historical justice and the liberation of indigenous Africans. George J. Sefa Dei articulates the starting point of such a pedagogy as follows:

> Afrocentricity is a commitment to a pedagogy that is political education . . . Afrocentric education uses African culture and cultural values as a weapon of liberation and as counterknowledge to fight Euramerican ideological domination in the schools. Afrocentric education however must be more than emancipatory or liberatory pedagogy. Afrocentricity as an intellectual paradigm must focus on addressing the structural impediments to the education of the African student by engaging her or him to identify with her or his history, heritage, and culture. To be successful the Afrocentric pedagogue must move away from a manipulation of the 'victim status and exploiting white guilt' to work toward finding solutions to pressing problems of educating students of African descent (1994: 17).

Afrocentric pedagogy is thus, by definition, a critique of Eurocentrism. It is a challenge to the centuries-old putative claim that to be a European ('Euramerican') is to be ontologically and qualitatively superior to other human beings. This challenge speaks to the recognition that the 'time has definitely come to ask' philosophers 'where they stand'. This critically interrogative time is our postcolonial present, in which the 'colonial asymmetries of the past are – at least in principle – not defensible any more' (Serequeberhan 2002: 64).

In order to illuminate the ethical and pedagogical issues arising from this challenge, Dei argues that special focus should be placed on the following major themes:

- solidarity;
- mutuality;
- collective responsibility;
- the obligation to share wealth with the rest of the community;

- the concept that the individual exists only within the context of the community – a thesis rendered by Bénézet Bujo as follows:

  For Black Africa, it is not the Cartesian cogito ergo sum ('I think, therefore I am') but an existential *cognatus sum, ergo sumus* ('I am related, therefore we are') that is decisive . . . It (*cognatus sum*) is not only a given; it is existential to such a degree that refusal to accept it must lead to the death, not only of the individual but even of the community itself (2001: 22–3);

- the fact that, according to Dei, 'to many Africans, the dichotomy is not between the *individual* and the *community*, but between the *competitive individual* isolated from his or her community and the *cooperative individual* enriched by community' (1994: 12);
- the status and role of the elders;
- religion, with particular reference to the African conception of the triadic constitution of community as including the living, the living-dead and the yet-to-be-born;
- the status and role of women;
- democracy/Bantucracy – according to Bujo:

  A hasty break with African traditions in favour of the Western model of democracy would be deadly, for this would mean repeating the same mistake made during the euphory of independence in the sixties. At that time, democracy and dictatorship, both of a Western kind, were adopted. Today, both models can be judged as having failed in Africa (1998: 15);

- poverty and Africa's foreign debt problem. According to Bujo, the idea of repayment of foreign debt by Africa is very questionable:

  The problem of the real debtor will have to be discussed anew. If the colonial past of Africa is reflected upon, the need for reparation in favour of the African people comes as an inevitable conclusion . . . Today it may be asked whether the tables should not be turned. Whoever recalls the history of black Africa cannot avoid thinking of reparation from the conquerors of this history . . . The history of those who were killed and exploited and robbed of their dignity is not yet buried. The unjust deeds of the past demand an *anamnestic* solidarity with the victims (1998: 176–7);

- disease and misfortune. Again, Bujo argues that African wisdom considers a disease as

  an indication that something in human relations is wrong . . . a disease can bring people to take the communal dimension seriously. Prescription of the appropriate medicine is not sufficient. In addition, the doctor or healer has to go beyond mere physiological and individual symptoms, until the proper psychological, moral and socially-conditioned cause is traced and discovered. Here, the patient's family relationships are studied and past conflicts interpreted anew. The sick person's social and economic relationships are thoroughly examined. The community of the deceased is also not forgotten since a disease might be caused by the disturbed relationship of the patient with the world of those who have passed away (1998: 182);

- HIV and AIDS: Having argued that historical, structural, systemic and systematic poverty has a direct contribution to the aggravation of the HIV and AIDS pandemic in Africa, Bujo argues:

  It ought to be stressed that the dramatic speed at which the disease is spreading in sub-Saharan Africa cannot be linked only to sexual contacts . . . To fight against AIDS in Africa, therefore, means also to create a just economic order, so that the widespread predicament within medical care can be corrected (1998: 191).

He continues: 'From an African perspective, it is to be stated that an indiscriminate distribution of condoms ultimately wipes out African culture. In dealing with AIDS, the main point is to change previous sexual behaviour. In the African tradition, there are many practices to prepare for sexual self-discipline' (1998: 192). Bujo concludes his commentary on sickness and HIV and AIDS thus:

In order to preserve the African understanding of sickness, not only with regard to AIDS, but in general, it is important that students of medicine in Africa intensively study the human person in their tradition. It is not enough for them to acquire technical know-how from the West. The African person has to be approached in his/her religiosity and understanding of the two-dimensional community of the living and the dead. There has, for instance, to be a special method of cure for a patient who links a severe headache to the dissatisfaction of a deceased uncle tormenting him or her (1998: 193);

- Ubuntu legal philosophy is by definition antithetical to the principle of constitutional supremacy (sovereignty) adopted as the legal foundation of the 'new' South Africa. The communal dimension of Ubuntu legal philosophy, coupled with the principle that *molato ga o bole* – prescription is unknown in African law – is but one illustration of the paradigmatic and ethical antithesis between Ubuntu and Western legal philosophies. The relevant provisions of the 1996 Constitution protecting property may be cited as an illustration of this antithesis. It is pertinent to consider this illustration in the light of the *baipei* and homeless peoples in South Africa. In an analysis of a similar phenomenon, the *favelas*, the Catholic Bishops' Conference of Brazil declared:

> The right to make use of urban land to guarantee adequate housing is one of the primary conditions for creating a life that is authentically human. Therefore when land occupations – or even land invasions – occur, legal judgments on property titles must begin with the right of all to adequate housing. All claims to private ownership must take second place to this basic need . . . We conclude that the natural right to housing has priority over the law that governs land appropriation. A legal title to property can hardly be an absolute in the face of the human need of people who have nowhere to make their home (May 1991: 122).

This conclusion is arguably deeper and more far-reaching than that in the well-known case of *Government of the Republic of South Africa and Others v. Grootboom and Others*.[2]

The themes articulated here may be construed as an incomplete list of ethical and political exigencies that demand recognition in the educational curriculum of South Africa. The continued exclusion of these issues from the curriculum is tantamount to the denial of justice as the recognition of Ubuntu. Such a denial is a recipe for instability since it contravenes the principles of human dignity and equality, including negative discrimination, deemed to be cardinal to the Constitution. It seems apposite to conclude this point with a citation from Leo XII's *Rerum Novarum*: 'If the citizens, if the families on entering into association and fellowship, were to experience hindrance in a commonwealth instead of help, and were to find their rights attacked instead of being upheld, society would rightly be an object of detestation rather than of desire.'[3]

The themes articulated here all relate to the question of justice in a much broader than juridical sense. At the same time, however, the realisation of this broader understanding of justice is limited by the very nature of the constitutional regime of the 'new' South Africa.

The transition to the 'new' South Africa

The struggle for a transition to the 'new' South Africa is predicated on the question of justice, arising from the conquest of the indigenous peoples of the country during the unjust wars of colonisation. It is thus historically short-sighted, even misleading, to speak of 'post-apartheid' South Africa since 1994 – as if apartheid, born formally in 1948, was the sole origin of the problem of justice in South Africa. On the contrary, there were many political organisations – such as the ANC, the Natal Indian Congress, the Pan-Africanist Congress, the South African Communist Party (SACP), the Black People's Convention (BPC) and the Azanian People's Organisation – engaged in this struggle, each upholding its own ideology. Two of the highlights of this struggle were the Rivonia and South African Students Organisation (SASO)/BPC 'political' trials. Steve Bantu Biko, one of the unforgettable and outstanding political martyrs in the struggle for the liberation, testified in court in the SASO/BPC trial and many luminaries of the same struggle, including Nelson Mandela, were arrested and testified at the Rivonia trial. Asked to clarify the relationship between the ANC and the SACP, Mandela explained that the ANC could work together with the SACP, despite the fact that they do not share the same ideology. Thus, once the ANC had achieved its objectives, the SACP would be free to pursue its ultimate objectives on its own. Of the standpoint and objectives of the ANC, Mandela had the following to say:

The ideological creed of the ANC is, and always has been, the creed of African Nationalism. It is not the concept of African Nationalism expressed in the cry, 'Drive the White man into the sea.' The African nationalism for which the ANC stands is the concept of freedom and fulfilment for the African people in their own land. The most important political document ever adopted by the ANC is the 'Freedom Charter'. It is by no means a blueprint for a socialist state. It calls for redistribution, but not nationalization, of land; it provides for nationalization of mines, banks, and monopoly industry, because big monopolies are owned by one race only, and without such nationalization racial domination would be perpetuated despite the spread of political power . . . Under the Freedom Charter, nationalization would take place in an economy based on private enterprise. The realization of the Freedom Charter would open up fresh fields for a prosperous African population of all classes, including the middle class. The ANC has never at any period of its history advocated a revolutionary change in the economic structure of the country, nor has it, to the best of my recollection, ever condemned capitalist society (1965: 178–9).

It is unlikely that this statement was absent from the minds of the architects of the 'new' South Africa. The transition was hailed as a 'miracle' from many quarters. The power of the 'miracle' seems to have been so overwhelming that few paused to pose the question: a 'miracle' by whom and for whose benefit? Obliviousness to this question gave birth to a new vocabulary, a new political discourse of the country being 'post-apartheid', 'non-racial' in 'our new democracy', of 'democratic' South Africa having one of 'the best Constitutions' in the world and so on. There are many other expressions belonging to this discourse, such as 'reconciliation', 'affirmative action' and, indeed, 'Ubuntu'. The birthday of the 'new' South Africa was 27 April 1994, confirmed by the Constitution of 1996. By 2012, the 'new' South Africa had attained the age of majority being thus an adult presumed capable of running its own life. Already as a teenager, South Africa was pricked to pose – in its own way – the question, a 'miracle' by whom and for whose benefit? It is to this question that I now turn.

Justice in the 'new' South Africa

The discourse on democracy in South Africa proceeds as if 'democracy' is an end in itself and as if oblivious to the fact that even before 1994, South Africa was a democracy just like ancient Athens, which had slaves and yet was considered a democracy. The widespread buoyant talk about the democracy of the 'new' South Africa appears to have failed to take into account the fact that democracy has long been overtaken (Hertz 2002: 13–15) by timocracy (Ramose 2010: 291–303). In the world today, we have the widespread reality of 'business-managed democracy' (Beder 2010) and that is the hallmark of our timocratic age. The glib talk about 'democratic values' is similarly misleading to the extent that it gives the impression that these values exist as metaphysical entities ready to be put to use. If 'democratic values' were so self-evident and readily accessible to use, surely the transition to the 'new' South Africa would have been unnecessary? Democracy is certainly not an end (Mancini 1998: 41) in itself, but a fragile means to an end (Weiler 1998).

The many varieties of democracy attest to its nature as a means to an end. Before 1994, South Africa was a parliamentary democracy. Many laws were passed and dehumanising measures taken in violation of the right to life of the indigenous peoples. Where were the 'democratic values' to come and redeem these peoples from the burden of inhuman laws? The power to make laws was vested in Parliament and no other superior legislator was recognised. Thus the principle of parliamentary supremacy was the foundation and pillar of South African constitutional history before 1994. Consonant with this principle, the courts had no jurisdiction to pronounce upon the substance of the law, as the famous Harris cases of the 1950s so eloquently demonstrate. It is evident then that parliamentary supremacy is, in principle, compatible with democracy. What then was the basis for the shift of paradigm from parliamentary to constitutional supremacy?

Some argue that the reason for the shift was to prevent, in advance, the abuse of the law by Parliament, as was the case before 1994. This argument is rather vacuous since, by analogy, it is doubtful that the best remedy to the abuses of the Bible is to throw it away and replace it with either the Koran or the Torah. On the contrary, the Bible as one of the sources of the theology of liberation – by every test, the proper use of the Bible – has not been thrown away, but the theology of liberation has been silenced for a long time. It follows that a solid plausible argument is required to justify the transition from parliamentary to constitutional supremacy in South Africa. If we leave aside for the moment the legal aspects of this transition, it would seem that the answer is to be found in the pertinent argument articulated by Terreblanche:

> For the MEC and the rest of the corporate sector the 'great prize' was to be
> exonerated of the huge apartheid debt that accumulated on their 'accounts'

as they exploited black labour relentlessly over a period of a hundred years. On this issue the MEC outmanoeuvered the leadership core of the ANC by clever deal-making in the process of which the South African corporations were empowered to metamorphose themselves unjustifiably from ugly apartheid ducklings with a heavy apartheid debt on their shoulders into South African corporations exonerated of their apartheid debt . . . The 'great prize' for the ANC political elite at the secret negotiations was that they, and they alone, would be declared previously disadvantaged individuals (PDIs) who would qualify to become political representatives with lucrative salaries or would become the beneficiaries of BEE [black economic empowerment] and AA [affirmative action] contracts . . . The 'great prize' to which the American pressure groups that participated at the secret negotiations aspired was to convince the ANC to accept the ideologies of neoliberal globalism and market fundamentalism, *so that South Africa could become a neo-colonial satellite of the American-led neoliberal empire* (2012: 72–3, emphasis added).

No wonder then that the property clause is the longest in the South African Constitution. It would seem that in order to safeguard the respective 'prizes', the transition from parliamentary to constitutional supremacy was the best option, an option that had nothing to do with putting in place the conditions to further the possibility of true justice for the indigenous peoples. It was a tactic to defend wealth gained and accumulated on the basis of unjust acquisition. Considerations of Ubuntu, even of the word itself, were more than remote in the hatching of this wealth-protection mechanism.

Constitutional supremacy thus entered for the first time into South African constitutional history. One wonders whether or not the architects of the 'new' South Africa considered that even the Constitution as the 'higher law' is not necessarily the best guarantor and defender of rights – even the fundamental right to life. Here it is sufficient to recall that the Supreme Court of the United States of America once held that slavery was consistent with the law of the country. It is therefore problematic to project and construe the Constitution as an omniscient infallible 'god'. The *trias politica* doctrine is by itself no solace since, under constitutional supremacy, it gives the courts power to strike down a law, even though the judges are not elected and therefore are not, strictly speaking, representatives of the people.

The 'independence of the judiciary' is a well-documented doctrine that requires no special discussion here. Compounding the problem is clothing the Constitution with the gird of eternity, by appeal to the 'essential features doctrine' – a problem that becomes even more complex when the Constitution is attributed with an immortality virtually greater than Thomas Hobbes's Leviathan, the mortal god. The point is simply this: a Constitution does not make a people. The reverse is true. Thus whatever subtleties may be brought to bear upon the concept of popular sovereignty, none is conceivable without taking seriously the actual living people as the authors of their own Constitution. Given the fact of conquest in the unjust wars of the colonisation of South Africa and the ensuing consequences of the questionable 'right of conquest' beyond 1994, the exclusion of Ubuntu from all constitutional dispensations in South Africa demands urgent and serious deliberation.

Ubuntu and constitutional supremacy

From an unspecified standpoint and in a context different from the present, the ANC has already averred that 'the constitution is not holy' (Joubert 2011). One implication is that the Constitution may not be treated as 'God' since it is not holy. Although the insight is correct, from the Ubuntu political-legal philosophical point of view (Ramose 1999: 102–28), the argument of the ANC nevertheless remains questionable. The correctness of the insight lies in the recognition that Ubuntu philosophy proceeds from the position that motion is the principle of being. Since everything is in incessant flow – a perpetual exchange – it is necessary to remain open to change and not to block it by imposing an arbitrary finality to life. In the perpetual flux of life, whatever is in a state of momentary endurance, being, is subject to change and evanescence. This is the *-ness* aspect of Ubuntu. It means that the Constitution may be construed as durable, but not as a fixed, eternal, immutable and immortal deity, deserving only of adoration from the human beings who are supposed to have made it in the first place. This philosophic statement takes cognisance of provisions to amend a Constitution. But such provisions do not necessarily detract from its putative trancendental status. One should understand Kéba M'Baye's argument with regard to a prescription that is foreign to African law (in Driberg 1934: 238). I suggest that his philosophic insight extends beyond prescription or the statute of limitation and therefore applies to the concept of a Constitution as a human-made deity. M'Baye avers:

Prescription is unknown in African law. The African believes that time cannot change the truth. Just as the truth must be taken into consideration each time it becomes known, so must no obstacle be placed in the way of the search for it and its discovery. It is for this reason that judicial decisions are not authoritative. They must always be able to be called into question (1974: 147).

It is therefore problematic to ascribe eternity, immutability and immortality, for example, to a human device such as the Constitution. From the point of view of Ubuntu philosophy, -*ness* is thus preferable to -*ism* as in 'constitutional-ism'. It is apparent that the principle of constitutional supremacy is incompatible with Ubuntu legal philosophy.

Furthermore, the Ubuntu understanding of community as a triad of the living, the living-dead ('ancestors') and the yet-to-be-born is not a metaphysics, but an ontology, extending to invisible beings. The emphasis is on beings, rather than the invisibility of the yet-to-be-born. After all, this latter group shares invisibility with the living-dead, who are understood pre-eminently in ontological terms. The import of this is that an ahistorical Constitution – written or unwritten – devoid of a living ontology and anthropology is merely an abstract metaphysical catalogue of rights and duties, with problematic implications for the adherents of Ubuntu philosophy. It follows that dialogue is necessary in order to reconstruct the 'new' South Africa into a home and not merely a space in which all may live. Deliberative democracy must recognise that to be different is not necessarily to stand in opposition to the Other. It is necessary to be open to the need to enter into dialectical learning. Such learning must be based on the postulates of 'comparable validity' and 'dialogical equality'. As Paul Healy puts it:

Briefly stated, these postulates stipulate that if we are to be genuinely responsive to difference in a manner conducive to promoting mutual understanding and learning, we need to allow others to articulate their own positions in their own terms and accord them the status of equal partners in the conjoint exploration of a topic, to the extent that we are prepared to allow their views actively to challenge our own 'settled opinion', to modify our preconceptions when they are found wanting, and to learn from what they have to tell us rather than simply asserting the superiority of our own viewpoint . . . The point of these postulates is to enjoin us to stop treating those who occupy different discursive standpoints either as mirror images of ourselves or as denizens of a deficient socio-cultural standpoint who need to prove themselves to us before we will accord them a respectful hearing, and instead recognize that they represent a position comparable in value to our own from which we can productively learn (2011: 302–3).

For those with an ear for African philosophy, the message of the citation has long been conveyed by Bujo and Ernest Wamba dia Wamba, among others. Palaver or *mbongi* is one of the means to be adopted in the search to remedy the 'new' South Africa from the deadly problems of unemployment, poverty and inequality.

Conclusion

I have identified the problem in the old and the 'new' South Africa as revolving around the question of fundamental natural justice, complicated by issues pertaining to historical justice. The exclusion of Ubuntu from all the constitutional dispensations of South Africa is far more than the accidental omission of a word. Accordingly, it is an exigency of justice to urge for the affirmation of the right to life of Ubuntu, first and foremost, in the country of the birth of the indigenous peoples conquered in the unjust wars of colonisation. This is one remedy that can be pursued through the gateway of the conduct of genuine dialogue, resulting in transformative learning for all.

Notes

1. This chapter is part of an *oeuvre* that has evolved over a number of decades and its use of 'Ubuntu' should not be read or interpreted in terms of the distinction between 'ubuntu' (praxis) and 'Ubuntu' (retrodicted, postcolonial philosophy) used elsewhere in this volume.
2. *Government of the Republic of South Africa and Others v. Grootboom and Others* 2001 (1) SA 46 (CC).
3. See http://www.vatican.va/holy_father/leo_xiii/encyclicals/documents/hf_l-xiii_enc_ 15051891 _rerum-novarum_en.html.

References

Asante, M.K. 2007. *An Afrocentric Manifesto: Toward an African Renaissance*. Cambridge: Polity Press.

Beder, S. 2010. 'Business-Managed Democracy: The Trade Agenda'. *Critical Social Policy* 30 (4): 496–518.

Bond, P. 2005. *Elite Transition: From Apartheid to Neoliberalism in South Africa*. Pietermaritzburg: University of KwaZulu-Natal Press.

Bujo, B. 1998. *The Ethical Dimension of Community: The African Model and Dialogue between North and South*. Nairobi: Paulines Publications Africa.

———. 2001. *Foundations of an African Ethic: Beyond the Universal Claims of Western Morality*. Nairobi: Paulines Publications Africa.

Dei, G.J.S. 1994. 'Afrocentricity: A Cornerstone of Pedagogy'. *Anthropology and Education Quarterly* 25 (1): 3–28.

Driberg, J.H. 1934. 'The African Conception of Law'. *Journal of Comparative Legislation and International Law* XVI: 230–45.

Healy, P. 2011. 'Rethinking Deliberative Democracy: From Deliberative Discourse to Transformative Dialogue'. *Philosophy and Social Criticism* 37 (3): 295–311.

Hertz, N. 2002. *The Silent Takeover: Global Capitalism and the Death of Democracy*. London: Arrow Books.

Joubert, J.J. 2011. '*Grondwet Nie Heilig*'. *Beeld*, 21 September.

Khan, K.R.N.P. 2007. 'The Origin of the Term "Africa"'. *Afuraka/Afuraikait Nanasom Nhoma, Afurakani/Afuraitkaitnit Ancestral Regional Journal*. Available at http://www.odwirafo. com/Afuraka-Afuraitkait_Nanasom-Nhoma_Obueakwan.pdf.

Makonnen, Y. 1983. *International Law and the New States of Africa*. Addis Ababa: UNESCO.

Mancini, G.F. 1998. 'Europe: The Case for Statehood'. *European Law Journal* 4 (1): 29–42.

Mandela, N. 1965. *No Easy Walk to Freedom*. London: Heinemann Educational Books.

May, R.H. 1991. *The Poor of the Land*. New York: Orbis Books.

M'Baye, K. 1974. 'The African Conception of Law'. *International Encyclopedia of Comparative Law* 1: 138–58.

Mills, C.W. 2009. 'Rawls on Race, Race in Rawls'. *Southern Journal of Philosophy* XLVII (S1): 161–84.

Osuagwu, I.M. 1999. *African Historical Reconstruction*. Owerri: Amamihe Publications.

Pilger, J. 2006. *Freedom Next Time*. London: Bantam.

Ramose, M.B. 1999. *African Philosophy through Ubuntu*. Harare: Mond Books.

———. 2010. 'The Death of Democracy and the Resurrection of Timocracy'. *Journal of Moral Education* 39 (3): 291–303.

Serequeberhan, T. 2002. 'The Critique of Eurocentrism and the Practice of African Philosophy'. In *The African Philosophy Reader*, ed. P.H. Coetzee and A.P.J. Roux, 64–79. London: Routledge.

Sparks, A. 1996. *Tomorrow is Another Country: The Inside Story of South Africa's Road to Change*. Johannesburg: Jonathan Ball.

Terreblanche, S. 2012. *Lost in Transformation: South Africa's Search for a New Future Since 1986*. Sandton: KMM Review Publishing Company.

Weiler, J.H.H. 1998. 'Europe: The Case Against the Case for Statehood'. *European Law Journal* 4 (1): 43–62.

CHAPTER 6

Utu, Usawa, Uhuru
Building Blocks of Nyerere's Political Philosophy

Issa G. Shivji

Dominant Eurocentric discourses either demonise or romanticise precolonial African cultures, ideologies and philosophies. Afrocentric reactions, on the other hand, tend to present them as harmonious wholes, predominantly characterised by positive qualities, such as humanness, kindness, sharing and generosity. After more than five centuries of European domination, this overly positive representation was perhaps necessary in order to 'strike a balance', so to speak, and for African historiography to celebrate what was called the African initiative. The challenge, however, is not so much to strike a balance in the abstract, but rather to understand the course of human thought and history and how it is constructed in actually existing struggles.

Constructing ideologies and philosophies

African cultures, ideologies and philosophies are socially and politically contentious terrains. They are constructed and reconstructed through arguments that have been and continue to be formed. It is also important to underscore that in the unequal power relations – between Africa and the West, but also within contemporary postcolonial African societies – so-called traditional cultures and ideologies are deployed in both domination and resistance, by those who exercise power as well as by those who resist it. Consider, for example, the following statement about Ubuntu made by Nelson Mandela:

> In the old days . . . a traveller through a country would stop at a village and he didn't have to ask for food or for water. Once he stops, the people gave him food, entertained him. That is one aspect of Ubuntu, but it will have various aspects. Ubuntu does not mean that people should not enrich themselves. The question therefore is: are you going to do so in order to enable the community around you to be able to improve?[1]

While the first aspect of Ubuntu mentioned here is common to many African (and for that matter non-African, pre-class societies), it is the other alleged aspect of Ubuntu that betrays its obvious reconstruction within a capitalist ethos: 'Ubuntu does not mean that people should not enrich themselves.' I am reminded of what Mahatma Gandhi once said: 'We invite the capitalist to regard himself as trustee for those on whom he depends for the making, the retention, and the increase of his capital.'[2] Gandhi, a moral, austere person, found nothing wrong with capitalists on condition that they recognise that they hold their property in trust for the people – indeed, an interesting definition and justification of the exploitative nature of capitalist formations! On these issues, as we shall see, Julius Nyerere was far more radical and insightful and much more consistent than either Mandela or Gandhi.

In this chapter, I explore the building blocks of Nyerere's philosophy and how they were reconstructed and deployed to develop his policy of socialism and self-reliance or *ujamaa na kujitegemea*. I also surmise how and to what extent his philosophical premises impacted on his political practice. As for deploying cultural or traditional resources, Nyerere explicitly argued that his variant of socialism or Ujamaa derived from traditional African society. In his own words:

> The word 'ujamaa' was chosen for special reasons. First, it is an African word and thus emphasizes the African-ness of the policies we intend to follow. Second, its literal meaning is 'family-hood', so that it brings to the mind of our people the idea of mutual involvement in the family, as we know it. By the use of the word 'ujamaa', therefore, we state that for us socialism involves building on the foundation of our past, and building also to our own design. We are not importing a foreign ideology into Tanzania and trying to smother our distinct social patterns with it (Nyerere 1968: 2).

Nyerere was astute enough to concede that 'socialism is international; its ideas and beliefs relate to man in society, not just to Tanzanian man in Tanzania, or African man in Africa' (1968: 2). But he emphasised that the international character of socialism did not mean, and ought not to mean, that all societies aspiring to build socialism would and should follow one single pattern of development. In his pragmatic political wisdom, he was doing this to distance himself from the power blocs and Cold War politics of the time.

Sources
Julius Kambarage Nyerere, Tanzania's nationalist leader and first president, did not write a long philosophical work as did Ghana's Kwame Nkrumah. He was more of a political thinker, rather than a philosopher. His political writings, though, are often infused with philosophical ideas. In fact, his rationalisations of politics are very philosophical. The first three volumes of his selected speeches, particularly the introductions, are a very good source of his political ideas. The 'Arusha Declaration' of 1967 is a concentrated form of his basic philosophical ideas. There are three elements in Nyerere's philosophical thought, which, I believe, can be extracted as building blocks of his philosophy. These are *utu* (dignity), *usawa* (equality) and *uhuru* (freedom).

Equality, dignity and justice
The idea of equality is central to Nyerere's thought. There is nothing unique about this. All great philosophers and thinkers have agonised and reflected on the idea of equality. As Friedrich Engels stated, the idea of equality is primeval, but it took thousands of years to arrive at the idea of equal rights in states and in society. What is special, and perhaps African, so to speak, in Nyerere's idea of equality is that it is inseparable from the idea of dignity or *utu* – which can be translated both as 'human dignity' and 'humanness'. The specificity of Nyerere's equality can best be appreciated by contrasting it with the idea of equality in bourgeois society (for a more detailed argument, see Shivji 1995).

As Evgeny Pashukanis (1978 [1924]) argued, equality forms the basis of the 'juridical outlook' of the bourgeoisie. Equality of individuals translates into equality before law, which in turn translates into equal rights. Thus all human beings are equal *because they possess equal rights*. Juridically speaking, all individuals in society possess or have equal rights. Needless to say, this political and legal equality is superimposed on the fundamental social and economic inequalities inherent in the capitalist system.

At work here is a double abstraction. First, the 'individual being' is abstracted from the 'social being' and second, this 'abstract individual' is then said to possess equal rights. Thus rights are quantified and become things to possess. They become commodities and their abstraction from actual social relations is thus disguised. Bourgeois philosophy and politics, as we know, are premised on several such abstractions and separations: the abstraction of individual from society (which separates the individual *from* society), the separation of politics and economics and the separation of the production of commodities from their circulation in the market. In the market, all commodity owners, sellers and buyers are equal. In production, the landlord and the tenant, the factory owner and the worker, the merchant and the retailer are all, of course, unequal. In the famous dictum formulated by Anatole France in Chapter 7 of *Le Lys Rouge* (*The Red Lily*), published in 1894: 'The law in its majestic impartiality forbids rich and poor alike to sleep under bridges, to beg in the streets, and steal bread.'[3]

For Nyerere, all human beings are equal – *binadamu wote ni sawa*. It is not that all human beings *have* equal opportunities or rights. They *are* equal. Coupled with the idea of *utu* (dignity or humanness), this idea of *usawa* (equality) per force imports the ideas of *equity* and *justice*, both of which, in Kiswahili, translate into the word *haki*, which also means rights. Here, rights are not separated from justice – unlike in the bourgeois understanding where 'right' connotes a legal right, so that justice merely translates into 'legal' justice. In Kiswahili, equity, justice and right are all connoted by this one word *haki*, which is often used interchangeably. *Utu* and *usawa* are inseparable in the sense that all are equal in their dignity. *Haki* is not equivalent to the concept of rights in bourgeois philosophy. *Haki* is not justice according to rights, but justice as social justice. Built into Nyerere's notion of equality are both *utu* (dignity) and equity/justice (*haki*). Only intellectuals, in certain contexts and circumstances, differentiate the three concepts. In the perception of the people, though, the term *haki* does not differentiate into equity, justice and right. I have found this again and again in my legal aid practice. After listening to a client – a worker, a peasant, etc. – I explain their legal rights in detail. Immediately and almost invariably, there is a retort: '*lakini hii sio haki!*' (but that is not justice!). In brief, then, for Nyerere, equality is a composite concept, incorporating both equity and justice:

> To say, for example, that a one-armed old man and active young man are equal if they each have ten acres of fertile land and a hoe would be to make a mockery of equality. There is, therefore, no absolute and simple rule which can be easily applied everywhere and to all aspects of life in relation to equality. Instead we are forced back to concepts of human dignity; every member of society must have safeguarded by society his basic humanity and the sacredness of his life-force. He must both be regarded, and be able to regard himself, as the human equal of all other members in relation to the society (Nyerere 1966: 15).

In the following sentence, Nyerere deals with the relation between dignity and rights in an interesting fashion:

> We have to work towards a position where each person realizes that his rights in society – above the basic needs of every human being – must come second to the overriding need of human dignity for all; and we have to establish the kind of social organization which reduces personal temptation above that level to a minimum (1966: 17).

One wonders how much the separation here, of dignity from equality, on the one hand, and the subordination of equality to dignity, on the other, arises from the use of the English language that Nyerere was writing in, thus betraying his own 'bourgeois' education. One wonders if, were he to render the same ideas in Kiswahili, he would have made such separation or even if there would have been a need to do so. But we will have to leave that to speculation. I am not aware of any of Nyerere's writing in Kiswahili on these or similar ideas.

In his major pamphlet on socialism, the 'Arusha Declaration' (of 1967), which was originally written in Kiswahili, the idea of *usawa* (equality) is a dominant theme and it is clear from the context that it imports both *utu* (dignity) and *haki* (equity or justice). In his English introduction to *Freedom and Socialism* (1968), it is interesting to see how Nyerere blends this philosophical unity of equality, equity and dignity in his understanding of socialism. Three quotes from this introduction demonstrate this point well:

> The equality of man may or may not be susceptible to scientific proof. But its acceptance as a basic assumption of life in society is the core and essence of socialism. No one who qualifies his belief in the equality of man is really a socialist . . . Socialism as a system, is in fact the organization of men's inequalities to serve equality. Their equality is socialist belief (4).

> The upholding of human dignity could be expected to follow automatically from these two basic characteristics of a socialist society . . . A socialist society would seek to uphold human dignity everywhere; and however limited its capacity in this respect, it could never act in such a manner as to be itself responsible for the denial of any man's humanity (4–5).

And none of these things is possible unless every other aspect of society – its economic, social and legal organization – is such as to emphasize and serve man's equality. A political democracy which exists in a society of gross economic inequalities, or of social inequality, is at best imperfect, and at worst a hollow sham (5).

Here we must pause a little. A careful reading of this text indicates that Nyerere has already modified his idea of justice or equity in a way that leads me to suggest that the concept of justice in Nyerere's thinking is *social* justice, as opposed to the bourgeois notion of *legal* or *individual* justice. My contention is that Western writers on Nyerere's philosophy – many being his personal friends and admirers – fail to see how this understanding of justice as *social* justice derives from equality, justice and equity. They invariably attribute to Nyerere a radical version of 'bourgeois' philosophy and, in some cases, even 'Christian humanness' (see, for instance, Huddleston 1995: 1–8). Trevor Huddleston argues that Nyerere was 'pre-eminently a Christian humanist' (6) and goes on to assert: 'I am sure that Nyerere would describe himself as a Christian socialist' (7). It is true that Nyerere was a deeply religious man – in fact, a practising Catholic. Yet, he would have never described himself as a 'Christian socialist'. Whether this was out of conviction or political astuteness or both, one cannot tell (after all, he led a nation of Christians and Muslims in almost equal numbers). It is easy to see how Huddleston could arrive at his claim given, for example, the following forceful statement Nyerere made to a Christian audience:

We say man was created in the image of God. I refuse to imagine a God who is poor, ignorant, superstitious, fearful, oppressed, wretched – which is the lot of the majority of those He created in his own image. *Men are creators of themselves and their conditions, but under present conditions we are creatures, not of God, but of our fellow men* (in Huddleson 1995: 6, emphasis added).

This could be a genuine philosophical contradiction in the man – as is often the case with profound thinkers – but it certainly does not lend itself to the conclusion that Nyerere was either a '*Christian* socialist' or a '*Christian* humanist'.

142

Freedom

The other fundamental premise of Nyerere's political philosophy is freedom. The first three volumes of the collection of his speeches are titled: *Freedom and Unity* (1966), *Freedom and Socialism* (1968) and *Freedom and Development* (1973). Nyerere's concept of 'freedom' operates at three levels: freedom from external domination, freedom from oppression and individual freedom. While he subscribed to individual freedoms or human rights, he argued that they could not override the collective right of the people to be free because only in a free society could human dignity be realised.

As a fervent nationalist and independence leader, the first political meaning of freedom for Nyerere was, needless to say, independence from colonialism. On this he did not compromise because no society can be free if it is ruled by an outside power. Nyerere was a great supporter of African liberation. He supported African liberation movements materially, militarily where necessary and also politically. Dar es Salaam was the headquarters of the liberation committee of the OAU (Organisation of African Unity, the predecessor of the African Union – AU). He also supported, morally and politically, freedom movements and various struggles against oppression on other continents – in Yugoslavia or Czechoslovakia in the Soviet bloc or Cuba or Vietnam against the United States. The bedrock of this understanding of freedom was his commitment to every peoples' right to self-determination – a right that formed the basis of independence movements in formerly colonised countries as well as the various United Nations declarations issued in support of those movements. In effect, it meant the right of a people to make their own decisions. For many African leaders, the right to self-determination was complete once a country attained formal independence in the sense of having its sovereignty recognised. Not so for Nyerere. Like Nkrumah (see his *Neo-Colonialism* of 1965), he argued that the threat of domination by foreign powers continued and in fact operated in many African countries, even after state sovereignty was achieved and formally recognised, in the sense that African governments were not free to make their own decisions. Only two years after independence, Nyerere warned of the second scramble for Africa:

> The question is still being asked 'Who is going to control Africa?' Those who are asking it do not expect the answer to be 'The Africans.' The events in the Congo have demonstrated that it is possible for a colonial power to leave by the front door, and the same or different external forces to

come in by the back. For let us make no mistake; as we are emerging successfully from the first 'Scramble for Africa', so we are entering a new phase, the phase of the Second Scramble for Africa, and, I believe, for Asia. As I have said elsewhere, this second Scramble will be conducted in a different manner from the first, but its purpose will be the same – to get control of our continent. This time we will not be subject to military invasions from countries outside our continent; foreign powers have no intention of fighting each other in this second Scramble. They will incite African to fight African, Asian to fight Asian, but always in their interests. The imperialists, old and new, will exploit the differences within African nations and between African nations, within Asian nations and between Asian nations (Nyerere 1966: 205).

Nyerere sought to translate his Ujamaa philosophy into a policy document on socialism and self-reliance. The doctrine of self-reliance followed from his philosophy on equality and freedom. A country or a people cannot be free and freely make its own decisions as long as it does not rely on itself, its own material and human resources, to develop in freedom. In many ways, therefore, self-reliance proclaimed by the 'Arusha Declaration' was a political summary of the ideology of Ujamaa, based on equality and freedom. The 'Declaration' argued that the government had overemphasised money as the vehicle for development when it was poor. In any case, if the country got money for development from foreign nations and investors, it would compromise its independence and freedom to choose its own policies. The 'Declaration' asked rhetorically: 'How can we depend upon foreign governments and companies for the major part of our development without giving to those governments and countries a great part of our freedom to act as we please? The truth is that we cannot' (Nyerere 1968: 241).

Finally, in discussing Nyerere's political philosophy one cannot ignore that he was a politician and head of state. While Nyerere, unlike many other leaders, often deployed his philosophical principles to rationalise and justify his decisions, he remained an astute pragmatist. He could thus be described accurately as a philosopher-king. It is interesting to note that Nyerere did not often philosophise about the character of state power or the inequality of power. He did not have a strong theory of state or class, both of which must have contributed to his lack of a deeper theoretical understanding of the state. Much of his discussion on politics is in relation to forms of power, democracy, participation and so on, rather than on the inequality of power. Yet there is one intriguing aspect of his discourse on politics that does not correspond with his philosophical precepts and that is the legitimisation of political power.

After stepping down from the presidency, Nyerere made a very interesting extemporaneous speech in which he warned his successors and the political class not to abandon the 'Arusha Declaration'. Here, for the first time, the author of the 'Declaration' discussed the legitimising role of his policy of socialism and self-reliance. It would not be totally correct to attribute Machiavellian motives to Nyerere in adopting the 'Arusha Declaration', but it is clear that he was quite conscious of its legitimating role. He said as much in this speech – of which we need to understand something about the occasion at which it was made.

The ruling party had organised a seminar on production, whose invitees were parastatal executives, entrepreneurs from the private sector – including the up-and-coming private compradorial capitalists – as well as top party and government leaders. The seminar came in the wake of the liberalisation policies that were adopted a couple of years previously and amid whispers that called for the renunciation of the 'Arusha Declaration'. The aim of the speech was to condemn the dependent nature of the Tanzanian economy, to expound on the North-South division and to urge South-South co-operation. These were not new themes in Nyerere's thinking, although what was new, in this particular instance, was the clarity and disarming frankness of their expression. On the one hand, he extolled the virtues of national capitalism – which he had rarely done during the heyday of the 'Arusha Declaration' – while, on the other hand, he underlined stability and peace in the country, which he had done repeatedly since stepping down. The translated speech is reproduced *in extenso* below because I think there is nowhere a better statement from the architect of Ujamaa on the role he envisaged for the ideology of Ujamaa in the Tanzanian political system. Arguing that peace and stability did not drop from heaven like manna, but were the product of the 'Arusha Declaration', Nyerere said:

> It is not that peace has come by itself. The source of peace in Tanzania is not that the Arusha Declaration has done away with poverty even a little bit. Isn't there this poverty we are still living with? This poverty is right here with us. Is it not the same economy we are grappling with? The fact is not that the Arusha Declaration has banished poverty even by an iota – nor did it promise to do so. The Arusha Declaration offered hope. A promise

of justice, hope to the many, indeed the majority of Tanzanians continue to live this hope. So long as there is this hope, you'll continue to have peace. Here in Tanzania we have poverty but no 'social cancer' [original in English]. It is possible it has just begun. But otherwise we don't have a social cancer. There isn't a volcano [in English] in the making such that if you pressed your ear to the ground you'd hear a volcano in the making, that one day it is bound to erupt. We have not yet reached that stage because the people still have hopes based on the stand taken by the Arusha Declaration. It did not do away with poverty but it has given you all in this hall, capitalists and socialists alike, an opportunity to build a country which holds out a future of hopes to the many . . . To be sure, you few Waswahili [a colloquial for, in this case, 'people'], do you really expect to rule Tanzanians through coercion, when there is no hope, and then expect that they will sit quiet in peace? Peace is born of hope, when hope is gone there will be social upheavals. I'd be surprised if these Tanzanians refuse to rebel. Why? When the majority don't have any hope you are building a volcano. It is bound to erupt one day. Unless these people are fools. Many in these countries are fools, to accept being ruled just like that. To be oppressed just like that when they have the force of numbers, they are fools. So Tanzanians would be fools, idiots, if they continued to accept to be oppressed by a minority in their own country . . . Therefore we cannot say that we have now reached a stage when we can forget the Arusha Declaration. Don't fool yourselves. This would be like that fool who uses a ladder to climb and when he is up there kicks it away. Alright you're up there, you've kicked away the ladder, right, so stay there because we'll cut the branch. You're up there, we're down here and you've kicked away the ladder. This branch is high up, we'll cut it. Your fall will be no ordinary fall either. Let me say no more. It is sufficient to say we should accept our principles, we should continue with our principles of building peace and peace itself. Tanzanians should continue to have faith in the Party, in the Government and in you in positions. Tanzanians should see you as part of them not their enemies. They should trust the Party, the Government and you who have opportunities for there is no country where everyone is equal. These fingers of mine are not equal, and in that sense there is no such equality anywhere (Shivji 1995: 159–60).[4]

In this speech, Nyerere has given a frank and lucid analysis of Ujamaa as a legitimising ideology. His argument that Ujamaa engendered hope and a vision around which the consensus between the rulers and the ruled was constructed, is incisive and disarmingly forthright for someone who had presided over the state for three decades. Ujamaa did not achieve equality, Nyerere admits, but held out a promise and the hope of building a society based on equality. This is indeed the role par excellence of a consensual, politically hegemonic ideology – as, for instance, the role of the 'rule of law' *qua* ideology in bourgeois society.

What about the ruled? What were their perceptions? What made them consent? Was it simply the *illusion* of hope? Or were there resonances between Ujamaa and the perceptions or world view of the people? It is my argument that there were such resonances and that they could be found in the African understanding of equality, dignity and justice propounded by Nyerere and discussed here. Equality thus understood – rather than the notion of equality in rights – had a powerful resonance with the people simply because the Western juridical construct has no historical roots in African society. The political ideology of Ujamaa as constructed by Nyerere on the bedrock of the notions of *usawa* (equality), *utu* (dignity) and *haki* (always 'social' justice, as I argued above) is a great example of how cultural resources, albeit reconstructed, were and can be deployed by a political leader to build a relatively stable and peaceful political order.

Conclusion: Nyerere, a political man

Nyerere was preeminently a political man, nay a politician in power. He was at the head of the state for more than a quarter of a century. His political practice was not always principled. Principles were sacrificed or deployed to justify and rationalise political decisions whose primary aim was political survival. His Western admirers often agonised over the contradictions between Nyerere's philosophical principles and political practice (see, for instance, the essays in Legum and Mmari 1995). For instance, Nyerere argued forcefully for voluntary movement of peasants to Ujamaa villages in the late 1960s and early 1970s, yet he also carried out the massive and forceful policy of villagisation by means of the hated Filed Force Unit, a paramilitary force (see Coulson 1982: Chapter 22).

In 1968, Nyerere could write in the *London Observer*: 'If the mass of the people of Zanzibar should, without external manipulation . . . decide that the union was prejudicial to their existence, I could not bomb them into submission' (in Dourado 2006: 74), yet throughout the history of the union between Tanganyika and Zanzibar, Nyerere was not averse to manipulating law and politics to preserve the union (see Shivji 2008). Undoubtedly, though, Nyerere stood head and shoulders above his peers, the first-generation African nationalists. He was first and foremost a nationalist, a radical nationalist and his preoccupation was with building a stable 'nation'. Although he did take some deliberate measures to address inequality in his country and inequality between nations, his philosophical world view was anchored firmly in idealism. He recognised social classes, but refused to characterise the state in class terms, thus dismissing the idea of class struggle (see, for instance, the debate in Shivji 1973, 1976; Cliffe and Saul 1973). He could not therefore mobilise the working people (peasants and workers) whom his Ujamaa exalted to defend through a vision of a society based on equality, social justice and freedom. When the crunch came and his country faced the massive onslaught of Western powers and the international finance institutions in the 1980s, his party abandoned the policy of socialism and self-reliance and took to neoliberalism with a vengeance. Neoliberalism triumphed. Nyerere's own lieutenants in the party and the state spearheaded the neoliberal transformation of the country (see Shivji 2006, 2009; Havnevik and Isinika 2010). If anything, neoliberalism proved the fragility and limits of Nyerere's radical national project. Today's Tanzania exhibits all the characteristics of a socially and economically unequal, polarised society, with fragmented politics and a fractionalised state headed down the road of instability. It is marred by religious and ethnic strife, with imperial exploitation aided by compradorial classes running roughshod over the rights and lives of the working people. Yet, Nyerere's philosophical ghost, the profound unity of *usawa*, *utu* and *uhuru* continues to haunt the rulers and the ruled alike. This is where its power lies. The king failed, but the philosopher lives on.

Nyerere's attempt at spinning a home-grown ideology drawing on the cultural resources of the African society was a valiant attempt. Yet, it proved to be fragile and its nationalist base, albeit radical, too weak to withstand the onslaught of the hegemonic construct of imperialism and neoliberalism. Compared to Ujamaa, Ubuntu in South Africa has been threadbare. South Africa's 'independence' was born into neoliberalism. Ubuntu can hardly be described as a hegemonic ideology at any point in time in the way that Ujamaa could be during at least one decade after its adoption. Perhaps time has come to ask: Can robust African philosophies be constructed on the narrow basis of colonially constructed so-called nations or do they require the whole continent as a base? If so, should we not return to pan-Africanism as the point of departure for building a truly African philosophy and politics?

Notes

1. See http://www.youtube.com/watch?v=RKjxgpuymVo. As elsewhere in this volume, the spelling 'Ubuntu' is used in this chapter to refer to the abstract postcolonial articulation of the living practice as philosophy.
2. See http://appliedgandhi.blogspot.com/2008/02/gandhi-on-socialism-capitalism-and.html.
3. See http://www.gutenberg.org/files/3922/3922-h/3922-h.htm.
4. Translated by the author; reprinted in *Mzalendo*, 21 May 1989.

References

Cliffe, L. and J. Saul (eds). 1973. *Socialism in Tanzania: An Interdisciplinary Reader*, Vol. 2. Nairobi: East African Publishing House and London: Heinemann Education Books.

Coulson, A. 1982. *Tanzania: A Political Economy*. Oxford: Clarendon Press.

Dourado, W. 2006. 'The Consolidation of the Union: A Basic Re-Appraisal'. In *Zanzibar and the Union Question*, ed. P. Chris and H. Othman, 73–105. Zanzibar: Zanzibar Legal Services Centre.

Havnevik, K. and A.C. Isinika (eds). 2010. *Tanzania in Transition: From Nyerere to Mkapa*. Dar es Salaam: Mkuki na Nyota.

Huddleston, T. 1995. 'The Person Nyerere'. In *Mwalimu: The Influence of Nyerere*, ed. C. Legum and G. Mmari, 1–8. London: Britain-Tanzania Society.

Legum, C. and G. Mmari (eds). 1995. *Mwalimu: The Influence of Nyerere*. London: Britain-Tanzania Society.

Nkrumah, K. 1965. *Neo-Colonialism: The Last Stage of Imperialism*. London: Heinemann.

Nyerere, J.K. 1966. *Freedom and Unity*. Oxford: Oxford University Press.

———. 1968. *Freedom and Socialism*. Oxford: Oxford University Press.

———. 1973. *Freedom and Development*. Oxford: Oxford University Press.

Pashukanis, E. 1978 [1924]. *Law & Marxism: A General Theory*. London: Ink Links.

Shivji, I.G. 1973. *The Silent Class Struggle*. Dar es Salaam: Tanzania Publishing House.

———. 1976. *Class Struggles in Tanzania*. Dar es Salaam: Tanzania Publishing House, New York: Monthly Review Press and London: Heinemann.

———. 1995. 'Rule of Law and Ujamaa in the Ideological Formation of Tanzania'. *Social and Legal Studies* 4 (2): 147–74.

———. 2006. *Let the People Speak: Tanzania Down the Road to Neo-Liberalism*. Dakar: CODESRIA.

———. 2008. *Pan-Africanism or Pragmatism: Lessons of Tanganyika-Zanzibar Union*. Dar es Salaam: Mkuki na Nyota.

———. 2009. *Where is Uhuru? Reflections on the Struggle for Democracy in Africa*. Oxford: Fahamu Books.

CHAPTER 7

Ubuntu and the Law
Some Lessons for the Practical Application of Ubuntu

Katherine Furman

This chapter seeks to assess Ubuntu's real-world applicability by looking at an area where it has already found some practical application in South Africa – the law. Other attempts have been made to give Ubuntu practical effect in South Africa, such as the corporate sector's enthusiasm over 'Ubuntu capitalism' and its incorporation into the government's Moral Regeneration Movement in the late 1990s (McDonald 2010: 142–3). However, these efforts have typically lacked theoretical substance and have often boiled down to being 'simply wishful and naïve' (140). By contrast, while legal scholars have struggled with the theoretical complexity of Ubuntu, a substantial body of academic literature on its incorporation into the law has developed, providing a theoretical node from which to explore a philosophical understanding of Ubuntu and its emancipatory potential.[1]

This chapter is divided into three parts. The first provides a very brief summary of the salient points in the genealogy of Ubuntu in the law, tracing its incorporation into South African legal culture from its initial inclusion in the interim Constitution of 1993 through to some key cases that subsequently made use of Ubuntu. The second provides a more thorough examination of whether Ubuntu has been *successfully* applied in the law. It compares two competing assessments of Ubuntu's legal inclusion – those of Johan van der Walt and Drucilla Cornell – selected because their respective positions seem to mark the outer limits of the debate, with the former questioning the usefulness of Ubuntu in the law and the latter celebrating its past use and potential future usefulness. The intention of the third section is to demonstrate that the way in which Ubuntu has been used in the law provides useful lessons for understanding its potential applicability in other spheres – first, by providing an understanding of Ubuntu in terms of ideal and non-ideal theory and second, by arguing for the need to combat the naivety often associated with Ubuntu-orientated projects.

Genealogy of Ubuntu in the law

It is worth tracing the development of Ubuntu in South African jurisprudence from its early incorporation in the interim Constitution through to some prominent Ubuntu-orientated judgments, including its initial inclusion in case law (*S. v. Makwanyane and Another*), its clarification as a legitimate jurisprudential value (*AZAPO and Others v. President of the Republic of South Africa and Others*), its extension into the socio-economic sphere (*Port Elizabeth Municipality v. Various Occupiers*) and what appears to be its eventual solidification in case law (*Afri-Forum and Another v. Malema and Others*).[2]

Ubuntu first appeared in the post-amble of the South African interim Constitution, which mandated the creation of the Promotion of National Unity and Reconciliation Act 34 of 1995 (known as the Reconciliation Act), thereby bringing the Truth and Reconciliation Commission (TRC) into existence:

> The adoption of the Constitution lays the secure foundation for the people of South Africa to transcend the divisions and strife of the past, which generated gross violations of human rights, the transgression of humanitarian principles in violent conflicts and a legacy of hatred, fear, guilt and revenge. These can now be addressed on the basis that there is a need for understanding but *not for vengeance*, a need for reparation but *not for retaliation*, a need for *ubuntu* but *not for victimisation*.

At this point in South Africa's jurisprudential history, Ubuntu's legal status was unclear. Ubuntu was not included in the final Constitution of 1996 and, in the interim Constitution, it referred specifically to the establishment of the TRC. It was therefore unclear whether Ubuntu would be legally applicable beyond issues of reconciliation or if the writers of the interim Constitution had intended for it to form part of South Africa's jurisprudence more broadly. It seems reasonable to assume that if the intention had been for Ubuntu to become a jurisprudential value that it would have been explicitly included in the main body of the text. This is similar to the point made by the Attorney General in *S. v. Makwanyane*, where he argued that if the writers of the Constitution had intended for the death penalty to be illegal, the interim Constitution would have stated this explicitly.[3] However, as the intricacies of the *Makwanyane* case confirm, constitutional interpretation is substantially more complex than literally applying the exact words of the text to the facts of a case.[4] Keeping this in mind, further cause for confusion was provided by Ubuntu's exclusion from the final Constitution (see Keep and Midgley 2007: 33; Motha 2009: 305). If the relegation of Ubuntu to the post-amble had not sent a clear message about Ubuntu's legal status, surely the absence of Ubuntu from the final Constitution should have been an obvious sign that Ubuntu was never intended to be central in the law or to its application in South Africa?

In 1995 this ambivalence was at least partially resolved in the case of *S. v. Makwanyane*, where the Constitutional Court had to decide whether the death penalty would remain a permissible sentence in the new constitutional order. The conclusion was that the death penalty was no longer appropriate and among the reasons provided was that it violates the spirit of Ubuntu. Ubuntu was explicitly included in the main judgment of Chaskalson P. and in the concurring judgments of Madala J., Mokgoro J., Mahomed J., Langa J. and Sachs J. However, Ubuntu was only one reason among many provided by the Court and it seems clear that the same decision *could* have and *would* have been reached without any reference to Ubuntu. Van der Walt (2005) questions whether Ubuntu formed part of the main rationale for the decision at all or whether it was simply *obiter* (an interesting aside with no actual bearing on the outcome of the case). He argues that the main rationale for the decision was that the death penalty is a disproportionate punishment, especially when one considers that there are alternative sentences available to the Court (105–6). This interpretation is particularly compelling in the light of Chaskalson P.'s judgment:

> Disparity between the crime and the penalty is not the only ingredient of proportionality; factors such as the enormity and irredeemable character of the death sentence in circumstances where neither error nor arbitrariness can be excluded, the expense and difficulty of addressing the disparities which exist in practice between accused persons facing similar charges, and which are due to factors such as race, poverty, and ignorance, and the other subjective factors which have been mentioned, are also factors that can and should be taken into account in dealing with this issue. It may possibly be that none alone would be sufficient under our Constitution to justify a finding that the death sentence is cruel, inhuman or degrading. But these factors are not to be evaluated in isolation. They must be taken together, and in order to decide whether the threshold set by section 11(2) has been crossed they must be evaluated with other relevant factors, including the two fundamental rights on which the accused rely, the right to dignity and

the right to life ... The carrying out of the death sentence destroys life, which is protected without reservation under section 9 of our Constitution, it annihilates human dignity which is protected under section 10, elements of arbitrariness are present in its enforcement and it is irremediable. Taking these factors into account . . . I am satisfied that in the context of our Constitution the death penalty is indeed a cruel, inhuman and degrading punishment.[5]

By contrast, when Chaskalson P. discusses Ubuntu, he uses it only as a counterweight to retribution in the law, meaning that it is incorporated only as a subsidiary element of the proportionality test. This is clear in the following excerpt from the judgment:

Retribution ought not to be given undue weight in the balancing process. The Constitution is premised on the assumption that ours will be a constitutional state founded on the recognition of human rights. The concluding provision on National Unity and Reconciliation contains the following commitment: 'The adoption of this Constitution lays the secure foundation for the people of South Africa to transcend the divisions and strife of the past, which generated gross violations of human rights, the transgression of humanitarian principles in violent conflicts and a legacy of hatred, fear, guilt and revenge. These can now be addressed on the basis that there is a need for understanding but *not for vengeance*, a need for reparation but *not for retaliation*, a need for *ubuntu* but *not for victimisation*.' Although this commitment has its primary application in the field of political reconciliation, it is not without relevance to the enquiry we are called upon to undertake in the present case. To be consistent with the value of *Ubuntu* ours should be a society that 'wishes to prevent crime . . . [not] to kill criminals simply to get even with them'.[6]

This quote illustrates Ubuntu's role as one of many factors to be taken into account when determining proportionality. This is worrying if one is of the view that Ubuntu should play a pivotal role in the Constitutional Court's jurisprudence because then it would be expected that Ubuntu should be dealt with more substantially in the judgments. However, the comparative absence of Ubuntu may not be surprising, given that it is, at best, a *value* to be used in the process of legal interpretation and not a legal rule to be transmitted via precedent.[7] However, it remains of concern that Ubuntu is dealt with in such a limited way, given the extent of the role that legal philosophers and the philosophical community more broadly attribute to it.

Importantly for the purposes of this genealogy, the quote from Chaskalson P. explicitly indicates that although the post-amble 'has its primary application in the field of political reconciliation', it is not strictly bound to the TRC and may be relevant to further legal problems. Although Chaskalson P. mentions briefly that the post-amble may have applicability beyond the TRC, for those concerned about Ubuntu's relegation to the post-amble (a section with supposedly less legal status than the main body of the interim Constitution), this provides little comfort.

This question of the post-amble's status was explicitly clarified in the 1996 case of *AZAPO v. President of the Republic of South Africa*. In this case, families of apartheid victims called into question the validity of section 20 (7) of the Reconciliation Act, which allowed for amnesty to be granted to those who had committed political crimes during apartheid. The applicants argued that the amnesty provision violated their constitutional right to a trial, as protected by section 22 of the interim Constitution, which states: 'Every person shall have the right to have justiciable disputes settled by a court of law or, where appropriate, another independent or impartial forum.'

The Court decided against the applicants for two reasons: first, the amnesty provision was necessary to gain information about crimes that were committed during apartheid, which normal criminal investigations would not have been able to uncover and second, the post-amble that empowers the Reconciliation Act is a legitimate part of the interim Constitution and is therefore capable of limiting the right to a trial as envisaged in section 22.[8] This unequivocally resolved the question of the post-amble's status in relation to the rest of the interim Constitution, with Mohamed J. explicitly stating: 'The epilogue . . . has no lesser status than any other part of the Constitution.'[9] It thereby provided some guidance about Ubuntu's legal status because it clarified that Ubuntu formed part of a legitimate section of the interim Constitution and was therefore available to the Court as a constitutional value. However, once again, this is an unsatisfying conclusion because Ubuntu did not play a substantial role in the decision-making process of this case. It did not form part of the two main reasons provided for the decision – constitutional consistency and evidentiary necessity – and the term 'Ubuntu' was only mentioned three times in the entire judgment (each time as part of an overall reference to the post-amble's establishment of the TRC and never as a value in its own right). This provides cause for concern because in both these cases Ubuntu is used in a very limited manner.

The case of *Port Elizabeth Municipality v. Various Occupiers* provided some hope that Ubuntu may perform substantive work in the law because it seems to have successfully extended Ubuntu into the socio-economic sphere in order to show that Ubuntu can form a meaningful part of the Court's reasoning process. The case involved two issues: whether the municipality can evict unlawful occupiers and whether there is an obligation for the party seeking an eviction order to find suitable alternative accommodation for the occupiers. This case may ease concerns that Ubuntu does not form a real part of the Court's reasoning process, because Sachs J.'s judgment seems to be fundamentally premised on Ubuntu (Keep and Midgley 2007). Sachs explicitly states:

> It [the Prevention of Illegal Eviction Act – PIE] is called upon to balance competing interests in a principled way and promote the constitutional vision of a caring society based on good neighbourliness and shared concern. The Constitution and PIE confirm that we are not islands unto ourselves. The spirit of *Ubuntu*, part of the deep cultural heritage of the majority of the population, suffuses the whole constitutional order. It combines individual rights with a communitarian philosophy.[10]

In a later interview with the Ubuntu Project about the case, Sachs J. stated that he would have been unable to reach his decision without recourse to Ubuntu (see Cornell 2009). However, Ubuntu's role in the case remains questionable, given that the above quote is the only time Ubuntu is mentioned in the judgment. Once again, given that Ubuntu is only an interpretive value and that the case fundamentally turned on PIE and the rights to property and housing, this may be understandable to a certain extent. However, there is still something deeply disconcerting about the almost complete absence of Ubuntu from the text of the judgment.

A more recent case provides some optimism about Ubuntu's applicability to the legal decision-making process. In the 2011 case of *Afri-Forum v. Malema*, the Equality Court had to decide whether the African National Congress (ANC) Youth League leader at the time, Julius Malema, was guilty of hate speech by publicly singing the words, 'Shoot the boer [farmer]', where the term 'boer' is taken to refer to Afrikaans-speaking farmers in particular and white South Africans more generally.[11] In contrast with the previous cases discussed, Ubuntu did seem to do substantial work in reaching a decision in this case. An entire section of the judgment is devoted to clarifying Ubuntu, with Lamont J. stating: 'An ubuntu-based jurisprudence has been developed particularly by the Constitutional Court. Ubuntu is recognised as being an important source of law.'[12] In the decision itself (that publicly singing the song does constitute hate speech), the judge specifically states that complying with the order is a matter of 'both law and ubuntu'.[13] Furthermore, Lamont J.'s trial process echoed the communitarian logic associated with Ubuntu. Evidence of this is provided by the following exerpts from the judgment:

> During the hearing I allowed much evidence to be led which would not normally be permitted in a Court of law as it appeared to me that it was proper to allow the parties to the dispute to fully and completely ventilate the issues between them . . .

> It appeared to me that in the course of the trial the parties should, as it were, be allowed to scratch the wound open, re-experience the pain and search for a solution.

> The public was entitled to see the events transpiring in Court so as not only be able to form its own judgment but also to re-live events as part of a process of healing. I directed that any party including a witness could at any time request the process to be stopped; that it was then to stop immediately pending further orders.[14]

This seems to indicate that Ubuntu played a fundamental role in the decision of this case, not only in Lamont J.'s reasoning, but also in the procedure adopted during the hearing. This suggests at least one case in which the law proceeded by way of both the letter as well as the spirit of Ubuntu.

How successfully has Ubuntu been incorporated into the law?

As can be seen, there has been a relative absence of Ubuntu in those cases that purport to have incorporated it as a value in their decision-making, with the one important exception of the *Afri-Forum v. Malema* case. Of course, there have been other cases (see Cornell and Muvangua 2012 for a more extensive and in-depth genealogy). The point here is not to be exhaustive, but rather to sketch the outlines of the context in which jurisprudence has found itself very divided on the question of Ubuntu's application in law (again, an extensive literature exists on the subject). I now want to address what appear to be some of the major critical issues to have emerged, with reference to the very different positions taken by Van der Walt and Cornell.

Van der Walt

Van der Walt identifies at least three problems with the use of Ubuntu in the law: a lack of conceptual clarity, a lack of African particularity and a lack of appropriate cultural context when making use of Ubuntu in the law. I want to briefly consider each of these in turn.

Van der Walt (2005: 111) is concerned that Ubuntu is employed in the law without any specificity about the term's meaning. In discussing Justice Langa's judgment in *S. v. Makwanyane*, which he initially takes to be one of the more promising legal accounts of Ubuntu, Van der Walt concludes that Justice Langa still leaves one with a nagging feeling that he offers no more insight than his colleagues regarding the specific and singular meaning of Ubuntu (110–11). Van der Walt argues that instead of a clear definition, the Court has provided a series of non-specific, feel-good phrases that 'would have had John Lennon (*Imagine All the People*) scrambling for new verses' (110). Van der Walt's assumption is that concepts need clear definition before they can be allowed to do legal work, which is an intuitively appealing position to hold. However, it is contrary to the history of legal practice, where concepts are frequently used before the court has settled on definitive meanings for them. The most famous example of this is provided by Justice Potter Stewart, in the case of *Jacobellis v. Ohio* in the United States, who while trying to settle on a clear definition for pornography concluded: 'I will know it when I see it.' The point is that legal praxis can (and often does) precede full theoretical understanding of the concepts employed – a comprehensive definition of pornography is not required in order to place a restriction on it in the law. Similarly, dignity is frequently deployed by the courts, despite the fact that its meaning remains conceptually unclear to those who invoke it (McCrudden 2008). This issue is revisited in more detail later in this chapter, so at this point it suffices simply to point out that Van der Walt's assumption that a lack of conceptual specificity is a problem for the courts is not as obvious as one might initially expect.

Van der Walt's second problem is that Ubuntu fails to add anything specifically African to jurisprudence. He states this problem as follows: 'A rigorous jurisprudence must be dissatisfied with the feel-good flavour of a jurisprudence that has done little more than add a local, indigenous and communitarian touch to the Christian, Kantian or Millsian respect for the individual that informs Western jurisprudence' (2005: 111).

The objection seems to be that if there is nothing distinctively African that Ubuntu can add to South African jurisprudence, why bother? A similar epistemological problem is encountered by all attempts to distinguish Ubuntu from other forms of communitarianism and/or humanism and our response should be similar: the problem is not *epistemological*, but *political*, in the sense that what matters is not that Ubuntu is epistemologically distinct, but rather that the lived experience of members of society needs to be taken into account when deciding what concepts will be used in the policies applicable to that society.[15] Taking lived experience into account is particularly important for the law, which requires that the majority of society buys into its central values if they are going to comply with it. Therefore, all that needs to be shown in order for Ubuntu to be applicable as a legal value is that it resonates with society, not that it is conceptually unique.

Van der Walt's third objection is that Ubuntu is thoughtlessly removed from its context in South African indigenous law when applied by the courts – that is, it is used as though it is a concept with no pre-existing legal context. He is particularly dissatisfied that in *S. v. Makwanyane*, the Constitutional Court failed to consider whether traditional communities in South Africa believe(d) that the death penalty is an appropriate punishment for certain crimes (2005: 111–12).[16] Van der Walt's thinking here can be interpreted in at least two ways. First, we can determine whether Ubuntu and the death penalty are compatible by looking at the beliefs of the community from which Ubuntu was taken: if they believed in both Ubuntu and the death penalty, they must be conceptually compatible. This is not an interesting objection because it assumes that people – or peoples – only ever hold conceptually compatible beliefs, which is clearly not the case. A second, more plausible reading may be that Ubuntu should be preserved as a culturally authentic value and that this authenticity is violated when Ubuntu is applied outside its cultural context. However, this is a politically dangerous understanding of 'authenticity' and clearly at odds with any relevant understanding of customary law as an evolving tradition and/or the extent to which all traditions are perpetual reinventions. Having examined Van der Walt's core concerns, it seems as if his objections are both limited and limiting.

Cornell

Cornell recognises the difficulties that have been faced by the courts in incorporating Ubuntu into the law (2009: 47). However, she argues that including Ubuntu in the law is necessary for the realisation of the Constitution's goals (2004: 274). She provides two justifications for holding this view: first, that Ubuntu offers an understanding of personhood that is distinct from that provided by Western jurisprudence and, second, that an Ubuntu-infused jurisprudence allows us to cope better with contradictions inherent in the law.

The first way that Cornell sees Ubuntu as being important for the law is that it brings an understanding of personhood that is absent from Western jurisprudence (2004: 668; 2009: 57). She provides a description of Ubuntu as interdependence, with all its metaphysical trappings. In particular, Cornell emphasises the importance of *serti* – 'the life force by which a community of persons are connected to each other' (2004: 674). It should be noted that it is problematic to adopt such a metaphysically laden account of Ubuntu, given the general applicability that we expect from the law. However, bracketing the supernatural elements of this account for the present moment, why and how might the insistence on our interdependence be useful for the law?

Cornell argues that it puts us in touch with the foundational values on which the legal system is premised – the 'Law of laws' in her terminology (2004: 670). The basis of Western jurisprudence is the social contract, with the individual at its core (668). In the case of the Hobbesian social contract, individuals only come together to co-operate because they fear each other and find security by transferring their right to violence to the state, who in turn commits to protecting them. By this account, it is not only the premise that individuals are atomised that is at issue, but also the fact that their relationships are inherently antagonistic. Cornell, following Mokgoro J., argues: 'Ubuntu provides us with a very different notion of the founding principle of law' (669). Her vision of a jurisprudence premised on Ubuntu, which she borrows from Mokgoro J., is expressed as follows:

> The original conception of the law perceived not as a tool for personal defense, but as an opportunity given to all to survive under the protection of the order of the communal entity; communalism which emphasises group solidarity and interests generally, and all the rules which sustain it, as opposed to individual interests, with its likely utility in building a sense of national unity among South Africans; the conciliatory character of the

adjudication process which aims to restore peace and harmony between members rather than the adversarial approach which aims to restore peace and harmony between members (Mokgoro J. in Cornell 2004: 669).

The second way in which Ubuntu can be understood to enrich South African jurisprudence is by allowing us better to cope with contradictions in the law – to use Cornell's phrase: the 'both-and' of the law. She describes this situation as arising when two opposing registers come into conflict that cannot (or perhaps should not) be brought into a coherent whole. For instance, one may simultaneously hold beliefs in ancestor worship *and* the legitimacy of the Constitution (Cornell 2004: 673). Her second example derives from *Soobramoney v. Minister of Health, KwaZulu-Natal*, in which Soobramoney's application for state-funded dialysis was rejected because he had too many additional complicating health problems to qualify for the transplant list and dialysis is prioritised for patients awaiting transplants.[17] Cornell concludes that the decision in *Soobramoney* is both 'just' and 'tragic' and that the inclusion of Ubuntu in jurisprudence allows us to cope with this result. This is because the logic of Ubuntu *qua* 'Law of laws' allows *both* for the sacrifice of the individual for the greater good *and* for our society to recognise that/when it is diminished by the loss of one of its members (674). Furthermore, Cornell believes that the 'both-and' scope of Ubuntu-engaged jurisprudence allows us better to deal with the unsatisfactory status of socio-economic rights in South Africa, which are simultaneously constitutionally guaranteed and unrealisable due to economic constraints – another example of what is both tragic and just. Both of Cornell's arguments are normative in the sense that they describe how South African jurisprudence may be enhanced by the inclusion of Ubuntu in legal reasoning. However, it remains unclear whether Ubuntu has already been successfully used in the law and whether it is possible to realise the goals that Cornell advocates.

At this stage, it should be clear that Ubuntu's inclusion in the law has had limited success. In three out of the four cases discussed, Ubuntu did not form a meaningful part of the Court's reasoning process. Furthermore, there are the concerns raised by Van der Walt: a lack of specificity, uniqueness and contextualisation – issues which, although undertheorised by him, are worth keeping in mind when assessing Ubuntu's inclusion in the law. Cornell has been more optimistic in advancing Ubuntu as 'Law of law' or *nomos*, capable of allowing us to rethink the fundamental premises of the legal system and allowing us to cope better with contradictions in the law – between that which is *both* just *and* tragic, that which is morally imperative *and* practically unachievable. However, these are forward-looking suggestions about what Ubuntu might achieve in the law, which do not help us to understand the limited success of Ubuntu's inclusion in the law to date.

Lessons from Ubuntu in the law

In this section I argue that we have learned at least two lessons from the manner in which the courts have grappled with Ubuntu.

Praxis preceding theory

The question of whether a correct theoretical understanding of Ubuntu should precede its application links to a broader philosophical debate about the connection between ideal and non-ideal theories of justice, a distinction first identified by John Rawls in *A Theory of Justice* (1972; see also Simmons 2010: 5). Rawls defines an ideal theory of justice as one that assumes that members of society will strictly comply with the requirements of justice, thus allowing the philosopher to work out the institutional framework of the 'well-ordered society' under ideal conditions. Non-ideal theory comes into play in order to practically realise the vision of ideal theory, particularly in determining what transitional steps need to be taken in order for society to be brought closer to the ideal (Rawls 1972: 245–6). In Rawls's description, ideal theory takes strict priority over non-ideal theory and must be fully worked out before any attention can be paid to the pragmatic concern of its applicability in society. Rawls's distinction is not applicable as it stands to the current discussion because the concern here is not with developing a 'theory of justice' as such. However, the distinction between an abstract, idealised political philosophy and its practical realisation in politics is useful to keep in mind as we grapple with the difficulties of trying to define Ubuntu and to find its application in the real world.

If Rawls is correct about the strict priority of ideal theory over non-ideal theory, it would be extremely difficult to understand Ubuntu's inclusion in the Constitutional Court's jurisprudence, given the problems associated with providing definitional content for Ubuntu. However, the fact that Ubuntu has found some application and the fact that it has been deployed to do political work suggest another way of thinking about all this, one in which the practical work suggested by a concept may sometimes precede our complete theoretical understanding of that concept.

Amartya Sen offers a helpful response to Rawls in *The Idea of Justice* (2009), in which he argues against Rawls's strict priority of the ideal over the non-ideal and suggests that an ideal theory of justice may not be necessary at all for dealing with real issues of social justice. Sen sees real-world decisions about justice as comparative: do we choose social arrangement A or social arrangement B? In making comparative assessments, it is not necessary to imagine an additional perfect alternative. For example, in determining whether a painting by Picasso or Van Gogh is superior, it is not necessary to have an idea of the perfect painting in order to make a decision (Sen 2009: 101–2). Similarly, when policy-makers choose between competing policies, they are unlikely to turn to Rawls or any ideal theory of justice in selecting their programme of action. The conclusion seems to be that we can, if not dispense with ideal theories of justice, at least allow the practical work of pursuing social justice in the real world to be guided or regulated by them – a willingness to prioritise political work over conceptual consensus or at least to recognise a dialectic or reciprocity between praxis and theory, which leaves the question of definition necessarily moot. Social policy development differs from aesthetic judgements in that considerations of justice do seem to play a role in selecting between alternative social arrangements, even though they may not amount to the kind of fully worked-out theory of justice that Rawls would require.

What we are left with is a suggested middle path between Rawls's strict priority of ideal theory and Sen's suggestion that we might dispense with theory entirely. This is helpful for understanding the courts' use of Ubuntu in that some use of the concept has occurred prior to obtaining a full theoretical grip on it. As I mentioned earlier, this is not the only instance of courts using a concept before it is fully understood. Courts across the world frequently make use of the concept of dignity, without necessarily having settled on a complete theoretical understanding of the term (McCrudden 2008). Naturally, the use of dignity in the law is at a distinct advantage over the use of Ubuntu, given that attempts to theoretically understand dignity in the context of the law date back to the Roman Law tradition (McCrudden 2008: 657) and, of course, having such a broad history of thought associated with dignity means that it has come to have a far more substantial role to play in the law than Ubuntu. The hope, however, is that as our theoretical understanding of Ubuntu improves, so courts may feel freer to make use of it in their reasoning.

Combating the naivety of 'Ubuntu-ists'

In the popular imagination, Ubuntu is unequivocally positive. Desmond Tutu provides a well-accepted account of a person 'with Ubuntu' as someone who is generous, hospitable, friendly, caring, compassionate, sharing, unjealous and so on (Tutu 2000: 31). These are all positive attributes. When this personal picture of Ubuntu is expanded to the political level, it becomes utopian. For instance, in the Department of International Relations and Cooperation's white paper, 'Building a Better World: The Diplomacy of Ubuntu', South African foreign policy informed by Ubuntu is described as follows:

> This philosophy translates into an approach to international relations that respects all nations, peoples, and cultures. It recognises that it is in our national interest to promote and support the positive development of others. Similarly, national security would therefore depend on the centrality of human security as a universal goal, based on the principle of Batho Pele (putting people first). In the modern world of globalisation, a constant element is and has to be our common humanity. We therefore champion collaboration, cooperation and building partnerships over conflict. This recognition of our interconnectedness and interdependency, and the infusion of Ubuntu into the South African identity, shapes our foreign policy (Department of International Relations and Cooperation 2011: 4).

This statement clearly indicates the overwhelmingly positive attitude that is expressed towards Ubuntu and its practical application. However, it ignores that incorporating Ubuntu into the political realm may involve negative consequences. Ignoring these potential consequences is a dangerous oversight and may signal, in advance, a shift away from the utopian Ubuntu ideal toward dystopia. What are these potential negatives and how does the legal application of Ubuntu forewarn us of them?

The negative potential of Ubuntu is that it may be possible for the individual to be sacrificed for the collective good (Mokgoro 1998). An early indication of this possibility in the law was provided in the case of *S. v. Magadani*.[18] In this case, the court took Ubuntu into account at the time of sentencing and found the crime to be such an infringement of Ubuntu that the accused was given a life sentence (Keep and Midgley 2007). This case at least indicates that the interests of the individual (to have a shorter sentence) may in some instances be sacrificed for the good of the group (to have particularly dangerous criminals in jail for longer).

A second case where we can see the logic of Ubuntu invoked in order to sacrifice the interests of the individual was, of course, *Soobramoney v. Minister of Health*, as discussed above. Interestingly, Ubuntu was not explicitly mentioned in this case. Instead, the reasoning is explicitly utilitarian – placing the emphasis on Department of Health budget restrictions and the moral obligation to maximise the good provided by the health system. However, this case is included in Cornell's discussion of Sach's Ubuntu-engaged jurisprudence (2004: 672) because his concurring judgment makes use of language very close to the language used when Ubuntu is explicitly invoked: 'Health care rights by their very nature have to be considered not only in a traditional legal context structured around the ideas of human autonomy but in a new analytical framework based on the notion of human interdependence. A healthy life depends upon social interdependence.'[19] Sachs clearly evokes the language that is typically associated with Ubuntu, thereby indirectly introducing it without explicitly naming it. Therefore, the *Soobramoney* case, despite not being directly premised on Ubuntu, provides a sense of the danger potentially associated with practically employing Ubuntu.

Ubuntu is not the first ethical theory to face the criticism that individuals may be sacrificed for the collective good. Utilitarianism in particular has been criticised for failing to take account of the separateness of persons – that is, the objection that one cannot make utilitarian calculations across persons as though they were assessments within a single life (Nozick 1974). This objection may be less problematic to those who already accept Ubuntu because they may be less committed to the separation of personal identity. However, Jonathan Wolff (2006) attributes utilitarianism's waning popularity to this objection and advocates of Ubuntu should therefore at least be aware of this concern.

The legal application of Ubuntu illustrates that those invoking Ubuntu need to at least be sensitive to the possibility and consequences of sacrificing the individual for the benefit of the group. This may not discredit endeavours to make use of Ubuntu practically, but those who do invoke Ubuntu in this manner should be aware of the possibility of sacrifice implicit in their activities and of the need to justify their sacrifices in terms of the same values that make those sacrifices desirable.[20]

Conclusion

This chapter argues that the application of Ubuntu in the law provides some guidelines for better understanding the practical application of Ubuntu. The initial assessment is that Ubuntu has played a relatively limited role in the law and that it is often mentioned in cases without actually being involved in the reasoning process of the courts. However, the final analysis considers some lessons we can take from the use of Ubuntu in the law for broader application – specifically by understanding the so-called problem of definition, more generously, in terms of a general tension between ideal and non-ideal theory.

Notes

1. It is beyond the scope of this chapter to grapple with the theoretical issues facing Ubuntu. Thus, for the purposes of this chapter, Metz's definition of an Ubuntu ethic is used: 'An action is right just insofar as it produces harmony and reduces discord; an act is wrong to the extent that it fails to develop community' (2007: 334). However, this is only one definition from among many suitable ones and the complexity of the definitional debate about Ubuntu should not be glossed over.
2. See *S. v. Makwanyane and Another* 1995 (3) SA 391 (CC); *AZAPO and Others v. President of the Republic of South Africa and Others* 1996 (8) BCLR 1015 (CC); *Port Elizabeth Municipality v. Various Occupiers* 2004 (12) BCLR 1268 (CC) and *Afri-Forum and Another v. Malema and Others* 2011 (6) SA 240 (EqC).
3. *S. v. Makwanyane*, para. 11.
4. Ibid., paras 13, 16, 18 and 19.
5. Ibid., paras 94–5.
6. Ibid., paras 130–1.
7. This maps onto Kennedy's distinction between 'rules' and 'standards', where rules are legal prescriptions and standards are the values used to narrow very broad, generalised rules to specific facts and to prioritise particular rules in instances where they may clash (1976: 1690–3).
8. *AZAPO v. President of the Republic of South Africa*, paras 36 and 12.
9. Ibid., para. 14.
10. *Port Elizabeth Municipality v. Various Occupiers*, para. 37.
11. *Afri-Forum v. Malema*, para. 49.
12. Ibid., para. 18.
13. Ibid., para. 111.
14. Ibid., paras 58 and 47.
15. Useful here is Janz's distinction between 'spatial' and 'platial' thinking, where spatial thinking is abstracted from lived experience, while platial thinking requires that lived experience is constitutive of the concepts themselves. Taking platial thinking into account helps us to understand why Ubuntu might be relevant, without necessarily being conceptually distinct (Janz 2004).
16. Van der Walt notes that Sachs J. does make some effort to determine what traditional communities believe about the death penalty. But he then goes on to argue that Sachs provides an incomplete account, as he only recognises that the death penalty would be inappropriate in cases of murder, but fails to recognise that the death penalty would be appropriate in cases of stock theft (2005: 112–13).
17. *Soobramoney v. Minister of Health, KwaZulu-Natal* 1998 (1) SA 765 (CC).

18. *S. v. Magadani* 2001 JDR 0321 (V).
19. *Soobramoney v. Minister of Health*, para. 54.
20. Van der Walt (2005) argues that all instances of the law involve sacrifice, but he also holds that recognising these sacrifices is better for the overall functioning of society.

References

Cornell, D. 2004. 'A Call for a Nuanced Constitutional Jurisprudence: Ubuntu, Dignity, and Reconciliation'. *SA Publiekreg/SA Public Law* (special edition, *Public Law in Transformation*) 3 (19): 666–75.

———. 2009. 'Ubuntu, Pluralism and the Responsibility of Legal Academics'. *Law Critique* 20 (1): 43–58.

Cornell, D. and N. Muvangua (eds). 2011. *Ubuntu and the Law: African Ideals and Postapartheid Jurisprudence*. New York: Fordham University Press.

Department of International Relations and Cooperation. 2011. 'Building a Better World: The Diplomacy of Ubuntu'. White paper on South Africa's foreign policy, 13 May.

Janz, B. 2004. 'Philosophy As If Place Mattered: The Situation of African Philosophy'. In *What Philosophy Is: Contemporary Philosophy in Action*, ed. H. Carel and D. Gamez, 103–15. London: Continuum.

Keep, H. and R. Midgley. 2007. 'The Emerging Role of Ubuntu-Botho in Developing a Consensual South African Legal Culture'. In *Explorations in Legal Culture*, ed. F. Bruinsma and D. Nelken, 29–56. Amsterdam: Reed Business BV.

Kennedy, D. 1976. 'Form and Substance in Private Law Adjudication'. *Harvard Law Review* 89 (8): 1685–788.

McCrudden, C. 2008. 'Human Dignity and Judicial Interpretation of Human Rights'. *European Journal of International Law* 19 (4): 655–724.

McDonald, D.A. 2010. 'Ubuntu Bashing: The Marketisation of "African Values" in South Africa'. *Review of African Political Economy* 37 (124): 139–52.

Metz, T. 2007. 'Towards an African Moral Theory'. *Journal of Political Philosophy* 15 (3): 321–41.

Mokgoro, Y. 1998. 'Ubuntu and the Law in South Africa'. *Potchefstroom Electronic Law Journal* 1 (1): 1–11.

Motha, S. 2009. 'Archiving Colonial Sovereignty: From Ubuntu to the Jurisprudence of Sacrifice'. *SA Publiekreg/SA Public Law* 24: 297–327.

Nozick, R. 1974. *Anarchy, State, and Utopia*. New York: Basic Books.

Rawls, J.A. 1972. *A Theory of Justice*. Oxford: Oxford University Press.

Sen, A. 2009. *The Idea of Justice*. Cambridge: Harvard University Press.

Simmons, A.J. 2010. 'Ideal and Nonideal Theory'. *Philosophy and Public Affairs* 38 (1): 5–36.

Tutu, D. 2000. *No Future Without Forgiveness*. New York: Doubleday.

Van der Walt, J. 2005. *Law and Sacrifice: Towards a Post-Apartheid Theory of Law*. London: Birkbeck Law Press.

Wolff, J. 2006. 'Making the World Safe for Utilitarianism'. *Royal Institute of Philosophy* 58: 1–22.

CHAPTER 8

Ubuntu and Subaltern Legality

Drucilla Cornell

As we know, the value of Ubuntu is disputed in South Africa. In all the burning debates, it is often deployed on both sides of the question. Part of the reason that Ubuntu is used in the streets as well as in the courts is that is remains an ethical force in the day-to-day life of South Africans. Ubuntu has an odd history in that it is a Zulu word that has often been combined with a Tswana word, *botho*, to yield the hyphenated value, *ubuntu-botho*. But then *ubuntu-botho* is picked up in just that form and not further translated. So it is already a 'South African' expression in the complexity of its meaning. This said, as I have repeatedly argued, *ubuntu-botho* defends itself as an appeal to our ethical humanness, which should be universally vindicated, not justified because of its roots in indigeneity (see Cornell and Muvangua 2012: 1–30).

There has been a flurry of recent articles in South Africa about the extremely troubling attacks on gays and lesbians, including the 'corrective rape' of lesbian women. Many of these articles point to the disconnection between the constitutional values and this seemingly aggressive rejection of those values by at least a part of the population, which uses violence against those who have sought and gained recognition of their dignity at the level of the Constitutional Court. Jean Comaroff and John L. Comaroff have powerfully argued that this kind of disconnection is not some mysterious force, but a basic trend of neoliberal capitalism, which has profoundly fractured the modern sense of the ideological mission of the nation-state and replaced it with what they call 'ID-ology' (2012: 65–90):

> In postcolonies, which are endemically heterogeneous, citizenship always exists in an immanent tension with policulturalism . . . As a result, it is a terrain on which increasingly irreconcilable, fractal forms of subjectivity, embodied in self-defined aggregates of persons, may seek to open up possibilities for social action, possibilities in pursuit of interests, ideals, passions, principles. It is on this terrain that the modernist sense

of ideology gives way to ID-ology, the quest for a collective good, and often goods, authorized by a shared identity. And, in the process, both the liberal modernist polity and the kingdom of custom are transformed (2012: 67–8).

I refer to this discussion for two reasons. The first is that we need to keep in mind the demand for a careful analysis of this kind of disconnection, for there is a profound danger that we may fall into diverse forms of 'Afro-pessimism', which have haunted the history of the struggle in Africa for decolonisation and liberation. But the second reason lies at the heart of this chapter: a defence of the reasons why the Ubuntu Project has insisted on the importance of the legalisation, including at the level of the Constitution, of the value of Ubuntu.[1] Comaroff and Comaroff argue that one type of ID-ology is a new form of what they call 'lawfare' and the use of the courts by many of the counterhegemonic movements in southern Africa. They do not, like some thinkers, argue that we can know in advance whether this turn to lawfare will have a liberating potential for the subaltern. Their focus is on a detailed analysis of why lawfare is a part of ID-ology and perhaps unavoidably so. To thoroughly understand this point, we have to return to why Comaroff and Comaroff associate ID-ology with what they call 'policulturalism':

Self-evidently, in this light, the term 'multicultural(ism)' is insufficient to describe the fractious heterogeneity of postcolonies. Demeaned in popular usage, it evokes images of Disney's 'Small World,' of compendia of the Family of Man, of ritual calendars respectful of human diversity, and the like; in short, of benign indifference to difference. Neither as noun nor as adjective does it make clear the critical limits of liberal pluralism: that, notwithstanding the utopian visions of some humanist philosophers, the tolerance afforded to culture in modernist polities falls well short of allowing claims to autonomous political power or legal sovereignty. In postcolonies, in which ethnic assertion plays on the simultaneity of primordial connectedness, natural right, and corporate interest, the nation-state is less multicultural than it is policultural. The prefix, spelled 'poli-', marks two things at once: plurality and its politicization. It does not denote merely appreciation on the part of the national majority for the customs, costumes, and cuisine of one or another minority from one or another elsewhere (2012: 77).

When we combine these insights into the relationship between ID-ology and policulturalism we can deepen our understanding of why the Ubuntu Project has engaged in both descriptive and prescriptive work on the importance of Ubuntu as an ethical and legal value in the new South Africa. All one has to do is pick up a newspaper in South Africa to see how Ubuntu and other indigenous values have been thoroughly politicised.

Let us turn to why the defence of Ubuntu is so important in the new dispensation, with a focus on the struggle over its legalisation. First is the defence of the importance in postcolonial societies of African ideals and values and, more comprehensively, of African or Africana philosophy. This defence is important for at least two reasons. The first is, as Comaroff and Comaroff have repeatedly reminded us, that African modernity is as *sui generis* as European modernity. It has made its own contribution to the world view of the modern, as has any of the other so-called geographies of reason that currently exist on our planet. In other words, Afro-modernity is not an 'alternative' modernity, if by that we mean an alternative to Europe and the United States, as if Europe and the United States and Africa could be so neatly separated.

Second, this recognition of African modernity is part and parcel not only of the struggle against Eurocentrism as a bias and a particularity that pretends to be universal, but also of a struggle to combat what Paget Henry (2000) has so elegantly described as Caliban's purported lack of reason. For many of the Afro-Caribbean philosophers, including Henry, Sylvia Wynter, Eduard Glissant, Lewis Gordon and many others, the struggle against anti-black racism is not only a political matter, but also a philosophical one, in that it challenges how philosophical conceptions of everything from reason and morality to humanity have been tainted by a thoroughgoing racialisation that 'whitens' the very philosophical notion of 'man'. Therefore, if there were to be a new humanism, as is called for in the struggle against anti-black racism, a humanism advocated from a wide range of thinkers in Africa from Frantz Fanon to Steve Biko, there must be a challenge, politically, ethically and philosophically, to racism and a defence of the human beyond the thoroughly racialised categories of philosophy.

Hence the first defence of Ubuntu. Despite all the struggles over its political and ethical meaning, Ubuntu points us to a new humanism, to a new ethical notion of being human that implies a thoroughgoing philosophical, political and ethical critique of racism. Let us throw the gauntlet down. To even take Ubuntu seriously, or more precisely, to demand that Ubuntu be taken seriously, is to challenge the racist assertion that somehow or another this African value, because it is so contested in its meaning, is too vague to have any moral, let alone legal purchase. The Ubuntu Project has been in a deep sense both descriptive and prescriptive because it has been advocating that an African ideal might be one that could and should universally inform us. To even hypothesise the reach of an African ideal in this manner implies an anti-racist stance and is therefore not neutral (as if such neutrality could exist in research), but is prescriptive as well. So the first aspect of the defence of Ubuntu is that it is indeed an important ideal and value in the day-to-day life of South Africa, which is also precisely why it is so contested.

The second defence derives from the fact that it presents itself as a new ethical way of being human together. We need to judge it then, not simply because it is an African or South African value or philosophy, but because it offers us the philosophical project of solidarity and, if one takes 'revolutionary Ubuntu' seriously, radical transformation. Abahlali baseMjondolo (as well as other movements of the poor in South Africa) coined the phrase 'revolutionary Ubuntu' in order to argue that Ubuntu is itself an anti-capitalist ideal and that capitalism cannot be rendered consistent with it. As I have written elsewhere (Cornell and Panfilio 2010: 125–50), Sampie Terreblanche (2002) describes 350 years of patterns of 'unfree black labour' to underscore that the transformation of South Africa could not be complete unless it completely undid that history. For Terreblanche, among other South African analysts, the transformation of South Africa could only take place if the destructive aspects of this long history of unfree black labour, which clearly began long before the institutionalisation of apartheid, were completely undone and this could only be achieved by some form of social democracy or socialism. My addition is that the expression Terreblanche uses, 'unfree black labour', should also be read as a *telos* that points towards a different history of free human beings. But it is important to underscore, for the purposes of this chapter, that the very term unites race and class and points to how the so-called modern project of neoliberal capitalism turns on forms of indentured servitude that continue to allow for the super-exploitation of a large majority of humanity. Terreblanche's powerful argument is that the failure to combat, in all its forms, the residues of unfree black labour in the name of a new humanity has completely undermined the transformation into a 'new' South Africa. I will not repeat his arguments here, but simply highlight two points: revolutionary Ubuntu points towards what it means to think the free human being, finally unchained from unfree black labour and, second, there can be no serious transformation of South Africa without a thoroughgoing economic transformation.

In his path-breaking work, *A History of Inequality in South Africa: 1652–2002* (2002), Terreblanche painstakingly describes the devastating economic effects in all forms of life for unfree black labour. He argues that therefore the shift in political and ideological power, represented by the electoral victory of the African National Congress (ANC), is incomplete. In *Lost in Transformation* (2012), he poignantly argues that the transformation may have faltered or indeed failed because of its refusal to take seriously what revolutionary Ubuntu demands: free human beings living together in an ethical community.

So far we have been discussing revolutionary Ubuntu as it has been explicitly associated with social ideals and anti-capitalist struggles on the ground in South Africa. Yes, Ubuntu can be used for conservative or even reactionary purposes. But so can dignity. The question then becomes, how and why can one advocate for revolutionary Ubuntu as a possible 'ideal' for transformative counterhegemonic struggles that are breaking out in South Africa and, furthermore, as a possible justiciable constitutional principle that might work as a form of subaltern legality to overcome the disconnection that is being described in the press between the Constitution and people on the ground? I should be clear that the Ubuntu Project did not start out as a project to reconstitutionalise Ubuntu as a justiciable principle in the new constitutional dispensation in part because, like many on-the-ground, collectively run research projects, the project developed over time in a number of different directions and still does. But the question of Ubuntu's legal status became pressing in the project early on because of the political furor over the removal of the post-amble of the interim Constitution, in which the word '*ubuntu*' was used broadly to justify the formation, indeed the mandated formation, of the Truth and Reconciliation Commission.

At first I thought perhaps it was the biographical coincidence that I am a lawyer and a founder of the Ubuntu Project that made law come to the fore. But I am now convinced that Comaroff and Comaroff are right about politics in South Africa and that lawfare is very much at the heart of it on all sides. But note that lawfare is a kind of politics and is therefore not based on the distinction between law and politics that is so familiar to us in the European or Anglo-American academy. Steven L. Robins (2009) also stresses this point and argues that both rights and liberalism are challenged by the complex discourse of movements on the ground in South Africa. He has carefully documented how the use of rights talk in South Africa, as well as appeals to ethnic identity, do not necessarily appeal to any discourse of 'injury', but rather are part of new mobilisations that are extraordinary in their creativity, given the ANC's attempt to render the subaltern governable:

> The case studies in this book have drawn attention to the ambiguous and contradictory character of rights-based approaches to political mobilisation in post-apartheid South Africa. They question assumptions about the individualising and depoliticising nature of rights discourses ... The cases also draw attention to the diverse political rationalities and identities that NGOs [non-governmental organisations] and social movements encounter in their daily work. These include hybrid political discourses that defy the enduring binary categories of citizens and subjects, liberals and communitarians, modernists and traditionalist and so on. The NGO and social movement activists discussed in this book appear to have recognised the profoundly hybrid, provisional and situational character of politics in post-apartheid South Africa (2008: 165).

My argument, then, is that the struggle over Ubuntu is part of this rich political discourse, which sometimes involves an appeal to law, very broadly construed. And this connects the Ubuntu Project with a larger project of subaltern legality, which by its very combination of terms, challenges the conventional definition of legality in Anglo-American jurisprudence as a set of institutionalised state structures that legitimise both coercive power and a recognisable system of rules and principles that can be known as law (as opposed to law and ethics).

In this manner, the battle over Ubuntu and its constitutionalisation became an important site for whether or not African values and ideals could be seen as thoroughly modern and therefore defensible within a modern legal system that would seem to foreclose them as outmoded forms of the 'kingdom of custom' (Mamdani 1996; Comaroff and Comaroff 2012). The defence of Ubuntu as a constitutional principle was and continues to be fraught with all the sweeping implications of the battle against anti-black racism, the struggle for the recognition of Afro-modernity and the engagement with Africana philosophy as one of the most important philosophical contributions to what we think of as modernity. This battle is, of course, about the constitutionalisation of Ubuntu, which has indeed become a frequently used constitutional principle through the post-1996 judgments of the Constitutional Court. Though there can be little doubt that emeritus justices Albie Sachs and Yvonne Mokgoro have played a crucial role in the struggle for the recognition of Ubuntu as a justiciable principle, they have not been alone (see Cornell and Muvangua 2012).

The question of whether the constitutionalisation of Ubuntu undermines its 'subversive' value as a form of counterhegemonic politics and legality remains. There can be no grand, sweeping answer to this question, other than in the day-to-day politics, ethics and reinterpretation of Ubuntu at the level of legality and politics in South Africa. And this, to some degree, is the central point in the path-breaking book, *Theory from the South* (Comaroff and Comaroff 2012). I would like to emphasise with them that the recognition of Afro-modernity, as well as a serious engagement with Africana philosophy, does not lead in any sense to a disavowal – in the Freudian sense of the word – of European philosophy. Obviously, Ubuntu changes when it is brought into the context of constitutional jurisprudence and it, in turn, changes constitutional jurisprudence. But it is exactly this untidy dialectic, to paraphrase Fanon's famous expression, which opens up the space for new forms of both politics and ethics and, yes, of subaltern legality. As Comaroff and Comaroff remind us, this way of thinking about the relationship between lawfare and ID-ology rejects the out-of-hand dismissal of battles for a subaltern counterhegemonic legality, to use Boaventura de Sousa Santos's telling phrase, because such a legality would necessarily inscribe 'bad traditionalism', conservative identity politics and the like. These questions cannot be answered apart from the struggle itself, including the struggle over the interpretation of Ubuntu at the level of law. But it is important to note here that the struggle over the legalisation of Ubuntu actually also challenges the notion of legality that is hegemonic in Anglo-American law. As Hylton White, among others, has emphasised, law is often brought to on-the-ground struggles by those, like sangomas, who have no institutionalised relationship to the state and indeed forsake it.[2] De Sousa Santos has argued, and I agree with him, that there is a profound difference between subaltern legality and conventional Anglo-American and European definitions of law because subaltern legality challenges the difference between politics and law and even the difference between legality and illegality. Much subaltern legality is illegal under the institutions of the state and that is part of the reason why it is counterhegemonic:

A strong politics of law and rights is one that does not rely solely on law or on rights. Paradoxically, one way of showing defiance for law and rights is to struggle for increasingly inclusive laws and rights. Manipulability, contingency and instability from below is the most efficient way of confronting manipulability, contingency and instability from above. A strong politics of rights is a dual politics based on the dual management of legal and political tools under the aegis of the latter (De Sousa Santos 2002: 187).

The most intense moments of cosmopolitan legality are likely to involve direct action, civil disobedience, strikes, demonstrations, media-oriented performances and so forth. Some of these will be illegal, while others will be located in spheres not regulated by state law. Subaltern illegality may be used to confront both dominant legality and dominant illegality (De Sousa Santos 2002: 467). Comaroff and Comaroff have underscored that the burning critical theoretical issues of the global South are, simply put, the burning critical issues that other nation-states all over the world are facing. Their point is that we have an evolution of Euro-America to Africa and, I would add, South America. It is not surprising that we find the challenge to reigning hegemonic definitions of politics, law, ethics and morality taking place in the global South in a manner that is forcing those involved in the struggles there to rethink their fundamental categories. So the struggle continues.

Notes
1. For more information, see http://www.theubuntuproject.org.
2. Hylton White's manuscript is on file with the author.

References

Comaroff, J. and J.L. Comaroff. 2012. 'Liberalism, Policulturalism, and ID-ology: Thoughts on Citizenship and Difference'. In *Theory from the South, or, How Euro-America is Evolving towards Africa*. Boulder: Paradigm Publishers.

Cornell, D. and N. Muvangua (eds). 2012. *Ubuntu and the Law: African Ideals and Postapartheid Jurisprudence*. New York: Fordham University Press.

Cornell, D. and K.M. Panfilio. 2010. *Symbolic Forms for a New Humanity: Cultural and Racial Reconfigurations of Critical Theory*. New York: Fordham University Press.

De Sousa Santos, B. 2002. *Towards a New Legal Common Sense: Law, Globalization, and Emancipation*. London: LexisNexis Butterworths.

Henry, P. 2000. *Caliban's Reason: Introducing Afro-Caribbean Philosophy*. New York: Routledge.

Mamdani, M. 1996. *Citizen and Subject: Contemporary Africa and the Legacy of Late Colonialism*. Princeton: Princeton University Press.

Robins, S.L. 2008. *From Revolution to Rights in South Africa: Social Movements, NGOs and Popular Politics after Apartheid*. Pietermaritzburg: University of KwaZulu-Natal Press.

Terreblanche, S. 2002. *A History of Inequality in South Africa: 1652–2002*. Pietermaritzburg: University of Natal Press.

———. 2012. *Lost in Transformation: South Africa's Search for a New Future Since 1986*. Sandton: K.M.M. Review.

CHAPTER 9

The Self Become God
Ubuntu and the 'Scandal of Manhood'

Siphokazi Magadla and Ezra Chitando

> We can discern two vital and intertwined processes inherent in European
> colonization of Africa. The first and more thoroughly documented of these
> processes was the racializing and attendant inferiorization of Africans as
> the colonized, the natives. The second process . . . was the inferiorization
> of females. These processes were inseparable, and both were embedded in
> the colonial situation. The process of inferiorizing the native, which was
> the essence of colonization, was bound up with the process of enthroning
> male hegemony.
>
> — Oyeronke Oyewumi, *The Invention of Women*

The attainment of democracy in South Africa in 1994 contributed to a growing
national interest in the recovery of indigenous ethics that place value on the
ways African people lived before European colonisation. More specifically, this
recovery can be seen in the attention that Ubuntu has received in these two decades
of democratic consolidation. Reuel Khoza observes that his own earlier reflections
on Ubuntu were prompted by the end of apartheid and that 'there was a heady
atmosphere of intellectual ferment' (2011: xxxv). Fainos Mangena notes that the
discourse on Ubuntu has largely focused on the 'distinctive nature of African ethics
when compared to Western ethics', specifically regarding how Ubuntu defines
'community, collectivism, reconciliation and restoration of relationships' as they
pertain to social justice (2009: 18). So far, it seems that this process has amounted
to the triangulation of the 'meaning of the work of ubuntu with reference to other
discourses on humanism, socialism, communitarianism to which it is always
found to be similar, yet different' (Praeg 2008: 374), motivated by the underlying
conviction that 'Ubuntu has much to offer to the wider world, in particular South
African society' (Bennett and Patrick 2011: 224).

In this chapter, we wish to contribute to a different debate about Ubuntu, one that seeks to investigate how, if at all, Ubuntu can/should contribute to reconfiguring masculinities and femininities that have been disrupted by the violence of colonialism. In the epigraph to this chapter, Oyeronke Oyewumi, referring to the colonial impact on the Yoruba gender system in Nigeria, argues that colonialism did not only produce a racialised African subject, but it also reconfigured the ways men and women related to one another by introducing a 'European system of hierarchy of the sexes in which the female sex is always inferior and subordinate to the male sex' (1997: 153). For us, both 'the work of ubuntu' and the discourse on Ubuntu (Praeg 2008: 374) invite questions about how to (re)imagine what it means to be a man and woman in the postcolonial moment and how we should 'do' the relations between men and women. We focus on the violence of 'male hegemony', evidenced by the persistence of sexual and gender-based violence in southern Africa. Despite the relative peacefulness of this region, in terms of the outbreak of civil wars, compared to other regions of the continent, such as the west and the Horn of Africa, countries in southern Africa have alarmingly high levels of criminal violence and gender-based violence. According to Philomena N. Mwaura:

> Gender based violence refers to any harm that is perpetrated against a person as a result of gender power inequalities that exist among males and females. It is an umbrella term covering any act of violence inflicted on a person primarily because of their gender. Gender based violence is often a display of male power which manifests itself in various forms including physical, psychological, cultural, economic and sexual (2010: 102).

The southern African region has one of the highest percentages of people infected with HIV and AIDS, many of them located in South Africa, Swaziland and Zimbabwe – a function of a 'social context in which coercive, unequal and violent sexual relations lie at the root of particularly high rates of female heterosexual HIV infection' (Vincent 2008: 433). Thus, despite the professed liberal democratic order, 'rights talk coexists with material practices which perpetuate a sexual division of labor and an overarching violent and unequal gender order' (356). In particular, we examine how Ubuntu can facilitate the emergence of transformative and dynamic masculinities that distance themselves from 'systems and cultures that privilege men over women' (Ramphalile 2013). Before we discuss the emancipatory possibilities of Ubuntu in this domain, it is important to revisit debates about the intersection between hegemonic masculinity and violence.

Men behaving badly: Masculinity, sexual and gender-based violence

Across cultures, men tend to enjoy dominance and privileges. For Raewyn Connell, it was the

> advent of Women's Liberation at the end of the 1960s and the growth of feminist research on gender and 'sex roles' as well as the 'advent of Gay Liberation and the developing critique of heterosexuality of lesbians and gay men' which paved the way for the growth of studies of masculinities (1993: 598–9).

Feminist epistemologies argue that although what it means to be a man and a woman differs across cultures and history, it is still possible to point out that in most cultures, 'gender differences signify relationships of inequality and the domination of women by men' (Tickner 1992: 7). These and other studies on masculinities, invoked by feminists in their search for ways to understand male violence, challenge the notion that men are naturally violent by arguing that there are 'categories of masculinity (dominant, complicit, submissive and oppositional or protest)' (Morrell 1998: 607). This distinction is helpful in recognising that sexual and gender-based violence is not somehow 'natural' to masculinity as such, but rather to a certain kind of masculinity that Connell labelled 'hegemonic masculinity', which 'embodied the currently most honored way of being a man, it required all other men to position themselves in relation to it, and it ideologically legitimated the global subordination of women to men' (Connell and Messerschmidt 2005: 832).

Importantly, Robert Morrell notes that 'in addition to oppressing women, hegemonic masculinity silences or subordinates other masculinities, positioning these in relation to itself such that the values expressed by these other masculinities are not those that have currency or legitimacy' (1998: 608). The key characteristics of hegemonic masculinity are 'misogyny, homophobia, racism and compulsory heterosexuality'. Morrell argues that the impact of imperialism was not only racial dominance, but also the destruction of 'indigenous gender regimes' (612). In fact, Oyewumi's primary contention is that in precolonial Yoruba society,

> the social categories 'men' and 'women' were nonexistent; hence no gender system was in place ... Rather, the primary principle of social organization was seniority, defined by relative age. The social categories

'women' and 'men' are social constructs deriving from Western assumption that 'physical bodies are social bodies' (1997: 31).

In her seminal African feminist text, *Male Daughters, Female Husbands* – an investigation of the Igbo gender system in Nigeria – Ifi Amadiume claims:

> The fact that biological sex did not always correspond to ideological gender meant that women could play roles usually monopolized by men, or be classified as 'males' in terms of power and authority over others. As such roles were not rigidly masculinized or feminized; no stigma was attached to breaking gender rules (1987: 185).

In South Africa, Nokuzola Mndende (2006) has argued that languages and traditional religions are genderless. She argues that the notion of *hlonipha* (respect), which underscores relations between individuals in the community, is not only practised by women, 'but *hlonipha* is also practised by men' (see also Hunter 2010). Furthermore, the marginalisation of women in religion today is not a reflection of an intrinsic patriarchal nature of African societies because if one examines African traditional religion, one finds that unlike in Western religion, 'in ATR [African traditional religion], the Creator is a genderless spirit' (Mndende 2006).

Interventions by African feminists have been instrumental in countering ideas about the universality of gender categories embedded within the globalised Western feminist discourse, which presumes that, as in Europe, anatomy everywhere determines one's social hierarchy. These interventions have also been used by African feminists to criticise the chauvinism that characterises the violent postcolonial state, which for most of the 1980s and 1990s seemed to have been at the mercy of the 'Big Men' to the exclusion of women, who were 'put back in their place' after independence (Hendricks 2011). In this regard, it is interesting that the invocation of Ubuntu as a 'return' to the culturally accepted ethic of social justice and fluid gender roles has been approached with scepticism by many feminists in South Africa, who see Ubuntu as the further legitimisation of a 'deep-seated patriarchy', which relies on a patriarchal order that places women as perpetually inferior to men (Keevy 2009: 36).

The current debate in South Africa about the adoption of the Traditional Courts Bill, which proposes to grant traditional chiefs the same powers as judges, has been heavily criticised for potentially marginalising rural women's chances at obtaining justice, due to their location at the bottom of the patriarchal order. Nomboniso Gasa argues that, if anything, the Traditional Courts Bill presents a manipulation of 'African customary practices and cultural philosophies', which are encapsulated in the 'belief that *umuntu ngumuntu ngabantu* – a person is a person because of others' because its interpretation is 'vested in power and privilege' and presents African systems as static and 'without any contradictions or inequalities' due to their innate 'pecking order' (2011: 24–7; see also Gqola 2012).

Examining violent masculinities and gender-based violence in post-1994 South Africa, Pumla Dineo Gqola says that even though women are legislatively empowered and have achieved commendable levels of female representation across sectors, 'discourses of gender in the South African public sphere are very conservative in the main' because

> they speak of 'women's empowerment' in ways that are not transformative, and as a consequence, they exist very comfortably alongside overwhelming evidence that South African women are not empowered: the rape and other gender based violence statistics, the rampant sexual harassment at work and public spaces, the siege on Black lesbians and raging homophobia, the very public and relentless circulation of misogynist imagery, metaphors and language (Gqola 2007: 115).

She concludes that the continued militarisation of ordinary life in democratic South Africa can be understood by 'making the connections between the various ways in which "normal" heterosexual "play" contains codes that inscribe feminine passivity and masculine aggression' (Gqola 2007: 115–17).

Tina Sideris (2007) has also argued that the language of 'culture' and 'tradition' has been used in South Africa to justify gender-based violence. She demonstrates from interviews with survivors of such violence that one of the major reasons women do not report these incidents to the police is due to pressure from their families to resolve the violence within the family structure. She cites the story of a woman who reported her husband to the police who, in turn, reported her to elders in his family (including elder females), who concluded:

> The woman had acted against tradition on two accounts . . . in the first place, they felt there was some justification in her husband's violence,

which they considered discipline rather than abuse. Second, it was felt that she should have brought her complaint to the elders rather than taking it to an outside agency. On these grounds, they imposed a fine on her (Sideris 2007: 240).

Thus, tradition in South Africa has largely symbolised the sordid legitimisation of violence in women's intimate lives, effectively undermining the formal equality that women experience in the public space. It should therefore not be surprising that evoking tradition as a response to transforming violent masculinity should be met with scepticism.

Similarly, in the case of post-independence Zimbabwe, it seems that even though 'women fought side by side with men in the struggle' (Lyons 2004: xxi), in the aftermath, 'nationalism and political independence did not translate into particular feminist benefits for women' as they became reinscribed into domestic roles (29). Instead, the postcolonial moment has been particularly frustrating for feminists in Africa as they see the nation-building process maintaining rigid gender roles. Sheila Meintjes, Anu Pillay and Meredeth Turshen argue that the 'impulse to women's social transformation and autonomy is circumscribed by the nationalist project, which constructs women as purveyors of community's accepted and acceptable cultural identity' (2001: 9).

Violence committed by men in southern Africa does indeed seem to be a strategy of 'putting women in their rightful place' (Gabaitse 2012: 308). The net effect has been dramatic: men 'doing' violence against women and children in homes, religious institutions, workplaces and so on. The theoretical understanding of the underpinnings of 'hegemonic masculinity' demonstrates overwhelmingly that this is not a simple matter of a 'few bad apples'; sexual and gender-based violence is not only committed by 'a few mad men' out there (Du Toit 2003: 65).

'The self became the god': The crisis of masculinity in post-apartheid South Africa

Sexuality is always political, in the sense of being saturated with the effects of power. Yet, in ways which are reminiscent of apartheid, South Africa has experienced extraordinarily intense public controversy, activism and confrontation in respect of sexual issues. More usually, however, the principal site of concern in the South African case has been the sexual propensies of men rather than women; indeed, the post-apartheid politicization of sexuality has been closely intertwined with a perceived crisis of masculinity. There have been two principal sites of public representation and argument along these lines: HIV/AIDS and sexual violence.

— Deborah Posel, 'The Scandal of Manhood'

Our understanding of the challenges posed by the transformation of the oppressive institutional culture of the colonial state after independence demonstrates that legislative transformation is but one aspect of this broader process of creating empowering postcolonial states. Profound shifts of mindsets are required if men's violence against women and children is to be addressed effectively. Deborah Posel's intervention in 'The Scandal of Manhood' (2005) reflects on the narratives that have been used to articulate the meaning of rampant sexual violence in South Africa by specifically looking at how the rising number of 'baby rapes' was narrativised as both reflective of a problematic masculinity and a 'moral violation of the new nation . . . the problem of sexual violence was reconfigured as a symbol of, and mirror upon, the fragile normative foundations of the post-apartheid order as a whole' (2005: 241). The rape of a nine-month-old baby girl known as 'Baby Tsephang' in Louisvale in the Northern Cape in 2001 – initially wrongly thought to have been committed by six men between the ages of 24 and 66 – became the 'first public sight into the close connections which had developed between sexual violence and AIDS' (246). This reflects the allegation that HIV-positive men are raping young girls in order to cleanse themselves of the disease (the so-called virgin myth). In South Africa, 'one in five of all rape cases reported to police are of children under age of 18 . . . In the year 2000, there were 21,427 reported cases of sexual assault of children' (Vincent 2008: 437). These reported cases offer only a glimpse of the extent of the crisis of sexual violence because the actual numbers are much higher, since majority of rape cases continue to go unreported.

The 'baby rape' scandals, the gang rape and mutilation of seventeen-year-old Anene Booysen, as well as the gang rape of twenty-eight-year-old Thandiswa Qubuda in 2013, contribute to the view that the moral crisis in South Africa is 'fundamentally a crisis of manhood' (Posel 2005: 249).[1] The rape crisis has challenged the view that rapists are social outcasts since most cases of sexual and gender-based violence towards women and children 'come from men closest to them: no longer protectors, fathers, husbands, relatives and friends had been exposed as predators' (249; see also Vincent 2008).

Neville Richardson (2003) argues that the articulation of sexual violence is indicative of a 'moral vacuum' due to the loss of values as a result of colonialism and apartheid. Thabo Mbeki points to this loss of values:

> There was a collapse of an acceptable level of morality in our society which resulted in the elevation of the self, and the serving of the interests of the self to the point that self becomes religion. *The self became the god we must all worship* ... In the vacuum individuals had to decide for themselves what was good and what was bad, and the good was defined as what would serve my interests (in Richardson 2003: 5, emphasis added).

Mark Hunter makes it clear that there are noticeable 'qualitative changes in sexual violence' in post-apartheid South Africa, such as the 'dramatic increase in "jackrolling" or gang rape ... One estimate is that a third of reported rapes involve gang rape' (2010: 173). Hunter sees this as part of 'an unmooring of gender norms' that sees many men in South Africa today failing in their social and economic role as providers and women moving into the labour force signifying a 'virtual ending' of the patriarchal bargain. Thus 'sex today holds an ambiguous position in the lives of many South Africans – it is a site of pleasure by right, a thing to exchange for necessities, and a site of intense gendered violence' (136). Similarly, Eusebius McKaiser, responding to the question, 'Why do South African men seem to hate women so much?' suggests that gigantic inequality has meant that 'millions of South African boys and men fail to respond healthily to their sense of despair, and deep disappointment, for not making it in the new South Africa' (2012: 123–8).

In *Three-Letter Plague* (2008), Jonny Steinberg claims that, for men, the HIV and AIDS stigma in South Africa presents a stumbling block as to how to manage the spread of the disease because they are too ashamed to discover their status. Hence, the majority of those participating in the country's AIDS treatment programme are women. Quoting Posel, Steinberg argues that men's shame derives from the fact that 'sex itself has become the vector of death ... It is the very intimacy of the home which has become comtaminated. And it is men particularly – fathers and sons of the nation – whose moral credibility is most acutely called into question' (326). It is in this light that Ubuntu has been framed as one of the possible ways of rethinking a return to an ethic of care that culturally defines manhood as a function of personhood – that is, premised on the community, as opposed to the self.

The view here is that using the language of an Ubuntu ethic of care to transform masculinities provides a culturally understood language that is not seen as imported from elsewhere. In particular, male African nationalists have resisted the call for gender transformation on the (spurious) grounds that it is a 'Western imposition' and African gender activists are routinely attacked for lacking authenticity and mimicking Western culture. Amina Mama has made the argument that for 'the most part the African intelligentsia has preferred to dismiss feminism as something alien and Western, to regard the international women's movement as resulting from the activities of a covey of sexually, abnormal, man-hating eccentrics far removed from the concerns of "real" African women' (1996: 5). The result has been that 'the "woman question" has generally been treated opportunistically and exploitatively by insecure regimes on the one hand wishing to retain credibility within the international community, but on the other, seeking to authenticate themselves with populist appeals to anachronistic notions of masculinity' (26). The assumption is that appropriating Ubuntu to challenge sexual and gender-based violence provides the African gender activist with an indigenous resource, thereby mitigating the accusation that they are using foreign concepts to address African existential issues. The cultural ideology that projects men as the defenders of African culture suggests that men would be more inclined to endorse the struggle against sexual and gender-based violence if it is couched in vernacular idiom and values. In short, men are more likely to embrace the quest for gender justice if it can be demonstrated that their own value system leads to gender justice. In the case of South Africa, Posel suggests:

> The intense eruption of public anxiety and argument about sexual violence which marked the post-apartheid period had relatively little to do with feminist analysis and politics (influential though this has been in some respects). Rather, the key to understanding this politicization of sexual violence lies with its resonances with wider political and ideological anxieties about the manner of the national subject and the moral community of the country's fledgling democracy (2005: 239).

The argument here is that the use of feminism to challenge violent masculinities might be inadequate in its language to have an impact on the protection of the individual bodily rights of women. In essence, it seems, respect for women must be intertwined with respect for community and nation, as opposed to being seen as a stand-alone issue. Posel's contention is that the language of moral regeneration appeals to a maleness that is dependent on its definition as provider and protector, instead of being premised on its ability to preserve individual freedom, in the Western sense. Perhaps this is the 'self' that Mbeki alluded to, which was elevated at the expense of the 'community'. It seems to us that the idea here with regard to transforming masculinities is *not* to call for a society without categories of 'men' and 'women' – as in the Yoruba case illustrated by Oyewumi (1997) – but rather to locate them in their appropriate order below the category of community first and self second. So, as in precolonial Yorubaland, Ubuntu offers a language through which

> the rights of the individual derived from group membership. This is an expression of the classic African conception of the individual in relation to the community, ever so beautifully expressed by the dictum, 'we are, therefore I am,' in contradiction to the Europe-identified Cartesian pronouncement, 'I think, therefore I am' (Oyewumi 1997: 143; see also Praeg 2008).

Posel argues that in the decade after democracy, the 'baby rape' crisis used this language of community as opposed to individual rights, because instead of asking, 'What is wrong with these men who rape babies?', the reaction of communities and the state to the 'moral vacuum' was to ask, 'Who are *we* that we can do such things to our children?' (2005: 248–9, emphasis added). The suggestion here is that if men fail to don the mantle of responsible fatherhood, they jeopardise the possibility of responsible nationhood. As noted by Rosinah M. Gabaitse, an appeal to '*botho*' (humanity) and not '*motho*' (human being) offers new ways of being (2012: 318). Gabaitse, who admittedly uses a very specific and contested image of deity, insists:

> When men are taught *botho*, they are taught to respect every living creature and to respect women on the basis that they are simply human, alive and bear the image of God. Whenever a man violates a woman he should know more than anything they are destroying the very essence and being of God. They will be taught to adopt the attributes of a human being that are life-giving and life-enhancing. *Botho* discourages violent masculinities, because they diminish life. As such, men who violate and kill women can

be characterised as lacking that value . . . If it means dissolving gender inequalities and doing away with our constructions of men and women, then so be it. *Botho* requires that men and women have life and have it in abundance, so much so that a community that has *botho* is a community that speaks openly and eloquently against gender injustices, especially violence against women (Gabaitse 2012: 318).

The 'curious coincidence of feminine and African moralities'

In 'The Curious Coincidence of Feminine and African Moralities', Sandra Harding argues that often what has been identified as the 'African World View', which is 'less interested in individual autonomy' – thus much more concerned with 'relations to others and to nature' – is 'suspiciously similar to what the feminist literature has identified as a distinctively feminine world view' (1987: 299). Therefore, the Western phenomenon defined above by Oyewumi (1997) of reducing physical bodies to social bodies is for Harding a 'masculine or androcentric' world view, rather than a Eurocentric world view. Harding further extrapolates the ways in which the 'African World View' and the feminine world view share 'similar ontologies, epistemologies, and ethics' (299):

> To Europeans and men are attributed ethics that emphasize rule governed adjudication of competing rights between self-interested, autonomous others, and epistemologies that conceptualize the knower as fundamentally separated from known, and the known as autonomous 'object' that can be controlled through dispassionate, impersonal 'hand and brain' manipulations and measures. To Africans and women are attributed ethics that emphasize responsibilities to increasing the welfare of social complexes, and epistemologies that conceptualize the knower as a part of the known, the known as affected by the process of coming to know and that process as one that unites manual, mental and emotional activity (Harding 1987: 303).

Harding challenges feminist theorists who 'attribute unitary world views to women and men', while ignoring the 'social contexts of being black or white, rural or industrialized, Western or non-Western' (1987: 300). She further argues that both the African world view and the feminine world view are 'categories of challenge', which seek to confront 'in the thinking and social activities of men and Europeans what is relegated to "others" to think, feel and do . . . the return of the repressed'.

The challenge Harding issues to feminist theory is important for our discussion on the intersection between an Ubuntu ethic of care and a feminist ethic of care. For one, it remains unclear how the Ubuntu framework can be 'cleansed' of its patriarchal baggage. Heidi Hudson argues that feminism in Africa has had to strike a balance between 'universal normative principles of gender equality and traditional values such as *ubuntu* (the interconnectiveness of each human being, consensus-building and social solidarity)' (2009: 293). According to Hudson, the particularities of the African continent mean that African feminists have had to consider 'using a notion of gender equality that embraces cultural difference but does not reinforce cultural subjugation', thus emphasising 'communitarian rather than individualist rights and duties toward family, community, the state, and the international community'. Hudson suggests that overtures made by women at both local and national levels in post-genocide Rwanda have relied on balancing liberal feminist agendas with traditional approaches to gender justice at legal, restorative and equity levels. It is therefore incorrect to assume a simplistic irreconcilability between traditional views and feminist emancipatory approaches.

Despite the gloomy picture painted above regarding the use of tradition to legitimise violence in South Africa, feminists such as Gasa and Mamphela Ramphele do not dismiss the utility of Ubuntu in the private and public sphere. In *Conversations with My Sons and Daughters*, Ramphele (2012) argues that the disconnect between the 'doing' and the 'being' in South Africa has resulted in excessive levels of corruption, loss of accountability and violence, symbolic of a loss of the values of Ubuntu. Critiquing Nkosi Phathekile Holomisa's *According to Tradition*, which argues that traditional leaders are custodians of African culture, Gasa argues that the contribution of patriarchs such as Holomisa have resulted in 'a narrative based on a distortion of historical legacies' of African tradition (2011: 25). This is because traditional leaders were never the sole custodians of tradition because 'people of different ranks and stature are custodians and repositories of knowledge, customs and practices'. In fact, Gasa argues that the problem of the distortion of African tradition today is not only detrimental to the role of women as citizens, but also that the manipulation of tradition has been characterised by the minimisation of the role of the entire community in governance, by attributing the majority of power to individual leadership. However, Gasa does not advocate throwing out the baby with the bath water. Instead, she argues:

Recognition of these inequalities and contradictions does not detract from the most valuable and positive aspects of what have been continually evolving African cultural processes and understandings. In any cultural milieu, there is that which is empowering and restrictive, enabling and disabling. As society develops we have to interrogate what is emancipatory and what hinders self-realisation in these cultural worlds (2011: 25).

This is a very different view from that represented by Ilze Keevy's contribution to this volume (see Chapter 3). For Keevy, African feminists 'perceive this fundamental value as a form of oppression and state that it regulates female-male relationships, ignores the welfare of women and exploits their sexuality'. In an earlier journal article, she states: 'Volumes of texts by African feminists and gender activists speak out against this ancient oppressive collective worldview with its shared traditional values and beliefs in which women play a central but inferior role' (Keevy 2009: 29). Following Gasa, we contend that it is simply incorrect to argue, as Keevy does, that the debate on Ubuntu has only focused on its positive aspects, thus 'conveniently ignoring the dark side of Ubuntu which erodes the human rights of women and others' (32).

Indeed, as the work of Drucilla Cornell demonstrates, to argue the contrary amounts to a very conservative understanding of the complexity of the Ubuntu debate. Unlike Keevy, who traces Ubuntu rigidly as a law based in African religion and ancestral spirits, Cornell argues that Ubuntu discourse is vibrant precisely because considered a *living tradition* – as opposed to sedimented traditional custom – its definition is so much disputed in South Africa. Cornell demonstrates that the reinvention of Ubuntu has resulted in an ethic that does not somehow 'belong' to traditional elders and the living-dead, but in a contemporary, revolutionary Ubuntu that very much expresses the reinvention of culture as a living tradition. Cornell has argued that this dynamism of Ubuntu can easily be gleaned in Jacob Zuma's ability to use

> Ubuntu to bolster his own claims that Zulu identity forecloses the rights of gays and lesbians as a decadent Western identity antithetical to what it means to be Zulu. On the other hand, radical gay and lesbian sangomas, who have organized into associations, have argued that it is as African to be a gay or a lesbian (or indeed a transgender) person as it is to be straight or heterosexual (2012).

The point here is that when it comes to engendering Ubuntu, the argument posited by Keevy provides us with a limited understanding of the intersection between

Ubuntu and constitutional values. This lens presents us with a binary opposition between, on the one hand, gays and lesbians who are completely unprotected by the ethic of Ubuntu and thus completely and only dependent on the supremacy of the Constitution and, on the other hand, the patriarchs who are all too eager to exploit tradition in order to chip away at such constitutional gains. Nowhere does an argument such as Keevy's capture the fact that many women, gays and lesbians also consider themselves custodians of Ubuntu (Hudson 2009; Gasa 2011).

In the context of women and peace-building, Hudson has also noted the importance of the intersections between traditional values and legal instruments that guarantee the protection of women's inclusion. Hudson argues that the liberal feminist focus on attaining legal and political equality for women to participate in different stages of peace-building contributes to women being included as an add-on to peace-building, thus assuming that 'they will behave like men when given men's roles and that the fundamental frameworks of peacebuilding, though they were created by men for men, are unproblematic and will remain intact' (2009: 291). Using as an example the limited success of United Nations Resolution 1325, Hudson argues that the top-down nature of liberal peace-building has resulted in a 'piecemeal' inclusion of women in conflict zones that continue to ignore gender analysis and that, at times, the resolution has 'brought about backlash in several conflicts' (301). It is in this light that Hudson argues that African feminism offers better insight into how feminist agendas can be reconciled with African women's special needs and the peculiarities of their context, informed by their own understanding and the utilisation of local knowledge and traditional values, such as Ubuntu.

Conclusion

Our contribution to this debate about the reinvention of Ubuntu as what Cornell (2012) calls 'subaltern legality' has been to examine how an Ubuntu ethic of care can offer answers to the question of the oppressive masculinity that has characterised much of postcolonial Africa. We have traced gender relations and debates in Africa, as shaped by the impacts of different periods: the precolonial, colonial and postcolonial. Examining gender relations in the postcolonial moment, we are able to suggest that these debates are characterised by the binary representation of tradition as preserving male hegemony versus liberal constitutional values that provide official or formal equality between men and women. In this binary, sexual and gender-based violence is outlawed publicly, while the private space is a site of extreme levels of violence, mostly perpetrated by men. While it is true that traditional values are routinely used to legitimate gender-based violence, we also recognise that Ubuntu, considered a living tradition, is a very dynamic and deeply contested construct. We therefore conclude that the emancipatory potential of Ubuntu is a function of this complexity, which allows it to be owned by the perpetrators of gender violence as well as advocates of gender justice. It is possible to aspire for legal equality that destroys the gender inequality inherent in the language of tradition, while *also* considering yourself a custodian of that same tradition. From this, it follows that there is indeed a space in which to claim and use Ubuntu in order to advocate for the reinvention of violent masculinity.

Note

1. The high rate of rape in South Africa is such that it is almost impossible to keep track of the cases. These were the cases that captured public attention at the time of writing, November 2013. Many more cases occur, but do not make news headlines.

References

Amadiume, I. 1987. *Male Daughters, Female Husbands: Gender and Sex in an African Society.* London: Zed Books.

Bennett, T. and P. James. 2011. 'Ubuntu: The Ethics of Traditional Religion.' In *Traditional African Religions in South African Law*, ed. T.W. Bennett, 223–42. Cape Town: University of Cape Town Press.

Connell, R.W. 1993. 'The Big Picture: Masculinities in Recent World History'. *Theory and Society* 22 (5): 597–623.

Connell, R.W. and J.W. Messerschmidt. 2005. 'Hegemonic Masculinity: Rethinking the Concept'. *Gender and Society* 19 (6): 829–59.

Cornell, D. 2012. 'Ubuntu and Subaltern Legality'. Rhodes University Thinking Africa Newsletter Issue 6. Available at http://www.ru.ac.za/media/rhodesuniversity/content/politics/June2012.pdf.

Du Toit, L. 2003. 'Rape Understood as Torture: What is the Responsibility of Men?' In *Rape: Rethinking Male Responsibility*, ed. E. Conradie and L. Clowes, 36–67. Stellenbosch: Institute for Theological and Interdisciplinary Research.

Gabaitse, R.M. 2012. 'Passion Killings in Botswana: Masculinity at Crossroads'. In *Redemptive Masculinities: Men, HIV and Religion*, ed. E. Chitando and S. Chirongoma, 305–21. Geneva: World Council of Churches.

Gasa, N. 2011. 'The Traditional Courts Bill: A Silent Coup?' *South African Crime Quarterly* 35: 23–9.

Gqola, P.D. 2007. 'How the "Cult of Femininity" and Violent Masculinities Support Endemic Gender Based Violence in Contemporary South Africa'. *African Identities* 5 (1): 111–24.

————. 2012. 'Respect Our Rights'. *City Press*, 5 May. Available at http://www.citypress.co.za/features/respect-our-rights-20120505/.

Harding, S. 1987. 'The Curious Coincidence of Feminine and African Moralities: Challenges for Feminist Theory'. In *Women and Moral Theory*, ed. E.F. Kittay and D.T. Meyers, 296–315. Totowa: Rowman & Littlefield.

Hendricks, C. 2011. 'Gender and Security in Africa: An Overview'. Discussion Paper. Uppsala: Nordic Africa Institute. Available at http://nai.diva-portal.org/smash/record.jsf?pid=diva2:458594.

Hudson, H. 2009. 'Peacebuilding through a Gender Lens and the Challenges of Implementation in Rwanda and Côte d'Ivoire'. *Security Studies* 18 (2): 287–318.

Hunter, M. 2010. *Love in the Time of AIDS: Inequality, Gender, and Rights in South Africa*. Bloomington: Indiana University Press.

Keevy, I. 2009. 'Ubuntu Versus the Core Values of the South African Constitution'. *Journal for Juridical Science* 34 (2): 19–58.

Khoza, R.J. 2011. *Attuned Leadership: African Humanism as Compass*. Johannesburg: Penguin.

Lyons, T. 2004. *Guns and Guerilla Girls: Women in the Zimbabwean National Liberation Struggle*. Trenton: Africa World Press.

Mama, A. 1996. 'Women's Studies and Studies of Women in Africa during the 1990s'. Working Paper Series 5/96. CODESRIA.

Mangena, F. 2009. 'The Search for an African Feminist Ethic: A Zimbabwean Perspective'. *Journal of International Women's Studies* 11 (2): 18–30.

McKaiser, E. 2012. *A Bantu in My Bathroom: Debating Race, Sexuality and Other Uncomfortable South African Topics*. Johannesburg: Bookstorm.

Meintjes, S., A. Pillay and M. Turshen (eds). 2001. *The Aftermath: Women in Post-Conflict Transformation*. London: Zed Books.

Mndende, N. 2006. 'A Genderless Faith'. *Mail & Guardian*, 13 April. Available at http://mg.co.za/article/2006-04-13-a-genderless-faith.

Morrell, R. 1998. 'Of Boys and Men: Masculinity and Gender in Southern African Studies'. *Journal of Southern African Studies* 24 (4): 605–30.

Mwaura, P.N. 2010. 'Gender Based Violence: A Pastoral Challenge for the Church in Africa'. *Journal of Constructive Theology* 16 (1): 102–19.

Oyewumi, O. 1997. *The Invention of Women: Making an African Sense of Western Gender Discourses*. Minneapolis: University of Minnesota Press.

Posel, D. 2005. 'The Scandal of Manhood: "Baby Rape" and the Politicization of Sexual Violence in Post-Apartheid South Africa'. *Culture, Health & Sexuality* 7 (3): 239–52.

Praeg, L. 2008. 'An Answer to the Question: "What is [Ubuntu]?"'. *South African Journal of Philosophy* 27 (4): 367–85.

Ramphalile, M. 2013. 'Looking Beyond the "Good Man" in Explorations of Positive Masculinities'. *Bokamoso Leadership Forum*, 23 September. Available at http://bokamosoafrica.org/2013/09/looking-beyond-the-good-man-in-explorations-of-positive-masculinities.html.

Ramphele, M. 2012. *Conversations with My Sons and Daughters*. Johannesburg: Penguin.

Richardson, N. 2003. 'Not Another Moral Summit! Problems and Possibilities for Moral Regeneration'. *Scriptura* 82: 3–14.

Sideris, T. 2007. 'Post-Apartheid South Africa: Gender, Rights and the Politics of Recognition'. In *The Security-Development Nexus: Expressions of Sovereignty and Securitization in Southern Africa*, ed. L. Buur, S. Jensen and F. Stepputat, 233–50. Uppsala: Nordiska Afrikainstitutet and Cape Town: HSRC Press.

Steinberg, J. 2008. *Three-Letter Plague: A Young Man's Journey Through a Great Epidemic*. London: Vintage and Johannesburg: Jonathan Ball.

Tickner, J. 1992. *Gender in International Relations: Feminist Perspectives on Achieving Global Security*. New York: Columbia University Press.

Vincent, L. 2008. '"Boys Will Be Boys": Traditional Xhosa Male Circumcision, HIV and Sexual Socialisation in Contemporary South Africa'. *Culture, Health & Sexuality* 10 (5): 431–46.

CHAPTER 10

Concluding Reflections
The 'Fierce Urgency of Now'

Danielle Alyssa Bowler

> I begin with a question: What sort of moment is this in which to pose
> the question of black popular culture? These moments are always
> conjunctural. They have their historical specificity; and although they
> always exhibit similarities and continuities with other moments in which
> we pose a question like this, they are never the same moment.
> — Stuart Hall, 'What Is This "Black" in Black Popular Culture?'

In the epigraph to this chapter, Stuart Hall (1993) examines the nature of the
particular historical moment to which he poses the question of blackness, in
relation to the emergence of 'black popular culture'. This desire to get to the heart
of the specificity of the moment, while acknowledging similarity, continuity and
conjuncture, is interrogated by the question of 'what *sort of moment*' this is in
which 'to pose the question of black popular culture'. To ask, in a similar fashion,
the same question of the contemporary moment and the need for Ubuntu, is to
attempt to delineate the historical particularity of the present, despite the fact
that it is contingent on the configuration of both the past and the future. The
configuration of past-present-future and the weight and value these epochs constitute
in contemporary nationalist discourse challenge both the act of remembrance and
the creative imagining of South Africa's future. Seeking to formulate a new South
Africa, the African Renaissance and 'rainbow nation' discourses sought to divorce
the new from memory and repetition, to cut it off from the past in a yearning
for the unprecedented. However, as Jacques Derrida reminds us, 'the new cannot
be invented without memory and repetition' (in Derrida and Beardsworth 1994:
40). Past and future are always caught up in the present, such that these different
epochs are difficult to distinguish because they are so complexly bound up with
and in each other (Farred 2012) – a reality that speaks to the conjuncture that

Hall identifies. The present emerges burdened by the weight of 'similarities and continuities' we recognise, both as memory and as present in the moment, as 'apartheid'. The invocation of apartheid, as Achille Mbembe (2002) argues, is in turn always shadowed by the memory of colonialism and slavery – converging in the triangulation of historic oppression, a layered oppression that the African self will always remember. The South African state's rainbow nationalism stifles this memory in favour of an anticipated ' "uncontaminated" newness' (Farred 2004: 593), with the promise of a miraculous future that will temper the past: a version of events possible only as a result of selective memory. Under the shadow of this selective memory, the question of Ubuntu makes its entrance.

In the context of a contemporary South Africa that continually faces inescapable questions about identity, the atmosphere in which this question emerges is urgent. For a student and young South African wrestling with these questions through political philosophy, Rhodes University's Thinking Africa project raises the current moment to a 'fierce urgency'.[1] This chapter and its consideration of Ubuntu is the outcome of addressing the challenges of thinking about ubuntu,[2] and simultaneously (and one could argue, inevitably) thinking about bigger questions such as: What does it mean to think from *within* Africa, against historical thinking *about* Africa for the sake *of* Africa? As such, this reflection is a continued conversation with Leonhard Praeg's contribution in this volume and an engagement with his insistence that a 'logic of interdependence' (2008) underpins all shifts in our contextual theorising of ubuntu as Ubuntu. This insistence on the primacy of the temporal, this positive embrace of the temporal dimension of the discourse, allows us to positively appropriate, instead of judge, the numerous inventions and imaginings of Ubuntu, thereby enabling us to explore the urgency of the current context and the future emancipatory potential of Ubuntu. I use 'potential' because, despite the assumed 'universality of citizenship', the experience of citizenship is clouded in particularity.

Under the weight of newness, the post-apartheid moment (which simultaneously functions under the weight of another proper name, 'postcolonialism') is that moment in which questions about being and belonging haunt the present with particular intensity – an intensity most acutely experienced in terms of the fault line of race that runs through it.[3] Imagined as the location of the possibility of liberation, the home of the not-yet free, contemporary South Africa provides the physical geography for questions of being and belonging, always articulated as a colossal complexity.[4] To question the shadow of historic oppression is to argue, in the manner of Hall (1993), that 'these moments are always conjunctural' because they project shadows onto each other. The recognition of historic contingency challenges our perception of temporality. Post-apartheid, conceived of as 'not-apartheid', suggests we think about the current moment in terms of political difference: the birthplace of the new political order. Imagined this way, the post-apartheid moment is emancipation guaranteed by virtue of its difference from the former political order. Caught in this oppositional system of thought, the post-apartheid moment gains its ontological significance from a negative formulation: the condition of being no-more, not-any-longer, not-apartheid. The reality, however, is less stark in its contrast, the difference less significant, perhaps not meaningful at all. Perhaps, then, it is less a question of difference than of in-difference (Praeg 2007: 140), in which the contemporary South African reality is not apartheid, but also not yet post-apartheid, having not delivered on either its emancipatory potential or promise. Contrary to the suggested binary apartheid/post-apartheid or old/new South Africa, the difference is unclear. The call for clarity, the demand to explain, 'What do we mean by Ubuntu?', occurs in a moment that begs for clarity itself, for an understanding of 'what *sort* of moment' this is in which we ask the question.

*   *   *

Postcolonialism is, paradoxically, an epistemology so deeply grounded in the temporal that its key historical events – or occasions – function not only as chronological signifiers but as markers (and producers) of meaning.

— Grant Farred, 'A Thriving Postcolonialism'

In an attempt to think about representational practices in historical, cultural and societal terms, Cornel West (1990) maps out a genealogy that identifies three general co-ordinates in which the (then) present moment was rooted, the context and intellectual traditions that gave rise to what he calls the 'new cultural politics of difference'.[5] The moment in question is found to have three general co-ordinates, three events that served as specific markers of change, displacements and shifts, variegated across the trajectory of cultural politics.[6] Hall's project in 'What Is This "Black" in Black Popular Culture?' gives further weight to these general co-ordinates by underscoring the conditions for the possibility of the shifts (the co-ordinates) in question. In terms of our concern with Ubuntu, in order to question the particularity of this moment in both its conjunctural nature and historical contingency, we require a genealogy of sorts, an identification of the 'general coordinates' (Hall 1993) of the present moment, as a first response to the dilemma of trying to think through the complexity of the question in the context of a postcolonialism that lacks clarity.

In mapping the specificity of this epistemological moment, a moment in which Ubuntu exists primarily as a question, three such 'general coordinates' make a persistent appearance. While constituted in divergent ways, the postcolonial moment is, for many, characterised by an acute fascination with colonialism, apartheid and slavery, and post-apartheid. The constellation of meanings attributed to these three events can be condensed as 'oppression' or expanded to 'multiple layers of oppression', differing in content, though compounding in effect, while generating almost infinite variations in the nature of this effect (as the contemporary history of 'post-apartheid' amply demonstrates).

The effect of these moments on African subjectivity has been and continues to be contested. The search for consequences, for signs of continued oppression upon the African subject, has led to conclusions that are not so much diverse as giving different weight to the signature of oppression and the possibility of freedom from the 'Tower of the past', to use Frantz Fanon's phrase (1967: 230). The interpretations of these three historic moments, conceived as outlining the process of becoming that constitutes African subjectivity, are never diametrically opposed, but rather shade off into differences that emerge as a result of contesting the imprint left on Africa(ns) by the continent's history. Understanding this moment, then, is a function of how we make sense of a past variegated by three historic moments or general co-ordinates and, in this regard, Mbembe's 'African Modes of Self-Writing' (2002) continues to speak to us.

*   *   *

The unprecedented is never possible without repetition, there is never something absolutely unprecedented, totally original or new; or rather, the new can only be new, radically new, to the extent that something new is produced, that is, where there is memory and repetition. The new cannot be invented without memory or repetition.
— Jacques Derrida, 'Nietzsche and the Machine'

The act of thinking about Ubuntu from within the present moment requires an acknowledgement of the archive against which we think: the realm of thought that reaches us by way of being pre-made, yet requires that we remake (rethink) it in terms of a critique of the archive. We find ourselves in the domain of historical memory, requiring an engagement with an archive that circumscribes knowledge, such that Ubuntu emerges as 'layered unthought' (Praeg 2008: 368). Understanding the present moment requires of us to think in retrograde, to retrace our steps through the historical retrodictions of ubuntu as Ubuntu. It represents an acknowledgement that Ubuntu, as it is now, is rooted in a *living praxis*, held together by a life world that has radical interdependence at the heart of its conceptualisation and configuration of society.

Mbembe's 'African Modes of Self-Writing' (2002) can be used to critique the various modes in and through which this praxis has been articulated as abstract philosophy. It is an extended lament on African philosophers' failure to make 'interesting sense of history' (2002: 241).[7] The primary offenders in his unforgiving critique are two intellectual currents, Afro-radicalism and nativism (as metaphysics of difference), which form part of a sterile African collective *imaginaire* whose characteristic theoretical mode is an obsession with the past. Mbembe argues that this obsession has impeded the development of a philosophy that 'might have explained the meaning of the African past and present by reference to the future'. Consequently, both these intellectual currents are said to be encumbered by their formulation of history, the interpretive activity involved in attributing 'canonical meanings' to the general co-ordinates of African being: colonialism, apartheid and slavery. Afro-radicalism, a current of thought dominated by a Marxist and nationalist character, is said to fail on three counts. First, Mbembe argues that there is a 'lack of self-reflexivity and an instrumental conception of knowledge and science, in the sense that neither is recognized as autonomous. They are useful only insofar as they are mobilized for service in partisan struggle' (243). Second, he accuses them of holding a 'mechanistic and reified vision of history', devoid of African agency and responsibility in the sense that 'causality is attributed to entities that are fictive and wholly invisible, but are nevertheless said to determine, ultimately, the subject's life and work'. These forces are held responsible for the trajectory of the African self, not only interrupted, but ultimately lost, the loss of 'that part of the African historical self that is irreducible to any other'. History is read as 'imposed' and the African subject's (read: 'victim's') response can only be under the conditionality of this subjugation – a naive and 'uncritical' response,

197

arising from a 'cult of victimisation', underpinned by a conception of 'history as sorcery' (245).

The nativists, preoccupied with a racialised conceptualisation of Africanity and 'the native condition' suffer the same fate as their Afro-radical counterparts. Mbembe's central critique is in the tension he identifies between their conceptual-isations of the African self – a tension fundamentally between a universalising move that claims shared membership in the human condition (sameness) that declares, 'We are human like everyone else', and an opposing, particularistic move that claims, 'We have a special kind of humanity that is native to the dwellers of the African continent'(2002: 252). Mbembe's concern here, in terms of the particularity of Africanness, is the easy slide into the 'principle of repetition (tradition) and the values of autocthony', a repetition of the Enlightenment dilemma of alterity, which converges on race-based thinking (243). A particular African humanity, distinct, recognisable and based in the past, is taken as the ontological starting point.

Central to both the nativist and Afro-radical traditions is a formulation of history and its vicissitudes as tradition left behind, being interrupted, such that progression is conceived as a journey to the past, which is seen as a 'necessary condition for overcoming the phase of humiliation and existential anguish caused by the historical debasement of the continent' (Mbembe 2002: 254). Given the infinite repetition of these interruptions, presented as indistinct, unrelenting and always external, the African self expresses and experiences existence 'almost always, as a stuttering' (252). In the challenge of remembrance and recall and the task of historical imagination, Mbembe finds African intellectuals wanting (258). Their configuration of colonialism, apartheid and slavery as 'all-purpose signifiers', formulated into a conception of being by way of interruption, is said to lack a creative engagement with being, offering only a mode of thought that is exhausted. At the heart of Mbembe's critique is a disagreement with the narrative that emerges in which the thematic of victimisation takes central place.

Ato Sekyi-Otu, in his characteristic prosaic style, offers an alternative and more generous interpretation of how African intellectuals have made sense of the 'living drama of African history and thought' (2003: 2). Rather than viewing the African collective *imaginaire* as a melodramatic lament on the African self and its loss, he suggests that African intellectuals 'say simply that the effects of that history impose limits on being, action and knowledge' (4). He writes:

They wonder aloud what the world and the drama of human life would look like, what promises and predicaments they might proffer, were they ever unshackled from the constraints of a particular time and place, a particular historical circumstance. A coherent historicism is predicated, has to be predicated, on a consciousness of the possibility of freedom, intimations of what the nature of things might have been (Sekyi-Otu 2003: 4).

Configuring colonialism, apartheid and slavery as (no more than) 'interruptions', Sekyi-Otu argues that the canon offers a 'meditation on things dislocated, displaced, disparaged, made instrumental and subservient to the requirements of racial vindication and political litigation with the white man', placing the African self within 'the schemata of interrupted histories' (2003: 4). The intellectual canon speaks more of constraint than victimisation, not of untimely endings and determinist notions of the future, but rather seeks to engage the repressed possibilities inhibited by way of interruption. Being is not understood as lost to the past, necessitating time-travel recovery, but rather as the site of 'existential deviation', to use Fanon's term (2008: 14). Being is considered influenced by a 'deviation from the regular predicaments of human intercourse, normal pathologies and prospects of the paths of liberty – promises and tragedies native, according to Ben Okri's book of aphorisms, to "a way of being free"' (Sekyi-Otu 2003: 6).

An engagement with history necessitates as critical historicism, at the heart of which there must be a *consciousness of the possibility of freedom*, intimations of what the nature of things might have been (Sekyi-Otu 2003: 4). This critical (and inevitably political) engagement with history and historicity demands an active imagination and critical perspective. At stake here, as Mbembe recognises in his epigraph, attributed to Gilles Deleuze, is the challenge of interpreting temporality *as subjectivity*.[8] To seal and contain Ubuntu in a way of thinking about the past from which it speaks, as if time was not interrupted, is alienating. Mbembe and Sekyi-Otu converge on a particular point, though configured differently: 'locality'. Mbembe, concerned with the 'cult of locality', points to views of the past that conceive of identity in territorial terms: committing citizenship to a 'consciousness of place' (2002: 266). The implication of this is an understanding of citizenship as emanating 'from a combination of ideological categories (membership and origins) and spatial categories (territory and locality)'. Sekyi-Otu's notion of locality is within the space of remembrance:

The challenge of remembrance resides, however, not only in its temporality, the complex manner in which the needs of the present and the call of the future fashion our relation to texts and contexts of the past; it is also a matter of place, *a function of the rememberer's location in the map of contemporary history*. For if all remembering is a political activity, a return to worlds and works occasioned by a community's circumstances and auguries of its destiny, that which we take to be the defining homestead in that community's expanse is decisive in framing the kind of questions we address to a text, to say nothing of the lessons we elicit from it (1996: 10, emphasis added).

Time remains the theoretical baseline from which meaning is contested, through which narratives emerge and from which historical attitudes emanate that serve to either locate Ubuntu within considerations of the possibility of freedom (reinvention proper) or to locate freedom's possibilities in a glorified past (reinvention as return). Ubuntu has been a site of rearticulation and reinvention, where time itself, temporality, has been the hallmark of reinvention.

*   *   *

... the relationship between *the work of ubuntu* and *the discourse on ubuntu*. While the former refers to everyday existence and gestures we recognise, in an everyday or common sense understanding of the term, as manifesting ubuntu, the latter refers to the self-conscious reflection on what we have to understand about being African that would explain or make such actions understandable.
— Leonhard Praeg, 'An Answer to the Question: What is [Ubuntu]?'

Considered as a static notion of community, with the perils of territoriality and race-based citizenship and igniting questions of Africanity, the mention of Ubuntu provokes questions of being and belonging. However, far from being an immobile notion of community, throughout South African history, Ubuntu has continually re-emerged, not as a repetition, but as a translation. In this sense, it is a historical concept, a discourse and, most fundamentally, a praxis that does not repeat through contemporary South African history. Rather, to quote Mark Twain, 'History doesn't repeat itself, but it often rhymes' (in Knoop 2009: 161). In translation, Ubuntu has been contextually reconfigured in the way that community is formulated in terms of contextual and subjective needs. Ubuntu exists in variegated forms across South African history, never changing in fundamental content – the 'logic of interdependence' – but malleable in its contextual reimagining. The 'logic of interdependence' that Praeg (2008) argues is at the centre of ubuntu, has historically reconstituted the notion of community – widened from precolonial communities (the first instance) towards the community of the South African nation (the contemporary instance). This contemporary imagining is not without its own internal shifts, in relation to the way different eras of governance have defined their own nationalist projects. Many would argue that Ubuntu is most explicit in the policies and outlook of Thabo Mbeki's era, haunted as it was by the question, 'Who is African?' (belonging). However, Jacob Zuma's era, with its focus on ethnicity, has seen a resurgence of race and the consequent rearticulation of the question, 'What is African?' (being) in terms of blackness. Within both these eras, however, Ubuntu emerges as a question of being and belonging that continues to be used as a catchphrase for the logic of being-together.

Challenging notions of Ubuntu as statically affixed to the precolonial era and radically immobile is the identification of the malleability and mobility of Ubuntu across time. Praeg (2008) and R.D. Coertze (2001) invite a consideration of Ubuntu *in motion*, an Ubuntu adept at contextual mobility. Praeg's distinction between ubuntu as work/praxis and the translation to Ubuntu as discourse represents a call to consider Ubuntu as split: with work and discourse existing in a mystical connection, registering both a perplexing similarity and difference that suggests thinking about ubuntu (work) as the origin and Ubuntu (discourse) as the origin reimagined and made mobile, according to the demands of time and context. This distinction registers the fascinating way that ubuntu and Ubuntu have their divergences and convergences, distinctions and meeting points – separate, but irrefutably related because one is rooted in the other. As ubuntu (praxis) shifts to widen the notion of community and embody the political needs of the time, so too does the discourse. Ubuntu is made in the image of the discourse privileged at the time, reinterpreted as underscored by the dominant need, what the subjective context needs ubuntu to do. In its original form, ubuntu as a precolonial praxis is not resurrected, but rather has been a site of continual reimagining. Thus Ubuntu-translated emanates from a past both imagined and removed, recent and remote, as it is caught up in historical articulations and imaginings of being and becoming, mobilised and invoked to do political work.

*   *   *

> 'Culture' has always been positioned in modernity either as the reconstruction of a lost authenticity (in its nostalgic or romantic mode) or a coming to terms with the loss of origin (in its ironic or high modernist mode).
>
> — Bill Readings, *The University in Ruins*

Ubuntu, in its first instance, finds its ground zero in the 'question of our humanity, of what it means to be human' (Gordon 2010). Thus, what is considered is 'the fundamentals of [Africans'] beliefs and behaviour, or their basic philosophical system' (Mudimbe 1997: 34). The precolonial is the oft-disputed, misinterpreted and perpetual site of contestation – the temporal space given unto 'the whitewashed wall' and how it 'paints the absence between sails, an illusory sea of unimaginable depth', which refers to the engagement with memory, necessitated by the absence of a definite origin (Wicomb 2002: 98). The geography of ubuntu-thought locates Ubuntu primarily within a logic of interdependence, held as a marker of precolonial African communities. This communal consciousness is held as underpinning interpersonal relations and positions all relationships within a 'political economy of obligation' (Chabal 2009: 86). To speak of the 'political economy of obligation' is to refer to 'the web of meaning within which [African] individuals and groups act in the world'. Thus, Ubuntu finds its genesis in social organisation conceived of interdependently, where questions of being and becoming are tied up in the communal, such that the communal enables the realisation of personhood. The ontological order and one's part within it are therefore premised upon loyalty to the communal – an acknowledgement of this kin network and the way in which it circumscribes being.

It is evident that rather than a simplistic, uncomplicated understanding of u/Ubuntu, from which naive rhetoric sprouts phrases such as, 'I am because we are', 'an injury to one is an injury to all' and 'a person is a person through other people' – often registering as unquestioned equality – what we have here is a precise constitution of society, functioning under the conventions of a very specific logic. This, critically, frames our understanding of ubuntu, not as truth, but as a conceptual analysis, from which to proceed – circumventing questions of authenticity and the problems of definition that often underscore engagement with ubuntu. Once ubuntu is made mobile, we recognise the seismic shifts that perpetually reconstitite it as Ubuntu, punctuated by the instability that comes with the radical alteration of the meaning of ubuntu, removed from its genesis, separated from the logic as it functioned in its habitus. From the Greek *seiein* (to shake), ubuntu is shaken, first by the move from real to local imagined communities (rural to urban) and second in the abstraction that comes with imbuing ubuntu within a nationalist teleology. Our search is therefore for the political instances that provided the possibility for what Praeg argues

> ... *de-territorialised* ubuntu from the domain or territory of cultural praxis and re-inserted or *re-territorialised* it in a different context as a trope, or philosophy, an abstract idea or perhaps a set of ideas in a way that sometimes and under certain conditions and in specific contexts, allows Ubuntu to function as legitimate sign for 'us all' (2014: 47).

Seismic shifts are also semantic shifts, shifts in both micro-geography and meaning, as the act of translation manifests the dilemma of dealing with the ghost of *ubuntu in a habitus* resuscitated. Simply put, to imbue ubuntu with ideology is the constant navigation of difference and sameness; Ubuntu in a new context is not the same as ubuntu – as (in difference) context shifts the content of what ubuntu is and means for interdependent conduct, while (in sameness) this Ubuntu cannot be radically different from ubuntu, or else what we are trying to do with it will dismally fail in the face of radical alteration.

*   *   *

> Because of the vicissitudes of history, Africans are supposed to have left tradition behind them. Whence the importance, in order to recover it, of moving backward, which is the necessary condition for overcoming the phase of humiliation and existential anguish caused by the historical debasement of the continent.
> — Achille Mbembe, 'African Modes of Self-Writing'

In the act of recovering tradition, the move backwards that Mbembe argues is characteristic of overcoming humiliation and existential questions, is precisely where we find Ubuntu playing a role in the nationalist project. Ubuntu has informed the post-apartheid national project, regardless of shifts in leadership, albeit in a way that can be argued has given us a different translation of sameness (Farred 2004). The move to the imagined community of the nation in the current

South African context represents the most ardent contemporary attempt to bring ubuntu from its *precolonial habitus* to a *postcolonial habitus*. This mobilisation has, as its chief factor, the abstraction of the transcendental element of ubuntu: the conditions for the possibility of the achievement of a united South Africa. Thus Ubuntu becomes linked with human rights, dignity and nation-building as part of nationalist teleology (Coertze 2001). Through Ubuntu, the nation begins to perform itself into being as a Derridean performative tautology, according to which 'we perform the nation to create the nation' (Praeg 2011: 344). Rather than 'developing and implementing reform programs', Christoph Marx argues there has been a 'convulsive attempt at nation building' (2002: 50), which paradoxically has occurred within a climate of radical cynicism – far removed from the hopes of reconciliation after the April 1994 election. Ubuntu has been positioned within the rhetoric-laden discourse of nationalism, unquestionably employed and imbued with the promise of a future that sounds much like utopia.

The post-apartheid state is not submitted to thought or action, underlined by the idea that the precolonial logic of interdependence can be transplanted into the postcolonial situation, determining how individuals must act and limit their actions, often by encouraging conformity to the nation (Marx 2002). The era of Nelson Mandela infused a way of being together that was saturated with Ubuntu rhetoric. In a climate of the most urgent subjective need for a way of being that would be fundamentally interdependent – the opposite of apartheid's ethos of separation – Ubuntu was all about forgiveness and reconciliation. Rather than a national project in itself, it became part of the discourse of liberation and fundamental equality. Following Mandela, Mbeki's African Renaissance project represented a more instrumental attempt to 'reincorporate and strengthen African epistemology and Ubuntu within an African postcolonial/post-apartheid era' (Swanson 2007: 57). In a move that was more rhetorical than active, Ubuntu represented an attempt at considering South Africa on a continental scale, appealing to a utopian idealism, to deal with the questions of belonging that still plagued the country in the wake of the thrill of liberation (Farred 2004; Swanson 2007). Here, interdependence was infused with the ideal of African identity beyond race, culture, religious affiliation and class. Thus, the shift was less about forgiveness and became an identitarian move that used Ubuntu to achieve the ideal of unity that goes beyond difference. The Zuma era has considered the question of Ubuntu more obliquely and in a more radically divisive manner. Ubuntu has been situated as fundamentally rhetorical in an ethnic-national project that lacks clarity. Ubuntu has now become about the dignity of the African self and Africanity – without consideration of the complex identitarian questions that Mbeki attempted to overcome with his universalising sameness. It is an Ubuntu that is fundamentally thrown off course by the pressing questions of citizenship and socio-economic equality in the face of an apartheid hangover.

What each era gives us is a different way of negotiating the same roadblock, represented in the question: 'How do we achieve a way of being together?' What is revealed in the process is a nationalism pitched to a tenuous citizenry, built upon a foundation that exists only as a fragment. The nation-building project suffers acute impediments as it comes up against multiple barriers. First, belonging is inhibited by the lack of a collective construction of a democratic South Africa. Second, ubuntu as praxis was not the act of creating community, but a way of enabling dwelling in the community through allegiance to the logic of interdependence and permeated all aspects of being. Insistent reminders of the lack of unity threatens the success of the nationalist project as Ubuntu fails to fully translate into the current context due to the manner in which ideology is problematised by reality. Fundamentally, as revealed earlier, Ubuntu runs into that taunting roadblock of unanswered questions, questions that resist easy answers, punctuated by history's effect on being and belonging. It is this tenuous being and belonging, evident in South African citizenship, that challenges the translation of Ubuntu in the nationalist project. It is this tenuous being and belonging that should then become the site of reconsideration.

*   *   *

The moment that went before, which will not permit a historically 'uncontaminated' newness . . .
— Grant Farred, 'The Not-Yet Counterpartisan'

To speak of the South African present is, in a sense, to speak of a perfidious present. The present is not, in and of itself, singular. In the place of singularity, what we have is a present that is constituted by being simultaneously both the present and the past. This notion is true of any context – the haunting of the present by the past and the future – and not unique to South Africa. However, it operates at an aggravated level in a country for which existence – being and belonging – is critical, making the dialogue between different temporal moments a dissonant and intense conversation. April 1994, the date of the iconic first democratic election, did not see the absolute move from the apartheid *nomos* to the post-apartheid *nomos*, the 'transformation from one historical epoch to another', but rather manifests a situation of historical continuity (Farred 2004: 593). History registers not as 'open and fluid', but rather as fixed, in the sense that the past is insistently present (Schmidt in Farred 2004: 591). The end of apartheid did not bring absolute autonomy – freedom from layered oppression in the form of colonialism, apartheid and slavery – nor the arrival of utopia and the rainbow nation. Freedom did not arrive as timeously as expected, but is rather experienced as delay.

The South African situation is therefore characterised by a neurotic consciousness of the history that preceded and informs the present, which can only be understood, in its truest sense, as 'the moment that is insistently not the past but that can only function politically – as a politics – because there is the historic epoch that went before – the past' (Farred 2004: 594). The past and the insistent way it constitutes the presenter are both a function of history, but also of our own inability to address the present, beyond surface attempts at nation-building. In history and not-yet-history (the past that is present), to use Farred's term, we are complicit. The situation has become a moment where

> after the initial, heady thrill of freedom and democracy is gone . . . for the historically disenfranchised the double temporality collapses, if only for a brief period, into a recognizable singularity: that occasion when the apartheid past and the post-apartheid present are experienced as an undifferentiated temporality, the reality of a black majority government notwithstanding – which, by force of its significance, allows the double temporality to retain its historical but not material difference; post-apartheid South Africa is a moment without a distinct historical innocence (Farred 2004: 595).

The challenge of making sense of the present, determining with precision the nature of this 'sort of moment' falls by the wayside. The promise of freedom, of new management, a promise understood as emancipation from that which was before, is reduced to a question on which the African National Congress (ANC) has failed to deliver. Questions of being and belonging, often bound up in questions of Africanity, have been met with a rhetoric that is often as vacuous as it is obsessive (Marx 2002: 49). This obsessisiveness precludes any real thinking of the postcolonial and post-apartheid state of being – configuring memory within a narrow conceptualisation of what has gone before and what is yet to come. Rather than an interrogation of the current context and its subjective need, we have nation-building, the 'situation where a state authority through a process of directed cultural chance, sometimes even forcibly, strives to promote a conscious sense of national identity' (Coertze 2001: 116). Falling into the trap of historical continuity, Ubuntu's resuscitation occurs at the level of discourse, slotting into the idealistic signifiers of newness that are self-consciously performed.

However, the general co-ordinates of African historical memory, the moment(s) that went before – colonialism, apartheid and slavery – will not permit a historically ' "uncontaminated" newness' (Farred 2004: 593) in the post-apartheid postcolony. Ubuntu, in its current reinvention and recognised as unrealised, operates contradictorily upon numerous temporal planes: it represents (1) the traditional, that which has gone before, which is at one level simply tradition, that which we have inherited, and on another level, the glorification of 'an imagined past'; (2) the self-consciously created pivot for national identity and community, existing simultaneously in the present and the future; and (3) the promise of the future as ' "uncontaminated" newness'. Signified by its uncertain temporality, Ubuntu becomes simultaneously tradition, tradition reinvented and anticipated newness – eviscerated of any certain locality. Nation-building, informed by Ubuntu, glorifies an imagined past, abstracting the transcendental to deal with the political, economic and social questions begged by this context, in a manner that is pure exteriority – not dealing with the interior questions that emanate from being contextually and subjectively located (Marx 2002: 49). Rather than truly *thinking* the post-apartheid state, the communal values central to Ubuntu are unquestionably employed as a value system to promote allegiance to the nation and achieve equal citizenship, as Ubuntu is made to dictate how one (as a citizen) should act *without thinking too much*. Thus, the precolonial logic of interdependence is transplanted into the postcolonial situation in the attempt to determine how an individual must act and limit their actions, by encouraging conformity to the nation-building project conceived in its name. In this instrumentalisation of Ubuntu, the rhetoric of nation-building is used in a way that any public discussion of the material conditions for the possibility of really being and belonging together is circumvented (50).

*   *   *

In its contemporary translation, the Ubuntu of the nation-building project is 'redolent with nostalgia and loss' (Farred 2012: 84) and, at the same time, punctuated by a return to the precolonial and imbued with aspirational new content. The project of nation-building *qua* Ubuntu seems 'content to define [the current context] in relation to values which preceded it' (Fanon in Farred 2012: 78). Rather than operating from the recognition of this radical conjuncture, recognising the Derridean imperative of 'memory and repetition', there is an evisceration of the past – a historical narrative that is selective, teleological and instrumental. But as Mbembe reminds us, in this 'historical innocence', 'existence is expressed, almost always, as a stuttering', registering in the dilemmas of citizenship, emancipation and existence that continually return in questions of the South African contemporary moment (Mbembe 2002: 252).

Ubuntu thus finds itself between the naivety of authenticity and the perils of invention – in abstraction speaking to different discourses, but forever remaining irreducible to them. Complicated by being made increasingly mobile, praxis becomes that which cannot be captured in Ubuntu discourse. This is the crucial dramatic moment that sees the entrance of the question, 'What is Ubuntu?' – a moment where the internal rumblings and ventriloquism cannot give a definitive voice to a praxis that, necessarily, perpetually finds itself lost in translation. Farred's citation of Martin Heidegger's views on loss of meaning thus become relevant to our situation, in light of the overuse and exploitation of Ubuntu:

> Heidegger . . . is concerned with what is lost in the overuse of terms so that starting over again for him recognises that 'true meaning falls easily into oblivion in favour of foreground meanings'. However, Heidegger also understands both the retrievability – the recovery, the making audible again – of the 'true meaning' and the kind of interrogation that is needed to achieve it (2012: 77).

Farred argues that 'there can be no (easy) hearkening to pre-coloniality' – the task of dealing with the present cannot be dealt with so easily; the easy answers, rather than providing catharsis, have been mere aids of the Convoluted Present (2012: 79). If we take seriously Heidegger's insistence that 'dwelling is nothing less than being' and Farred's interpretation that dwelling is everything because 'human beings consist in dwelling' (78), Ubuntu cannot be the answer to questions of the South

African/African self, as long as nation-building precludes any real interrogation of being, not asking questions of being and becoming, or any question about the nature of this particular moment.

Ubuntu can thus not operate in a situation that limits the interrogation of the nature of this context. This is not to say that Ubuntu cannot provide a framework for the achievement of dwelling, but to insistently argue that in its current formation, Ubuntu as potential critical humanism, is punctured by translation, sucked of its potential, eviscerated and excised of all it could achieve by not considering this context as one that requires a commitment to thinking itself – a commitment that must depart from the acceptance that the question 'What is Ubuntu?' must necessarily remain unanswered. In a nation so divided, fragmented and, in some instances, splintered, there is little commonality to be found, whether in being or in experience. To be effective as renewed praxis, u/Ubuntu would have to be engineered to those interests *that cannot be anything but common.*

*   *   *

> This relation to the future is active, it is affirmative; and yet, however active it is, the relation is also a passive one. Otherwise the future will not be the future.
>
> — Jacques Derrida, 'Nietzsche and the Machine'

Taking seriously the task of dwelling in the contemporary South African present is to commit oneself to complexity, a complexity that evidences itself in the constitution of time – that which is not, that which is and that which is yet to come. In facing a present that is a complexly constituted moment, it seems the current South African ontology is a disillusioned, complex double temporality (Farred 2004). Considering emancipation cannot be the simple task of positioning the future, the unprecedented, as that which has no sense of the way history rhymes and the force of conjuncture. The site of 1994 in popular imagination did not present the freedom hoped for in the ecstatic moment of the transition. Rather, freedom appeared as a Trojan Horse (Farred 2004), a potentiality once saturated with the hopes of a population for whom repression had been the marker of being and belonging.

In the present moment, we dwell in the interstices: of the past-present (given the past's insistent presence in this historic moment) and the present-future, the hope of a future that will shake off the odour of the past, the dream of a reality where freedom will not be experienced as restriction. We dwell in an uneasy present. However, as Derrida argues, the relation to the future needs to be active in the sense that it allows for the future of decision (a future in which decision can 'take place') and passive in the sense that it is not fully anticipated (Derrida and Beardsworth 1994: 40). This relation allows for 'the future to arrive as the future (and not a future present)'.

The current positioning of Ubuntu in state discourse anticipates a future that arrives as pre-made and is experienced within this moment as future present. Incompatibly contradicting the South African reality, this translation of Ubuntu presents an easy and uncomplicated road to the future, devoid of the hard work of making sense of what sort of moment this is, to recall Hall's question in the epigraph to this chapter. The current translation of Ubuntu has a problematic sense of time that, in its obsession with progression, cannot address the present as present (a moment that understands its constitution by way of conjuncture) and in so doing also cannot experience 'the future as future'. This is not to say that Ubuntu has no place in the contemporary moment, or in that which is yet to come, but rather to argue that the question we need to address to this context cannot be subject to the immediate answer of a 'convulsive attempt at nation-building', to quote Marx (2002: 50). Rather, the question that necessitates direct address can only be: What sort of moment is this in which to pose the question of Ubuntu to the contemporary South African reality? – a question with a sense of history and time and, most importantly, an acute sense of the way in which memory and its repetition paves the road towards the unprecedented.

Notes

1. The title of this chapter is taken from Martin Luther King Junior's speech 'The Fierce Urgency of Now: Beyond Vietnam', in which he refers to the action demanded by the present moment, action that will prevent the declaration that it is now 'too late'. See http://www.jillstein.org/mlk_speech.
2. This is 'ubuntu' as the praxis that will 'always remain heterogeneous to our attempts to name it' (Praeg 2008: 367).
3. This is most acutely evidenced in popular culture and media – particularly mediated debates that reveal the pre-eminence of race in public consciousness. See, for example, (a) Brett Murray's painting *The Spear* was followed by weeks of debate about the president's genitalia (see http://www.zapiro.com/Sponsored-by/Brett-Murray-Why-I-painted-the-Spear/) and (b) A tweet, perceived as racist, by model Jessica Leandra dos Santos caused national uproar,

fuelled by another tweet by model Tshidi Thamane (see http://www.iol.co.za/pretoria-news/all-a-twitter-in-wake-of-racist-tweets-1.1291927#.T_Q4EJEkmQo).

4. Farred (2004) explores the subtleties of this dilemma in 'The Not-Yet Counterpartisan', premised upon the notion of the double temporality of the present.

5. West's controversial article considers the shift 'in the sensibilities and outlooks of artists and critics'. He argues that 'a new cultural worker is in the making, associated with a new cultural politics of difference', new ways of understanding vocation and critique (1990: 1).

6. Hall summarises these general co-ordinates as: (a) 'the displacement of European models of high culture'; (b) 'the emergence of the United States as a world power' and (c) 'the decolonisation of The Third World' (1993: 104).

7. Unlike its Jewish messianic and German existentialist counterparts, Mbembe argues that 'governed though it has been, for the most part, by narratives of loss, such meditation on divine sovereignty and African people's histories has not yielded any integrated philosophico-theological inquiry systematic enough to situate human misfortune and wrongdoing in a singular theoretical framework' (2002: 239).

8. Mbembe's epigraph reads: 'The only subjectivity is time . . . Gilles Deleuze, *Cinéma 2: L'image-temps*' (2002: 239).

References

Chabal, P. 2009. *Africa: The Politics of Suffering and Smiling*. London: Zed Books.

Coertze, R.D. 2001. 'Ubuntu and Nation Building in South Africa'. *South African Journal of Ethnology* 24 (4): 113–18.

Derrida, J. and R. Beardsworth. 1994. 'Nietzsche and the Machine: An Interview with Jacques Derrida'. *Journal of Nietzsche Studies* 7: 7–66.

Fanon, F. 1967. *The Wretched of the Earth*. Translated by C.L. Markham. New York: Grove Press.

———. 2008. *Black Skin, White Masks*. Translated by C.L. Markham. London: Pluto.

Farred, G. 2001. 'A Thriving Postcolonialism: Towards an Anti-Postcolonial Discourse'. *Nepantla: Views from South* 2 (2): 229–46.

———. 2004. 'The Not-Yet Counterpartisan: The New Politics of Oppositionality'. *South Atlantic Quarterly* 103 (4): 589–605.

———. 2012. 'To Dwell for the Postcolonial'. *Journal of French and Francophone Philosophy* XX (1): 75–86.

Gordon, L. 2010. 'The Brotherwise Dispatch vs Lewis Gordon'. Available at http://www.lewisrgordon.com/selected-articles/interviews/v-2-lgordon_brotherwise_dis.pdf.

Hall, S. 1993. 'What Is This "Black" in Black Popular Culture? (Rethinking Race)'. *Social Justice* 20 (1–2): 104–14.

Knoop, T. 2009. *Recessions and Depressions: Understanding Business Cycles*. Santa Barbara: ABC-Clio.

Marx, C. 2002. 'Ubu and Ubuntu: On the Dialectics of Apartheid and Nation Building'. *Politikon* 29 (1): 49–69.

Mbembe, A. 2002. 'African Modes of Self-Writing'. *Public Culture* 14 (1): 239–73.

Mudimbe, V-Y. 1997. *Tales of Faith: Religion as Political Performance in Central Africa: Jordan Lectures, 1993*. London: Athlone Press.

Praeg, L. 2007. *The Geometry of Violence*. Stellenbosch: Sun Press.

———. 2008. 'An Answer to the Question: What is [Ubuntu]?' *South African Journal of Philosophy* 27 (4): 367–85.

———. 2011. 'Philosophy, and Teaching (As) Transformation'. *South African Journal of Philosophy* 30 (3): 343–59.

———. 2014. *A Report on Ubuntu*. Pietermaritzburg: University of KwaZulu-Natal Press.

Readings, B. 1996. *The University in Ruins*. Cambridge: Harvard University Press.

Sekyi-Otu, A. 1996. *Fanon's Dialectic of Experience*. Cambridge: Harvard University Press.

———. 2003. 'Fanon and the Post-Colonial Imagination'. Paper presented at the Codesria Symposium on Canonical Works and the Continuing Innovation in African Arts and Humanities. Accra, University of Ghana, 17–19 September. Available at http://abahlali.org/files/Sekyi_Otu.pdf.

Swanson, D.M. 2007. 'Ubuntu: An African Contribution to (Re)search for/with a "Humble Togetherness"'. *Journal of Contemporary Issues in Education* 2 (2): 53–67.

West, C. 1995. 'The New Cultural Politics of Difference'. In *The Cultural Studies Reader*, ed. Simon During, 257–67. London: Routledge.

Wicomb, Z. 2002. *David's Story*. New York: CUNY Feminist Press.

Notes on the Contributors

Ama Biney has more than twenty years of teaching experience in the United Kingdom. She has taught courses in African history (ancient and modern), Caribbean history, the history of pan-Africanism and the history of black people in Britain. Her most recent publication is *The Political and Social Thought of Kwame Nkrumah* (2011).

Danielle Alyssa Bowler is working on her Master's degree in the Department of Political and International Studies at Rhodes University and is a recipient of the 2012 Mandela Rhodes Scholarship, based on leadership, education, entrepreneurship and reconciliation.

Ezra Chitando is affiliated to the Ecumenical HIV and AIDS Initiative in Africa (EHAIA), the World Council of Churches (WCC) and the Department of Religious Studies, Classics and Philosophy at the University of Zimbabwe. He has published widely on the topics of religious ethics, HIV and AIDS and masculinities in southern Africa.

Drucilla Cornell is a professor of political science, women's and gender studies and comparative literature at Rutgers University. Her most recent book, with Nyoko Muvangua, is *Ubuntu and the Law: African Ideals and Postapartheid Jurisprudence* (2012). A collection of her essays, *Reflections on Revolution in South Africa: Ubuntu, Dignity, and the Struggle for Constitutional Transformation*, is forthcoming in 2014.

Katherine Furman was a Master's student in the Department of Political and International Studies at Rhodes University. She has a Master of Science degree in philosophy and public policy from the London School of Economics and Political Science (LSE) where she is currently pursuing her Ph.D.

Lewis R. Gordon is professor of philosophy and Africana studies, with affiliations in Caribbean, Latino and Latin American studies and Judaic studies, at the University of Connecticut at Storrs. He is also Europhilosophy visiting professor at Toulouse University and a Nelson Mandela visiting professor in the Department of Political and International Studies at Rhodes University. His website is http://lewisrgordon.com/.

Ilze Keevy is head of the Department of Constitutional Law and Philosophy of Law at the University of the Free State and has been admitted as advocate of the High Court of South Africa. She is the author of, most recently, '*Ubuntu*: Ethnophilosophy and Core Constitutional Values' in *Ubuntu, Good Faith and Equity: Flexible Legal Principles in Developing a Contemporary Jurisprudence* (2011).

Siphokazi Magadla is a lecturer and Ph.D. candidate in the Department of Political and International Studies at Rhodes University. She is a Fulbright scholar and has a Master's degree in international affairs from Ohio University. Her research interests include the security-development nexus in Africa in post-conflict reconstruction, gender and militarisation/demilitarisation and the postcolonial African diaspora.

Leonhard Praeg is associate professor in the Department of Political and International Studies at Rhodes University and is the author of, most recently, *A Report on Ubuntu* (2014). He is series editor of the Thinking Africa Series, published in collaboration with University of KwaZulu-Natal Press.

Mogobe B. Ramose is extraordinary professor at the University of South Africa (UNISA) and has published numerous articles in theoretical and applied ethics, social and political philosophy, the philosophy of liberation, African philosophy and the philosophy of international relations.

Issa G. Shivji has served as advocate of the High Court and the Court of Appeal of Tanzania since 1977 and of the High Court in Zanzibar since 1989. He has spent most of his life addressing the exploitation of Tanzanians. He occupies the Mwalimu Julius Nyerere Research Chair in Pan-African Studies at the University of Dar es Salaam and has published widely on the political economy of reforms in Tanzania.

Abahlali baseMjondolo   7, 49, 170
Abraham, Willie E.   65
abstraction of individual from society
        139–40
Achebe, Chinua   61
aesthetic judgements   162
affirmative action   130
    contracts   132
Africa   13, 41
    invention and imposition of name
        123–4
Africana philosophy   10, 169, 172–3
African Charter on the Rights of Women,
        Protocol to   77
African diasporic philosophy   see Africana
        philosophy
African 'High Law of Life'   62
African humanism (Ubuntu)   3, 10, 28,
        42–3, 49
    definitions   30
    curating of   29–40
African indigenous law   58, 78
'Africanisation'   41
Africanity   124, 200, 206
African law   74, 77
    and African religion   76
    and ancestors   62–3
    definition   56–8
    and legal thinking   58–60
    group rights   61
    patriarchal basis   62, 63

spiritual dimension   61, 63
and taboos   62–3
and ubuntu   64
unwritten   58
versus customary law   59–60
versus Western law   61–2
African National Congress (ANC)   129–30,
        133, 171–2, 206
'leadership core'   123
Africanness   124
African philosophy and trends   135
    Bantu philosophy   65
    ethnophilosophy   65–6
    folk wisdom   65
    hermeneutical trend   65
    literary trend   65
    political philosophy   65
    professional philosophy   65
    sage philosophy   65
    understood as 'historical essay' by African
        philosophers   124
African Renaissance project   44, 193, 204
'African Socialism'   32, 39
African spirit world   67, 76
    spiritual forces of   77
African Union   143
African Women's Protocol   71, 72, 78
African World View   65, 186
Afri-Forum and Another v. Malema and
        Others   151, 155–7
Afro-Caribbean philosophers   169

Afrocentric pedagogy   125

Afrocentrism   124

Afro-modernity   169, 172, 173

Afro-pessimism   168

Afro-radicalism   197

   Marxist and national character   197

Afro-radical traditions   198

al-Bashir, Omar   40

Alexandria   12–13

alienation   38

Amadiume, Ifi

   Male Daughters, Female Husbands   179

Amnesty International   43

ancestors   62, 76

   and African spirit world   56–7, 76

   legislators in traditional societies   62

   worship   160

   see also living-dead   56

ancestral spirits   61, 63

Anglo-American jurisprudence   172

Anglo-American law   173

Angola   40

   survivors of land-mines   40

anthropology

   philosophical   15, 21

   theological-naturalistic to secular   14

anti-apartheid struggle   106

anti-imperialist emancipatory praxis   48

apartheid   60, 129, 183, 194, 196, 197,
   198, 199, 206, 207

   ethos of separation   204

   political crimes   154

apartheid/post-apartheid binary   195

   old/new South Africa   195

'Arusha Declaration'   35, 39, 139, 141, 144,
   145, 146

association   96

   contractual understanding of   97–8

Athens   12–13

Azanian People's Organisation   129

AZAPO and Others v. President of the
   Republic of South Africa and Others
   151, 154

Bantu law   58

Bantu-speaking peoples of Africa   121

Batho Pele (putting people first)   163

behaviour, morally good and bad   97

being   199

   African way of (communalist)   109

   and becoming   201, 209

   Western way of (individualist)   109

being and belonging   99, 194, 200, 201,
   205, 206, 209

   logic of being-together   201

   meaning of   99

   relationship   96–9

beliefs   78

   of communities   68

   traditional   76

belonging   96–7

Bhe v. Magistrate, Khayelitsha and
   Others   58, 60

Biko, Steve Bantu   50, 129, 169

Bill of Rights, South African   54–5, 72, 77,
   78

black economic empowerment

   contracts   132

Black People's Convention (BPC)   129

Bond, Patrick

   Elite Transition   122–3

botho   *see* humanity

Brazil

   Catholic Bishops' Conference   128

   favelas   128

British pressure groups   123

'Building a Better World: The Diplomacy of Ubuntu', Department of International Relations and Cooperation's white paper   163

Bujo, Bénézet   126–7, 135

'capability' and freedom   42

capitalism   6, 28, 31, 37, 145, 170

Caribbean   13

Césaire, Aimé   27
   on Hitler's crime   41

Chaskalson P.'s judgment   152–5

chiefs' status   67

children   67, 68–9
   abduction   71–2
   forced marriages   71
   marriages   70–1
   rape of   39
   sexual assault of   182
   stereotyping   78

Christiandom   13
   in Afro-Arabic form   13

Christianity   4, 21, 106–7

circumcised males and females   68

citizenship   199
   equal   207
   race-based   200
   universality of   194

civil disobedience   174

civil liberties   19

civil wars   40

clan   103

class   170, 204
   struggle idea   148

closed societies   75

codified customary law   59, 61

Cold War   39

collective good   164

collective philosophy   78
   eroding human rights   72
   shared values and beliefs   65–6
   sub-Saharan traditional societies   76
   traditional African people   64

collective responsibility   125

collective shame as deterrent for offenders   61–2, 63

collective solidarity   64

collectivism   103, 176

colonialism   11, 31, 40–1, 103, 105, 109, 114, 183, 194, 196, 197, 198, 199, 207

colonial laws   59

colonial rule   60

colonisation   12, 17, 21, 125, 129
   'right of conquest'   125, 133

'Coloureds'   122

Comaroff, Jean and Comaroff, John L. 167–9, 171–2, 174
   on policulturalism   168
   Theory from the South   173

commercialisation of services   42

commodity owners, sellers and buyers   140

communal consciousness   202

communalism   2, 109

communitarianism   104, 176
   African   62, 64, 97, 100
   African versus Western individualism   108
   Western   100

communitarian logic associated with Ubuntu   156

communities of political practice   106

community   176
   contemporary   201
   hierarchy and status   67
   life force (*serti*)   159
   of living and living-dead   61, 134

precolonial 201

universal 18

Constitution, South African 4, 54–5, 72,
76–7, 78, 104, 114, 122, 125, 129,
130, 133, 134

equality clause 73

goals 159

inclusion of Ubuntu 150

interim 122, 149, 151, 154, 171

legitimacy 160

pivotal moment of modernity 115

property clause 132

Constitutional Court 54–5, 77, 152, 158,
167, 172

jurisprudence 153–4

constitutionalisation of Ubuntu 173

constitutionalism 107–8

republican 115

constitutional supremacy in 'new' South
Africa 121, 132, 134

constitutional values and Ubuntu 189

Cornell, Drucilla 150, 159–61, 164

'A Call for a More Nuanced
Constitutional Jurisprudence' 7

'Ubuntu, Pluralism and the Responsibility
of Legal Academics' 7

corruption 187

Côte d'Ivoire 39

compensation fund 43–4

dumping of toxic waste 43

see also Trafigura oil-trading company

counterhegemonic movements in southern
Africa 168

crime 39

Cuba 143

'cult of victimisation' 198

cultural resouces of African society 148

culture 202, 204

black popular 193

and tradition, language of 180

customary law 58, 59–60, 77, 158

customs, traditional 76

'Dark Ages' 13

death penalty 151–2, 158

decolonisation 21

struggle in Africa 168

dehumanism 40

deification of epistemic or social order 14–15

Deleuze, Gilles 199

democracy 122, 144–5, 176

business-managed 131

discourse 130–1

liberal political 47

'new' 130

theology of free market economics 47

varieties of 131

democracy/Bantucracy 126

Democratic Republic of the Congo 38, 40

democratic South Africa 130, 205

democratic values 131

demonstrations 174

Derrida, Jacques 193

imperative of 'memory and
repetition' 208

'Nietzshe and the Machine' 196, 209

De Sousa Santos, Boaventura 173

dialectical learning

'comparative validity' 134–5

'dialogical equality' 134–5

difference 98

new cultural politics of 195

of opinion 96

as violence 96

dignity (utu) 139–42, 147, 157, 162, 171,
204

'human dignity' and 'humanness'   139
    and rights   141
    subordination of equality to   141
Diop, Cheikh Anta   109
discrimination   72, 78, 129
disease and misfortune   127
dominant legality and dominant
        illegality   174
Du Bois, W.E.B.   15, 110
    double consciousness   22, 110
    potentiated double consciousness   15–16,
        22
Dworkin, Ronald
    Law's Empire   54
    metaphor of chain novel   54

economic transformation   170
education
    adult in community   50
    curriculum of South Africa   129
    right to   124
Egyptians   13
elderly people's status   67
elders
    as sages and judges in communities   67
    status and role   126
election, first democratic   206
emancipation   3, 206, 209
enculturation   104
Engels, Friedrich   139
Enlightenment dilemma of alterity   198
enslavement and colonialism   41
epistemology   124
equality (*usawa*)   75, 100, 115, 121, 129,
        139–42, 144, 147–8, 202
    in bourgeois society   139
    of human beings   6–7
    and human dignity   55, 66

of rights   6
    traditional versus legal discourse   8
Equality Court   155–6
equal rights   139
equity and justice   140
ethical activism potential   5
ethics   17–18, 74, 124
    of care, feminist   187
    of care, Ubuntu   184, 187
    of communities   68
    indigenous   176
    Western   176
ethnic conflicts   38
ethnic groups, diverse   39
ethnic identity   171–2
ethnicity   68, 103
ethnophilosophers   109
ethnophilosophy   65–6
    see also collective philosophy
Euro-America to Africa (and South America)
        evolution   174
Eurocentric world view   186
Eurocentrism   125, 169
Euro-Christian Africa   31
European colonial laws   61
European enslavement   40–1
European laws versus 'traditional' laws   15
European legal system   59
European-made customary law   59
European philosophy   173
'existential deviation'   199
extended families   78

Fanon, Frantz   4, 21, 110–11, 169, 173,
        199, 208
    'Algeria Unveiled'   110
    'Tower of the past'   196
    'zone of nonbeing'   15

female genital mutilation   70–1

feminine world view   186

feminism   178, 184, 187, 189

feminists, African   66, 70–1, 179, 188

Ferdinand, King   13

folk philosophy

   and cult of silence   73–4

   and sexism   66

folk wisdom   65

foreign debt repayment by Africa   126–7

foreign policy, South African   163

foreign powers, threat of domination by   143

Foucault, Michel   102

France, Anatole

   Le Lys Rouge (*The Red Lily*)   140

freedom (*uhuru*)   21, 115, 143–8, 206, 210

   consciousness of the possibility of   199, 200

   from external domination   143

   individual   143

   as instrument of oppression   48–9

   from oppression   143

   as Trojan Horse   209

free human being   170

Freire, Paulo   50–1

Gandhi, Mahatma   138

gang rape   72

   'jackrolling'   183

   and mutilation of Anene Booysen   182

   of Thandiswa Qubuda   182

Gasa, Nomboniso   180, 187–8

gays   189

   attacks on   167

gender

   activists   70–1

   equality   77, 78

   inequality   8, 70

   relations in postcolonial moment   189

   stereotyping   66

Gender and Development, SADC Protocol   77

George III, King   40

Ghana   39, 48

globalisation   49

Government of the Republic of South Africa and Others v. Grootboom and Others   128

Greeks   13

Greek Sophists   64

Greenpeace   43

groups

   rights and duties   63, 75, 76

   solidarity   62, 69, 74

Guinea   39

Guinea-Conakry   39

haki (Kiswahili)   *see* social justice

Halacha   *see* Judean laws

Hall, Stuart   193–6

   'What Is This "Black" in Black Popular Culture?'   193, 195–6

Harding, Sandra   186–7

   'The Curious Coincidence of Feminine and African Moralities'   186–9

harassment 72

hate speech 72

   'Shoot the boer [farmer]'   155–6

health services, lack of access to   42

Heidegger, Martin   208–9

hermeneutical trend   65

Herodotus, writings of   13

heterosexuality, compulsory   178

'historical innocence'   208

historicists   108–9

   a priori   102–3

'history as sorcery' 198
HIV and AIDS 127, 177
   antiretroviral drugs 44, 45
   crisis in South Africa 29
   distribution of condoms 127–8
   female heterosexual HIV infection 177
   Mbeki government's position on 44–6
   pandemic 43
   stigma 183
   treatment programme 183
hlonipha *see* respect
Hobbs, Thomas
   expectation of social order 16
   Leviathan, mortal God 133
   social contract 159
Holomisa, Nkosi Phathekile
   According to Tradition 187
Holy Roman Empire 13
homeless people, South Africa 128
homophobia 178
homosexuals 76–7
   stereotyping of 78
hospitality, 'fundamental African value' of
   71, 74
Hountondji, Paulin J. 65
Houston, Charles 19–20
Huddleston, Trevor 142
human being (*motho*) 185
human beings are equal (*binadamu wote ni
   sawa*) 140
human dignity 129
humanism 169–70, 176
   African 28–9, 40, 100
   secular forms 109
   Western 100
humanity (*botho*) 185–6
   African 198
   super-exploitation of majority 170

humanness and wholeness 124
human rights 4, 29, 106–7, 204
   individual 106
   international mechanisms 77
   international organisations 46
   and traditional African values 75
   Western notion of and African humanism
      46–9
Human Sciences Research Council 73
human solidarity 7
human subordination 16

identity 21, 194
ideologies and philosophies, constructing of
   137–8
'ID-ology' 167–9, 173
image of deity 185–6
imaginaires 98, 117, 197
   African collective 198–9
imperialism 17, 33, 148, 178
indentured servitude 170
Indians 122
indigenous gender regimes, destruction of
   178–9
indigenous law
   for the people 58
   of the people 58
indigenous peoples 10, 129
   liberation of 125
   problem of justice for 123
   of the New World 14
individual 126
   abstract 139
   being 139
   competitive 126
   cooperative 126
   rights and liberties 75

individualism   105–6, 109
    advancement with group welfare   33
    in Africa before colonialism   111
    Western   33
individualist a priori   98
industrialisation   105
industrial revolution, South Africa   105
inequalities   20, 78, 135, 141, 180, 183,
        186, 187–8
    and disadvantages   19–20
    gender-power   177
    political   50
    social   6, 139
    socio-economic   50
initiation   112–14
    personhood and humanness   112
    social status   113
injustice   69
intellectuals, African   198
interdependence   99, 159, 204
    capitalist system   116
    see also logic of interdependence
Isabella, Queen   13
Islam   13, 21
    sharia, response to Christendom   14
Islamic Africa   31

Jacobellis v. Ohio (United States)   157
Japanese colonialism in Asia   41
Jerusalem   12–13
Jesus of Nazareth   12
Jews   13, 14
    burials   17
    identity of   12
    normative framework   17
Judah, conquest of   11–12
    Judea (Romans and Greeks)   12

Judaism   17, 21
    Rabbinic   12, 13–14
Judean laws (Halacha)   12, 17
    and Roman law   13–14
Judeans in Rome   12
'juridical outlook' of bourgeoisie   139
jurisprudence
    African   59, 60
    Anglo-American   172
    'both-and' scope of Ubuntu-engaged   160
    democratic approach to   54
    revenge permitted by   69
    Ubuntu-engaged   164
    Ubuntu-infused   159–60
    Western   75, 159
justice   5–7, 21, 78, 122, 129, 139–42
    fundamental natural   135
    historical   125, 135
    legal or individual   142
    real-world decisions   162
    retributive   116
    social   176
    in traditional African societies   63
    and Ubuntu   19
    universal translatability of English word
        18

Kagame, Alexis   59–60, 65
Kant, Immanuel   158
    expectation of social order   16
    rational beings model   18
Kaunda, Kenneth   3, 40, 49
    Christian humanist   36
    humanism as ideology   36–7
    social morality   36
    'Zambian humanism'   30, 36–8
Kenya   48

Khmer Rouge, Cambodia   41
Khoi and San peoples, exclusion of   122
'kingdom of custom'   172
kinship   68, 74–5, 98
kinship-based cultural practices and rituals
      104
kinship-based unity   98
Kmt/Egypt   11

Lamont J.'s trial process   156
Langa J.   152, 157
law and Ubuntu
      genealogy   151–6
      incorporation   156–61
      naivety of 'Ubuntu-ists'   162–4
      praxis preceding theory   161–2
lawfare   168, 171
Law of laws (nomos)   20–1, 22, 104, 159,
      160–1
legalisation of Ubuntu   168, 169
legitimisation of political power   145
Leo XII
      Rerum Novarum   129
lesbians   76–7, 189
      attacks on   167
      'corrective rape' of   167
      stereotyping   78
liberal constitutionalism   4
liberalisation policies   145
liberalism   171
liberal rights discourse   8
liberation   21, 38, 194, 204
      Bible and theology of   131
      struggle in Africa   106, 168
Liberia   40
liberties   20
literary trend   65
lived experience and the law   158

living   126
      customary law   58
living-dead   56, 58, 63, 96, 112, 126
locality   199
      cult of   199
      within space of remembrance   199–200
      territory and   199
logic of interdependence   98–9, 101, 102,
      103, 104, 115–17, 194, 201, 202
      empathetic and antipathetic manifestations
            post-apartheid   116
      historicist a priori   102–3
      precolonial   204, 207
      relativist a priori   102–3

MacIntyre, Alasdair
      After Virtue   114
Madala J.   152
Mahomed J.   152
male-dominated or patriarchal societies   56
Malema, Julius   155–6
males
      African nationalists   184
      hegemony versus liberal constitutional
            values   189
      status of adults   67
Mali   31, 38, 39
management theory   37
Mandela, Nelson   40, 129–30, 137–8, 204
manhood as function of personhood   183
Marx, Karl   34–5
masculine or androcentric world view   186
masculinities and femininities   177, 178
masculinity   178–81, 190
      anachronistic notions   184
      categories   178
      crisis of in post-apartheid South Africa
            181–6

hegemonic   71, 177, 178, 181
oppressive   189
patriarchal   87
reinvention of violent   190
and violence   177
see also sexual and gender-based violence
Mauritania   31
Mazrui, Ali   61
Mbeki, Thabo   29, 40, 43, 44–5, 183, 185, 201, 205
Heritage Day address   39
on Moral Regeneration Campaign   39
reference to Ubuntu in speech   30
see also African Renaissance project
Mbembe, Achille   194, 197–8
'African Modes of Self-Writing'   196, 197, 203–4
historical innocence   208
On the Postcolony   20–1
Mbiti, John S.   65
media-oriented performances   174
Menkiti, Ifeanyi
'Person and Community in African Traditional Thought'   111–12
mental enslavement of African people   50
meta-critiques of reason   21
Mgqolozana, Thando
A Man Who is Not a Man   112–13
micro-geography and meaning   203
migrant thinking
first global a priori: colonialism   102–4
first local a priori: urbanisation   104–8
second global a priori: dialectic of recognition   108–11
second local a priori: constitutionalism as 'liberation'   111–17
minerals-energy complex   123
misogyny   178

modernity, modernities   3, 10–16, 172
African as *sui generis* as European   169
European outlooks   11
indigenous peoples of the Americas outlooks   11
Western   106
Mokgoro J.   152, 159–60, 172–3
moral regeneration, language of   185
Moral Regeneration Movement   150
morals of communities   68, 78, 112
motho   see human being
Mozambique   40
survivors of land-mines   40
Mudimbe, V-Y   109–10
On African Fault Lines: Meditations on Alterity Politics   2
'multicultural(ism)'   168
Muslims   14
control of trade across Mediterranean   13
Muthu u bebelwa munwe (a person is born for the other) Venda proverb   105
mutuality   125

Natal Indian Congress   129
nationalism   204
nation-building   204, 205, 207, 209
qua Ubuntu   208
nation-statism   38
Native American Indian   121
Native Americans   40
nativism   197
nativists and 'the native condition'   198
Negritude (*négritude*)   39, 110
neocolonialism   28, 33, 45
neocolonial state   40–6
neoliberal capitalism   167, 170
neoliberalism   28, 33, 45, 117, 148

neoliberal modernity   98

nepotism   116

'network society'   98

'new democracy'   130

'new' South Africa   129–30

   justice in   130–3

   palaver or *mbongi*   135

   transformation into undermined   170

   transition to   129–30

New World of North America   40

Nigeria   31, 38

   Igbo gender system   179

   Yoruba gender system   177, 185

   Yoruba society   178–9

Nkrumah, Kwame   3, 31–4, 35, 36, 38–9, 40, 49, 65, 139

   'African Socialism Revisited'   32

   call for social revolution in Africa   34

   Neo-Colonialism   143

   see also 'philosophical consciencism'

non-governmental organisations

   foreign-funded   46

   local   46

normative concepts   18–19

North-South division   145

Nyerere, Julius Kambarage   3, 36, 40, 49, 65, 106–7, 139–47

   Filed Force Unit, paramilitary force   147

   Freedom and Development   143

   Freedom and Socialism   141–2, 143

   policy document on socialism and self-reliance   144–5

   policy of socialism and self-reliance   138

   political ideology of Ujamaa   147

   political man   147–8

   political philosophy   6, 143, 144–5

   practising Catholic   142

   socialist society   34

socialist Ujamaa project, Tanzania   2, 6, 30

Ujamaa ('familyhood' in Kiswahili)   30, 35, 38, 144, 145–7

ujamaa na kujitegemea (socialism and self-reliance)   138

'*Ujamaa*: The Basis of African Socialism'   34–6

obligation   96

   historical praxis of   115

   political economy of   97–8, 100, 101, 113, 115

   reciprocal   97

Oduyoye, Mercy A.   66

Okri, Ben   199

oppression   196

   historic   194

oral tradition   56

Organisation of African Unity   143

Oruka, Henry Odera   65

   African philosophy trends   65–6

'Othering' of non-European cultures and peoples   46–7

outsiders

   differential treatment of   75

   discrimination and oppression   75

Oyewumi, Oyeronke   177, 185

pan-Africanism   38, 40, 148

Pan-Africanist Congress   129

parliamentary supremacy   131

   to constitutional supremacy   131–2

patriarchal hierarchies   66–9, 76–7, 78

   discrimination and human oppression   69

   gender, age, seniority in birth   68

patriarchal order   179

patriarchs   189

patriarchy   55, 66, 70, 77–8
personhood   159
'phallo-primocentric values'   100
'philosophical consciencism'   30, 34, 39
Pilger, John
    Freedom Next Time   122–3
poeticists   108–9
'policulturalism'   168, 169
political economy
    of individual freedom   115
    of obligation   202
political parties, African   42
political philosophy   65, 194
polygamy   70–1
pornography, defintion of   157
Port Elizabeth Municipality v. Various
    Occupiers   70, 77, 151, 155
Posel, Deborah
    'The Scandal of Manhood'   182
post-apartheid   130, 194, 195, 196
    state   204
postcolonial Africa   37
    state   27–9
postcolonialism   194, 196
postcoloniality   8, 109
postcolonial politics   96
postcolonial situation   204
postcolonial states   39, 40–6
post-independence development projects   3–4
post-independent experiences   40
'potentiated double consciousness'   15
poverty   127, 135, 146
power   144–5
    inequality of   145
Praeg, Leonhard   3
    A Report on Ubuntu   2
praxis preceding theory   161–2
Prevention of Illegal Eviction Act   155

previously disadvantaged individuals   132
'processual personhood'   112
professional philosophy   65
Promotion of National Unity and
    Reconciliation Act   *see* Reconciliation
    Act
Provincial Commission of Inquiry, Limpopo
    Province   73

Rabbinic Judaism   12, 13–14
race   47, 74, 98, 121, 130, 152, 170, 194,
    201, 204
    Bantu races   57
    critical theory   110
race-based thinking   198
racial dominance   178
racialisation, anthropological order of
    modern   15
racism   68, 178
    anti-black   28, 169, 172
    violence as legacy of colonialism   41
rainbow
    nation   193
    nationalism   194
Ramodibe, Dorothy   66
Ramphele, Mamphela   187
    Conversations with my Sons and
    Daughters   187
rape
    of African women   70–1
    baby rape scandals   182, 185
    'Baby Tsephang', Northern Cape   182
    cases unreported   182
    'corrective'   72, 167
    marital   70–1
    see also gang rape
Rawls, John   18, 19–20
    A Theory of Justice   121
    The Idea of Justice   161–2

Readings, Bill
    The University in Ruins   202
rearticulation and reinvention   200
reciprocity   98
reconciliation   69, 130, 176
Reconciliation Act   151, 154
relationality of the human being   20
relativist a priori   102, 103–4
religion   12, 126
    African   76, 77
    African traditional   60, 179
    marginalisation of women   179
religious affiliation   204
religious law   77
respect (*hlonipha*)   179
restoration of relationships   176
restorative justice   115, 116
    and consensus   69
retribution as collective right   69
revolutionary Ubuntu   7, 170, 171
rights   47–9, 100, 122
    economic and social   48
    individual   6
    and justice   6, 69
    to life   6
    to property and housing   155
    socio-economic   6
    in traditional societies   66–7
    use of talk in South Africa   171–2
Rivonia trial   129
Roman Empire   11–12, 21
    concepts of *relegere* (to read again) and
        religare (to bind)   12, 21
    laws   12–13
Romanisation of West Asian laws and values
        13
Roman Law tradition   162
Romans   13

Rome   12–13
Rwanda
    genocide   40
    Hutu-led government and Tutsis   40
    post-genocide   187

Sachs J.   172–3
    judgment   152, 155, 164
sage philosophy   65
SA Human Rights Commission and Others
        v. President of the Republic of South
        Africa and Others   58
sangomas   173
    muti murders   73–4
    as spiritual leaders   74
    status   67
scramble for Africa   143–4
seiein (Greek for 'to shake')   203
Sekyi-Out, Ato   198–200
self-accountability   17
self-determination   103, 109, 143
Senghor, Léopold Sédar   38, 49, 109
    'Négritude and African Socialism'   30, 65
separation
    of politics and economics   139
    of production of commodities from
        circulation in market   140
serti (life force)   *see under* community
sexual and gender-based violence   8, 177,
        178–81, 184, 189–90
sexual orientation   72
sexual violence
    and AIDS   182
    loss of values   183
    qualitative changes post-apartheid   183
sharia   *see under* Islam
Sierra Leone   40
slavery   132, 194, 196, 197, 198, 199, 207

slaves
  and descendants 67
  trade 125
social being 139
social contract 159
social democracy 170
social hierarchy 179
socialism 31, 34–5, 37, 170, 176
  African 100
  international character 138
  Western 100
social justice (*haki*) 140, 142, 147–8, 162
social order, Hobbesian and Kantian
    expectations 16
social policy development 162
socio-economic rights 160
solidarity 105–6, 125, 170
Soobramoney v. Minister of Health,
    KwaZulu-Natal 160, 163–4
South Africa 177
  indigenous law 158
  post-apartheid 49–50
South African Communist Party (SACP) 129
South African Students Organisation (SASO)/
    BPC trials 129
Southern African Development Community
    (SADC) 77, 78
South-South co-operation 145
Soviet bloc 143
Sparks, Allister
  Tomorrow is Another Country 122–3
Steinberg, Jonny
  Three-Letter Plague 183
Steward, Justice Potter 157
stokvel 116, 117
strangers, stereotyping of 78
subaltern counterhegemonic legality 173–4
subaltern legality 172, 173, 189

subjectivity, African 196
subjugation 50
sub-Saharan Africa 57, 58–9, 65, 71, 72,
    73, 75–6, 77, 127
  traditional societies 76
Sudan 31, 38, 40
S. v. Magadani 163
S. v. Makwanyane and Another 54, 58, 60,
    64, 77, 151, 152, 157, 158
Swaziland 177

Tanzania 39, 49, 146, 147–8
  economy 145
  imperial exploitation 148
  religious and ethnic strife 148
Tempels, Placide 97
  Bantu Philosophy 65
temporality
  perception of 195
  as subjectivity 199
Terreblanche, Sampie 122–3, 131–2, 170
  A History of Inequality in South Africa:
    1652–2002 171
  Lost in Transformation 171
theodicy of new era 14
theory of justice
  non-ideal 161–2, 165
  vision of ideal 161–2, 165
Thinking Africa Series, African studies
    project 1–8, 194
time as theoretical baseline 200
TINA ('there is no alternative') 45
tradition 8, 21–2, 78, 190, 198, 207
  as 'the savage slot' 10
traditional African society 31–2, 158
  egalitarian principles 33–4
traditional African values 63
traditional chiefs 179–80

Traditional Courts Bill   179–80

traditional laws   16, 76

traditional leaders   187

Trafigura oil-trading company   43
    dumping of toxic waste in Abijan   43–4

Treatment Action Campaign   44, 45

tribalism   68

tribe   103

Truth and Reconciliation Commission (TRC)
    49–50, 117, 151, 154, 171

Tubman, Harriet (African-American 'Black
    Moses')   28

Tutu, Archbishop Desmond   49–50, 162–3
    South Africa as 'rainbow nation of God'
    50

Twain, Mark   200

ubuntu
    as African Constitution   75–7
    as 'basis of African law'   55–64
    as 'constitutional law'   76
    as cultural praxis   100
    as ethnophilosophy   65–9
    hierarchy and status   66–9
    historical praxis   4–5
    jurisprudence   69, 75
    justice, hierarchy and status   69
    as moral philosophy   77
    oppression of homosexuals, lesbian,
        witches   72–4
    oppression of women   70–2
    as precolonial praxis   201
    in state discourse   210
    strangers and outsiders   74–5
    as/and Ubuntu   197, 201
    unadulterated forms of African social life
        3
    versus regional human rights
        mechanisms   77

as work/praxis   201
    see also African law

Ubuntu
    as abstract philosophy   3, 106
    as constitutional principle   172
    and constitutional supremacy   133–5
    contemporary, retrodicted reinvention of
        philosophy   5
    contemporary, South African context
        16–22
    definitions   29–30
    as ethical and legal value in new South
        Africa   169
    forgiveness and reconciliation   204
    as glocal phenomenon   114–15
    'I am because we are'   96, 97
    'I exist because of others'   96
    in a habitus   203
    in motion   201
    intellectual philosophical discourse   49
    legal application of   164
    legal philosophy   55, 62, 64, 128, 134
    legal status   154
    as living tradition   188
    as philosophical practice   100
    philosophical understanding of   150
    philosophy   124, 133
    as postcolonial philosophy   5
    precolonial habitus to a postcolonial
        habitus   204
    Project   155, 168, 169, 170, 171, 172

Ubuntu/African humanism as philosophy   28

ubuntu/botho   104, 106, 167

'Ubuntu capitalism'   37

ubuntu praxis to Ubuntu philosophy   115
    translation or codification   115

Uganda   38

uhuru   see freedom

ujamaa   *see under* Nyerere, Julius Kambarage

ukungena   71

uMona (jealousy) concept   67

umuntu ngumuntu ngabantu (a person is a
    person through other persons)   29, 36,
    65, 180

unemployment   135

unfree black labour   170

United Nations
    declarations   143
    Resolution 1325   189

United States of America
    pressure groups   123
    problem of race   121

unity   98
    ideal   204
    value of   98

Universal Declaration of Human Rights   46

universalising
    elements of Ubuntu   21–2
    human rights   46
    and universal practices   15

universalistic ethos   43

universality, hegemonic conceptions of   22

unofficial customary law   58

urbanisation   105, 106

usawa   *see* equality

utilitarianism   164

utopian Ubuntu ideal toward dystopia   163

utu   *see* dignity

values   78, 99–100
    of communities   68
    and meaning   11
    premodern temporal location   10
    traditional   8, 76

Van der Walt, Johan   150, 157–8, 160
    *Law and Sacrifice: Towards a Post-
        Apartheid Theory of Law*   7

Vietnam   143

violence   187, 190
    criminal   177
    gender-based   70–1, 190
    hegemonic masculinity and   177
    of male hegemony   177
    women and children   181
    see also sexual and gender-based violence;
        sexual violence

violation of human dignity   78

virginity testing   70–1

virgin myth   182

virtue ethics   100

Wamba dia Wamba, Ernest   135

wealth, obligation to share with community
    125

welfare of the collective   31

Wells, Julia
    *The Return of Makhanda: Exploring the
        Legend*   1–2

Western feminist discourse   179

Western ideologies and philosophies   100–1

Western individualism   2

Western legal philosophy   128

Western philosophy   107

white people, *abelungu* or *makgowa*   104

widow inheritance   71

Wiredu, Kwasi   19
    Cultural Universals and Particulars   19

witches   73, 76–7
    burning and victimisation of   71, 73
    stereotyping   78

women   76
    domestic violence   39
    economic injustice   72
    formal equality   181
    human dignity   71–2

individual bodily rights   184–5

as inferior to men   67

legal and political equality   189

oppression of   70–1

and peace-building   189

reproductive rights   72

status and role of   126

stereotyping of   78

violation of human dignity   70

wife-beating or 'correction'   70–1

yet-to-be-born   126, 134

Yugoslavia   143

'Zambian humanism'   39

Zanzibar   147–8

Zimbabwe   177

   post-independence   181

   Ubuntu and Hunhuism 30

Zoe-Obianga, Rose   66

Zuma, Jacob   188, 201, 204–5